The Archaeology of the Industrial Revolution

The Archaeology of the Industrial Revolution

BRIAN BRACEGIRDLE BSc FRPS FIIP
Principal Lecturer in Science and Learning Resources
The College of All Saints, London

with

BRIAN BOWERS BSc(Eng) CEng MIEE
Assistant Keeper, The Science Museum, London

NEIL COSSONS MA FSA FMA
Director, Ironbridge Gorge Museum Trust

W. K. V. GALE FRHistS
Past President, Newcomen Society
Metals Editor, The Engineer

CHARLES E. LEE FCIT CIMarE
Past President, Newcomen Society

A. RIDLEY BSc
Senior Lecturer in Science,
The College of All Saints

L. T. C. ROLT MA FRSL CIMechE
Vice-President, Newcomen Society

WILL SLATCHER MA MSc PhD
lately Leverhulme Research Fellow, Imperial
College, London

JENNIFER TANN BA PhD
Lecturer in Modern Economic and Social History
The University of Aston in Birmingham

REX WAILES FSA FIMechE
Past President, Newcomen Society
Consultant on Industrial Monuments,
Department of the Environment

Text figures by
STANLEY PAINE ARCA

Research Assistant
PATRICIA H. MILES BSc ARPS

 HEINEMANN · LONDON

Heinemann Educational Books Ltd

LONDON EDINBURGH MELBOURNE AUCKLAND TORONTO
KUALA LUMPUR SINGAPORE HONG KONG
IBADAN NAIROBI JOHANNESBURG
NEW DELHI

ISBN 0 435 32990 1

NOTE ON THE SECOND IMPRESSION

A new printing has been called for only a few months after publication, but the temptation to add new material has been resisted. Some typographical errors have been corrected, two captions altered, and a completely new index made.

1974   B.B.

Published by Heinemann Educational Books Ltd
48 Charles Street, London W1X 8AH
Filmset and printed in Great Britain by
BAS Printers Limited, Wallop, Hampshire

Colour plates printed by
Colour Reproductions Limited, Billericay, Essex

Preface

INDUSTRIAL ARCHAEOLOGY emphasizes the physical remains of past technologies, and offers great opportunities for the photographer. The camera can, of course, record invaluable information on a site scheduled for re-development, for example; it can also capture something of the evocative beauty of the abandoned mine or derelict canal. This book has been built round some of my photographs chosen to illustrate the wide variety of industrial relics that may be encountered; selection has not been easy, and much that deserved a place had to be omitted for lack of space. I have included full map references for all sites visited, and provided each picture with a caption describing the technical and historical significance of the site. I have been fortunate in persuading well-known experts to give me technical advice and write the linking text which puts the illustrations in their historical, economic, and technological context.

I hope the book will perform two functions. In the first place, specialist readers may find the photographs and captions a useful reference source for key sites, some of which they may have been unable to visit, and some of which have been destroyed since the pictures were made. Secondly, I have tried to communicate the visual appeal and intellectual fascination of industrial archaeology to readers who are relative newcomers to its study.

I owe a great debt of gratitude to all those listed on the title page, but especially to my colleagues Tony Ridley and Pat Miles for their unfailing support and encouragement. Less obviously perhaps, but no less important, I am grateful to all those very many people who have admitted me to their property to make my photographs; without exception, my reception has been most cordial, and many happy memories remain of sites visited and people met on them to turn a day into an event.

My publishers have been a further source of strength. In Alan Hill and Hamish MacGibbon I have found every facilitation of my aims, and I am most grateful to them and their staff for the care and interest they have lavished on this book.

1973   B.B.

Contents

List of Colour Plates

1. An Introduction to Industrial Archaeology

BRIAN BRACEGIRDLE

BRITAIN'S PLACE IN TECHNOLOGICAL HISTORY is unique, for it was the first country to pass through an industrial revolution. Many of the crucial improvements in manufacturing techniques on which further progress was based were initiated within these islands. It is hardly too much to claim with Samuel Smiles that 'our engineers may be regarded in some measure as the makers of modern civilization'.

To the historian of industry this rich heritage is both a challenge and a responsibility. Countless avenues of research open up before him; many sites of great intrinsic interest await his exploration and recording. Unfortunately, however, apathy is still sometimes encountered in the matter of preserving industrial monuments. Without continuous vigilance much of importance may be needlessly swept aside. There is an urgent need to record those sites which are in jeopardy.

The drama of the changes wrought in Britain between the years 1760 and 1830 was quite apparent even to those living close to the events. An ancient way of life had been overthrown and the country's economy transformed. England was more altered by the adoption of machines and factory methods than was France by the Reign of Terror and the regime of Napoleon. As early as 1837 Blanqui could refer to what had happened as the 'Industrial Revolution' – a description which has stuck ever since. The importance of industrialization as an historic process was therefore swiftly realized and the sustained success of Smiles' *Lives of the Engineers* (1861) indicates an abiding popular interest in the men behind the events. But although the study of industrial history had an early beginning, attention was for long mainly focused on personalities and economic theories; the detailed analysis of changing techniques and processes was seldom attempted and the significance of industrial monuments often went unnoticed. Since the beginning of the twentieth century these deficiencies have slowly been remedied. Of recent years there has been a growing concern with the physical remains of the factories, plant, and transport systems left behind by the onward march of progress. Such relics are the province of the industrial archaeologist.

The term 'industrial archaeology' was first coined in the early 1950s to describe what is perhaps best thought of as the field study of technological change. Anything concerned with past methods of manufacture and distribution lies within its scope. Nothing is too old nor too recent. With metals or textiles many important remains may date back several centuries; with plastics or electronics interest will be confined to the immediate past.

Perhaps the best way of gaining an insight into the methods and subject matter of industrial archaeology is to join one of the many societies devoted to the study and preservation of industrial monuments. Within groups of this kind a newcomer will find a wealth of knowledge and expertise which will help him direct his energies along worthwhile lines. As new societies are frequently formed and the officers and addresses of existing ones are continually changing, the current edition of the *Industrial Archaeologists' Guide* should be consulted for up-to-date information. Some description of the range of societies available may, however, be helpful.

1

The premier society in this country for the study of the history of engineering and technology is the Newcomen Society, which was formed as a result of the James Watt Centenary Celebrations in 1919. All those who have worked in industrial archaeology since the foundation of the Newcomen owe it a great debt, for its *Transactions* are a gold mine of authoritative papers while its early pioneer work has done much to ease the way for later researchers. The headquarters of the Society are at the Science Museum in London, where papers are read each month during the winter. The out-of-town summer meeting is held at a different location each year, local members taking parties around places of interest in the neighbourhood. Membership of this great society is open to people from all walks of life.

There are also several national societies which cater for those with a more specialized range of interests. The Cornish Engines Preservation Society (now part of the Trevithick Society) is an outstanding example and so is the Railway and Canal Historical Society. The Wind- and Water-mill Section of the Society for the Protection of Ancient Buildings is another national body of great importance.

Many people prefer, however, to join a more locally-orientated society of the kind which has been springing up all over the country. Most such groups work on the complete industrial spectrum within their area but some confine their attention to one particular activity. A good example of this latter type is the Northern Mill Engine Society, which preserves engines from Lancashire and Yorkshire mills and is responsible for the preserved engines at Dee Mill in Shaw [see *6.19* and Plate 31(a)].

One of the great merits of belonging to a society is the help which becomes available from fellow members. The recording of a site is often a hurried affair. Once a decision has been made to demolish a structure, the wreckers can move in very rapidly, leaving a lone worker at a serious disadvantage. The various skills of different members may also be complementary, so that each may contribute something of value to the work of a team. A single individual is unlikely to possess a complete mastery of every technique used in analysing and recording an industrial complex.

Perhaps the most valuable record which can be made on any site is a set of dimensioned drawings. Usually these need not be works of fine engineering draughtsmanship; for most purposes all that is required is a resonably accurate sketch. The important thing is that all drawings should be carefully dimensioned. Once demolition has occured the opportunity of making measurements will have gone for ever.

Photography is another important recording technique. Today's photograph may well represent the nearest approach to a first-hand experience which a future worker can obtain. It is therefore vital that the highest possible standard should be achieved. With a little extra care and a minimum of additional equipment the quality of record photographs may be improved immensely (see relevant chapter in *Industrial Archaeologists' Guide 1971–73*).

Industrial archaeology can sometimes be spotted in the making – where a factory is one of the last of its type or where an entire industry is in a state of flux. Plate 1(a) shows a dyeworks which still dyes and weights silk in the traditional way. The advent of synthetic fibres has, however, drastically reduced demand for its products, so that this works is unlikely to continue its present mode of operation for much longer. Photographic records were made before the opportunity was lost.

A cine camera can be an invaluable tool in recording the movements involved in an obsolescent industrial process. There can be few societies which do not number one or two enthusiastic cinematographers amongst their members but if a really ambitious

1.1
MODEL WATER-MILL (from the Abbot's Hall Museum of Rural Life, in Stowmarket, Suffolk). Museum exhibits often help to identify objects found on site. It is worthwhile comparing this superbly detailed model with some of the photographs in chapter five. It was made in the mid-nineteenth century by an apprentice, using his master's mill as pattern. (I am indebted to the Curator of the Museum for permission to photograph this model, and for his generous co-operation in removing its cover.)

project is planned then it might be better to seek the co-operation of a local photographic society.

Sound recording can also play a part. It can save time and trouble in, for example, taking down the account of an elderly ex-worker who still remembers how some long-vanished plant was operated. For such purposes a portable battery machine run at slow speed is quite adequate, so that the making of a tape involves very little expense.

Museums can help the industrial archaeologist in a number of ways. The major national collections, like the Science Museum in London and other museums of science and technology in the larger manufacturing cities, need little in the way of introduction. They contain many superb exhibits of great historical interest covering a wide range of industrial activities and publish much useful information. But the small local museum can also be invaluable. Its curator often possesses a wealth of knowledge about the surrounding district and his advice can be of immense assistance in preventing false starts. Local collections may be specialized in nature; for example, in the north a number of museums concentrate on the textile industries. Private companies sometimes maintain works museums, with very worthwhile contents – Holman's museum in Camborne is an excellent example of such a collection [6.10]. A full list of relevant museums may be found in the current edition of the *Industrial Archaeologists' Guide*.

From the industrial archaeologist's point of view, one of the most useful exhibits to be found in either the local or the national museum is the accurate scale model. Because its small size allows all to be seen at once, it can frequently give a better idea of the arrangement of a machine, building or plant than could be got on the site itself, even if everything were intact and visible [1.1]. The overall picture gained from a model can thus be of great help in interpreting remains discovered during field-work.

The outdoor museums now under development in several parts of the country will perhaps have even more to offer than their conventional counterparts. They will not only contain transplanted buildings and machines but will provide the industrial archaeologist with the stimulating experience of being able to watch long out-moded processes in action. Some smaller-scale local museums, of which Abbeydale in Sheffield is an excellent example [9.16 and Plates 27(a), (b) and (c)], have already been opened. These, however, are devoted to one particular trade, whereas the developing regional museums will attempt a fuller representation of the manufacturing activities of their

1.2

ONE-INCH ORDNANCE SURVEY MAP
OF 1833 – COALBROOKDALE AREA
The first edition of the Ordnance Survey
series, of which this is an example, shows
much detail of interest to the industrial
archaeologist, for it can be directly compared
with later editions, of which there have been
several, to trace the development of a site or
confirm the identity of remains. Original
copies of the first edition are difficult to find
nowadays, although a number of libraries
have them. However the entire series of the
first edition for England and Wales has been
reissued, with some minor additions, by David
and Charles Ltd. Soon reprints will be available
for the Scottish section thus completing coverage of the whole country. Apart from this
particular copy, the author has copies of a
printing of ten years later which was revised to
include a railway making its way down
towards Coalbrookdale, but stopping at Light-
moor. The David and Charles version shows
this railway complete, so that with the current
modern version shown in *1.3* much of the
history of the area from 1833 onwards can be
traced very easily.

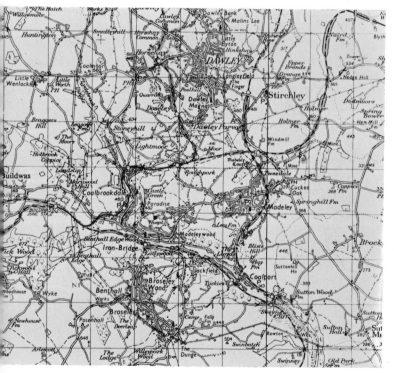

1.3

ONE-INCH ORDNANCE SURVEY MAP
– CURRENT SERIES OF COALBROOK-
DALE AREA (Reprinted with the permission
of the Director-General, Ordnance Survey).
This reproduction has been made to match
the portion of the 1833 edition shown
in *1.2*. It is obvious that direct comparisons
can be made between present-day topograph-
ical features and those of nearly 150 years ago.
This is a fascinating exercise, whatever one's
interest, particularly in one's home area, and
it is invaluable for the industrial archaeologist.

districts. The museum being built up at Beamish Hall in County Durham will have a magnificent array of exhibits covering all aspects of industry in the North-East, as the currently-open exhibition centre makes clear. In a similar way the Ironbridge Gorge Museum Trust is re-establishing many former industries and bringing together important examples of early engineering. One of its main areas is the Blists Hill site, which includes the Hay inclined plane on the Shropshire Canal and the nineteenth-century blast furnaces. This site will show, amongst other things, charcoal burning, various furnaces and forges, clay industries, coal getting, and numerous exhibits concerned with transport. Another site in the same Trust's area is already established and contains the Old Furnace of Abraham Darby I. This furnace is of such fundamental importance in industrial history that it will not be removed from its original position; other exhibits will be taken to it. The Trust has a most ambitious and imaginative programme, which will need a great deal of money if it is to succeed. Restoration of the Iron Bridge alone may cost almost £100 000 and many other things are planned. The eventual conservation of the whole area, with shops, churches, inns, schools etc to make a complete living complex, will take many years. As the sponsor of a project devoted to so massive and unique an aim, the Trust deserves the fullest support.

Concern with physical remains should not, of course, blind the industrial archaeologist to the fact that he is attempting to contribute to the study of industrial history as a whole. Background reading which serves to set a particular site or factory in its wider context will help make work in the field all the more meaningful. Documentary sources should not be ignored, although their authority should be regarded as subservient to evidence from the site itself. The industrial archaeologist is an historian who is prepared to get his feet wet and his hands nettled but there is no reason why he should not also use the traditional methods of historical research.

The most useful kind of document is perhaps the map and Britain is very well-provided for in this respect. A good start can be made with the Ordnance Survey maps of the various series and scales. The earliest are in the one-inch first edition published between 1805 and 1873. Occasionally sheets from this first issue turn up in antique shops but they are becoming increasingly rare and expensive finds. Fortunately, however, the publishers David and Charles have now reprinted those for England and Wales in 97 sheets and have inserted some later material, mainly on railways. First edition maps, whether original or reprinted, may be used in conjunction with the current series to clarify all manner of problems [*1.2* and *1.3*]. With the added help of intermediate editions, which are easily obtainable secondhand or seen in the local library, the history of a site can be traced from mid-nineteenth century to the present day. Larger-scale maps are even more valuable. The most notable is probably the two-and-a-half inch to the mile provisional edition, now being replaced by a more up-to-date set. This provisional edition was made by reduction from larger-scale sheets and included much detail omitted from more recent versions. The larger scale allows for greater precision in tracing the location of a building or other relic and is the normal working tool for a local group. Really large-scale plans, at twenty-five inches to the mile, are proportionately more useful still; they may often be consulted at a local library.

The Ordnance Survey series is not the only source of trustworthy maps. After about 1850, railway maps and plans appeared in profusion and sometimes showed details found nowhere else. Accurate local maps prepared for directories and estate agents may sometimes be acquired. Access to earlier maps is often difficult but here David and Charles have again come to the rescue. They have recently published an exact facsimile

port China Works.   W. S. Allcock, Photographer.   Post Card, No. 25.

1.4
POSTCARD OF COALPORT CHINA WORKS. Browsing through local junk shops one can often find a pile of postcards. Many of them will be of little interest, but occasionally one or two will be valuable finds. Such an example is this picture of the Coalport china works, made probably just after the turn of the century. It is known that the canal ran from the bottom of the inclined plane [Plates 6(a) and 7(c)] above flood level of the Severn through the Works and on to the wharf at Coalport. The exact line of the canal could be deduced on both sides of the works, but in between it had been thoroughly obliterated. This postcard shows where it ran, and will be helpful in making the reconstruction which the Museum Trust hopes to carry out (see page 32).

of the Royal English Atlas, first printed in 1762. Tithe and enclosure maps may also be available to help piece together a picture of a district in the eighteenth century.

Written evidence concerning a site may have to be sought in a number of quarters. County record offices may be helpful, although many have only recently come to realize the importance of the industrial past. If particular documents are required and their whereabouts are not obvious, the National Register of Archives will usually be able to suggest the appropriate collection to visit. Company archives, if accessible, may prove a major source of information but all too often records were either never kept or have been subsequently thrown away. To finish off a piece of work on a site it may sometimes be necessary to delve into the back-numbers of local newspapers to study advertisements, notices of sale, and even the columns dealing with births, marriages, and deaths. Public libraries frequently maintain complete sets of all newspapers published in their areas.

A useful collection of information peculiar to industrial archaeology itself is contained within the National Record of Industrial Monuments, originated by the Council for British Archaeology. Workers who have investigated a site send in a card to the Centre for the Study of the History of Technology at Bath University of Technology, where it is copied and returned to the sender. The file of such copies now exceeds 7000 and gives details such as map reference, description of site, any records made, danger of demolition, name of reporter etc. If this system could be further developed it would be most valuable, since it would give a list of monuments deserving preservation. Unfortunately the present reliance on individual reporting produces a very uneven coverage from county to county. Individual workers can consult the Record to make sure they are not duplicating the work of others and should certainly complete record cards when they have discovered something of interest.

Another means of communicating one's findings to fellow enthusiasts is to contribute to the bulletin of the local society. Some amateur magazines of this sort are very well produced, running to over fifty pages and containing short articles as well as news items. More ambitious articles may be submitted to such journals as *Industrial Archaeology*. Success in obtaining publication in a professional periodical is a mark of both careful investigation and good reporting.

The expertise needed to carry through a satisfactory investigation is not easily acquired and the apprenticeship may be long and arduous. Recently, however, a number of extra-mural university departments have eased the situation by providing courses in the techniques of industrial archaeology. The Field Studies Council has done likewise and offers one-week residential courses at two of its centres, that at Flatford Mill being concerned with the use of photography. Local societies help their members by arranging occasional lectures.

The study of industrial history makes many demands on time and energy but in return it can be immensely rewarding. Great opportunities for original research still abound, because certain aspects of industry have never attracted widespread attention. Neglected topics include ports and harbours, the clay industries, quarrying, roads, and the smaller workshops and factories. Detective work on the site has a thrill all its own while there is a quieter satisfaction in developing and using the skills needed for accurate recording. Small things which would have seemed hardly worthy of notice begin to assume new significance. Plate 1(b) shows some old timbers embedded in the mud of the Thames. Although of no particular interest at first glance, these have been recognized within the last few years as remnants of the slipway timbers used by Brunel in the launching of the historic *Great Eastern*. Such dramatic discoveries are, of course, rare but the shape of a window, the form of a factory chimney, the winding gear of a pit, each has its own story to tell. To the eye of the initiate the industrial landscape takes on an additional dimension.

To strike a more personal note the author hopes that this book, with its background chapters and carefully captioned illustrations, will contribute in a small way to the growing interest in the preservation and study of the relics of by-gone industry. We owe it to future generations to save those industrial monuments possessing genuine significance and to record those lesser remains which for economic reasons cannot be preserved.

FURTHER READING

BRACEGIRDLE, B. *Photography for Books and Reports* (Newton Abbot: David and Charles, 1970)

BRACEGIRDLE, B. 'Industrial Archaeology and Photography: an Account of a Course at Flatford Mill'. *Industrial Archaeology*, Feb. 1971, **8**, 14–24.

COSSONS, N. AND HUDSON, K. *Industrial Archaeologists' Guide 1971–73* (Newton Abbot: David and Charles, 1971)

HOSKINS, W. G. *Local History in England* (London: Longmans, 1959)

HOSKINS, W. G. *Field Work in Local History* (London: Faber, 1967)

HUDSON, K. *Handbook for Industrial Archaeologists* (London: John Baker, 1967)

PANNELL, J. P. M. *The Techniques of Industrial Archaeology* (Newton Abbot: David and Charles, 1966)

In addition, David and Charles publish a series of books each dealing with the industrial archaeology of a particular region. After a general introduction to the industry of the area, a fairly comprehensive gazeteer lists most of the important sites, although regrettably often without map references. If the volume for a particular area has been published, it will be a good introduction to the industrial archaeology of the district.

First edition of the one-inch Ordnance Survey has been reprinted by David and Charles in 97 sheets covering England and Wales.

The Royal English Atlas, originally published in 1762, has been republished in exact facsimile by David and Charles.

Plate 1(a)

INDUSTRIAL ARCHAEOLOGY IN THE MAKING – SILK-DYEING WORKS (*110/SJ 919722 – London Road, Macclesfield*). The machinery and processes in this dye-works, one of the last in England still dyeing and weighting real silk, have changed very little in the past eighty years, and not much in the last century and a half. The vats themselves are of the original thick timber construction, made by a local firm of wheelwrights still in existence and still maintaining their work. The porcelain spindles on which the skeins are rotated in the baths are of an early pattern, as is the ironwork in the winding handles and gearing. The only touches of modernity are the plastic buckets and, in the foreground, the stainless steel vat which has been installed to deal with other fibres. It is likely that the near future will see the closure of this works and the loss of all the expertise which goes with it. Other examples of industrial archaeology in the making can be found in fibre processing and other industries, like fuel and transport, where technological changes have been rapid.

Plate 1(b)

THE SIGNIFICANCE OF THE INSIGNIFICANT – LAUNCHING SITE OF THE *GREAT EASTERN* (*camera position 171/TQ 375780; site itself across the Thames at TQ 376783*). Quite recently the owner of the timber yard has had a notice fixed on to his wharf to commemorate this momentous event but previously all that remained to remind us of the launching of the *Great Eastern* were the few timbers exposed at low water. These are visible immediately at the foot of the wharf under the notice. The ship was at least forty years ahead of her time and her construction and launching posed many new problems. A number of the methods designed to solve them were engineering breakthroughs. For example, an experimental tank was used by William Froude to test the stability and resistance of the hull; steam-operated steering gear was developed by J. M. Gray, and the launch itself gave the Tangye brothers their great opportunity in hydraulic engineering. Timber launching-ways and cradles were used and after seven partially successful attempts, the ship was finally launched on 31 January 1858. The timbers seen in the plate are all that remain of the launching-ways – their insignificance being significant indeed.

8

WATERBEACH LEVEL BANK, TOLLS
PAYABLE HERE
For Every Horse or other Beast except an ass
or asses Hauling any Boat or Boats
For every Ass Hauling
For Horse Mule or Ass not Hauling any vessel
For every Score of neat cattle the sum of
But if under five for each Beast
For every score of Calves Swine sheep
or Lambs the sum of
And so in proportion for every
greater or less number.
Musgrave Francis, clerk to the commissioners

Plate 2(a)
BARGE WEIGHING MACHINE AT STOKE BRUERNE (*146/SP 743499 – about 7 miles south of Northampton*). Tolls were levied on barges by the ton-mile, according to the commodity carried. In order to decide the tonnage, gauging rods were used to measure how deep the barge lay in the water, and this was tabled against the barge and the commodity. The tables were made up originally by actually weighing the barge plus load, and a machine designed to do this has been re-erected at Stoke Bruerne, near the British Waterways Museum. The machine, which has been preserved in excellent order, is in an unusual lock with cast-iron gates.

Plate 2(b)
WORKING BOATS AT NORBURY JUNCTION (*119/SJ 793228 – about 8 miles west of Stafford*). The junction of the Shropshire Union with the now derelict Newport branch has been turned into an important basin for pleasure craft. It is a British Waterways depot, and working narrow boats can sometimes be seen amidst the cruisers.

Plate 2(c)
TOLL-BOARD (*preserved at Stretham Old Engine – 135/TL 516730 4½ miles south of Ely*). The use of the river's banks as a through land route was especially apposite in the Fens, since they were both above water level throughout and went in straight lines – hence the heavy tolls exacted!

Plate 2(d)
HARECASTLE TUNNELS ENTRANCE (*110/SJ 837541 – in the middle of Kidsgrove*). On the right is the entrance to Brindley's original tunnel, the eighth wonder of the world when it was being cut between 1766 and 1777. The only precedent for such an engineering work was the underground canal system at Worsley, and because of this lack of experience great difficulties were encountered in the digging. The tunnel is 2897 yd long, but the diameter is so small that boats were unable to pass and consequently it was always a great bottleneck. On the left is the new tunnel, started in 1825 under Telford. Fifteen shafts were sunk in its digging, allowing work to proceed from thirty points at once. The tunnel, opened to traffic in 1827, is 2926 yd long and, unlike the old one, wide enough for a towpath. It is still in use on the Trent and Mersey canal.

2. Inland Waterways

L. T. C. ROLT

BRITAIN'S INLAND WATERWAY SYSTEM has been called with some truth the Cinderella of the transport world. Although commercial trading on our waterways persisted stubbornly in the face of mounting competition, first from the railways and then from the roads, they were virtually forgotten by a public dazzled by these newer forms of transport. Latterday travellers by rail or road, if they glimpsed our waterways at all in the course of their hurried journeys, took them for granted as part of the landscape. They never troubled to inquire whither they led or who had built them and when.

It is only since the last war that there has been a great awakening of public interest in our inland waterways and it is ironical that such a revival should have been accompanied by a most disastrous decline in their commercial use. This may not be co-incidental for, as the poet W. B. Yeats so truly wrote: 'Man is in love and loves what vanishes'.

Despite all that has been written on the subject in recent years there is still much to be learned. For the industrial archaeologist our inland waterways make a fascinating and fruitful subject for study, being not only vast in their physical extent but in their date range also. In recent years diligent research among original sources such as company minute books has revealed a great deal about canal history, but this is only half the story. Properly to appreciate the works of our great waterway engineers, to understand the magnitude of their achievement with the rudimentary means at their disposal, historical knowledge must be used to supplement and illuminate the careful study of the actual artifacts upon the ground: locks, inclined planes, tunnels, aqueducts, canal bridges, wharves and warehouses, even the humble lock cottage, all are meaningful. This is what industrial archaeology is all about.

What makes our inland waterways so significant is that, in the three-dimensional language of earth, timber, stone, brickwork and cast-iron, they can tell us the complete story of the development of the art of civil engineering in this country over a period of more than two centuries. It is a story that begins with individual 'engineer-undertakers' like Arnold Spencer, who made part of the Great Ouse navigable in 1618, and ends with the highly professional expertise of Thomas Telford. Telford's last canal was completed in 1835, shortly after his death, and reveals a mature 'cut and fill' technique which had been evolved during the age of canal construction and was part of the legacy of experience that passed on to the builders of railways and, through them, to those who build our motorways today.

To make the Great Ouse navigable, Spencer made use of an ancient device commonly known in East Anglia as a staunch [2.1] and elsewhere in England as a flash lock or a watergate. Very briefly, this consisted of a masonry weir across the river having within it a movable portion which, when removed, left a gap through which boats could pass. This movable portion could consist of a vertically rising 'guillotine' gate [2.2], a hinged gate opened against the current by a winch, or – most primitive of all – an arrangement of poles (rimers) and boards (paddles) which had to be removed piecemeal.

10

2.1

STAUNCH, MILDENHALL (*135/TL 708743 – in Mildenhall, 8 miles north-east of Newmarket*). No remains of the timbers of staunches are still to be seen, but in several places the masonry walls have survived, as at Mildenhall. The fall on the river here is small, and this was typical of a staunch. A vertical paddle of wood was raised when a craft approached, allowing the pent-up waters to flow swiftly through the gap. If the boat was going downstream, it was swept through the small opening; if upstream, it had to be pulled through against the current. Either way it could be an operation attended with some danger.

2.2

A STAUNCH. When the wheel (A) was turned, the gate (B) was raised, thus allowing water to flow from (C) to (D), and giving clearance for the boat to pass beneath.

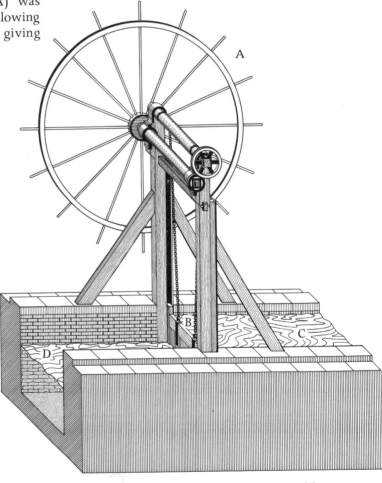

11

Plate 3

PONT CYSYLLTE AQUEDUCT (*117/SJ 271420 – 3½ miles east of Llangollen*). Designed by Thomas Telford for the proprietors of the Ellesmere Canal Company, this is probably the supreme achievement of canal engineering. It was completed in 1805, as recorded by the plaque on the pier to the south of the river. Telford's original plans for this aqueduct were modified by William Jessop. At first a long approach embankment was envisaged, so that the crossing could be made on eight spans of 53 ft. Finally, however, it was decided to build a shorter embankment, necessitating the present nineteen spans of 53 ft – a total of 1007 ft at a maximum height of 127 ft above the river Dee. The embankment, rising to a height of 97 ft, is an impressive achievement, and would be famous in its own right if it were not overshadowed by the aqueduct. The cast-iron trough is 11 ft 10 in. wide, with a 4 ft 8 in. tow path carried above it on iron plates. This leaves only some 7 ft free for navigation, but the additional width beneath the tow path allows for easier movement of water past the boat and avoids spillage of water when a craft of maximum beam passes through. The stone piers, which are hollow above seventy feet, are still in excellent condition. The ironwork was cast by William Hazeldine at his Plas Kynaston Ironworks close to the site. There is a great improvement in quality of casting compared with the Longdon aqueduct of ten years before.

Plate 4(a)

LONGDON-ON-TERN AQUEDUCT(*118/ SJ 618156 – about 3½ miles north-west of Wellington*). Built by Thomas Telford, newly-appointed engineer to the Shrewsbury Canal Company, in late 1795, this structure is the first substantial cast-iron aqueduct in the world. It was a considerable achievement in its own right, besides acting as a trial run for the magnificent Pont Cysyllte aqueduct of ten years later. The 187 ft long cast-iron trough is carried over the river Tern by three triangulated cast-iron bearers on masonry foundations. Extra cast-iron columns are taken from these foundations to support the towpath, which is carried alongside the main channel. The trough was cast by William Reynolds at Ketley. As may be seen from the abutments, it was built after the newly built masonry aqueduct on the same axis had been swept away by a flood.

Plate 4(b)

TAVISTOCK CANAL TUNNEL PORTAL (*175/SX 462724 – about 1½ miles south-west of Tavistock*). The Morwelldown tunnel, like the rest of the Tavistock Canal, was engineered by John Taylor. Although only 8 ft high by 6 ft wide, it is 2 miles long and took 14 years of hard work to finish (the inscription 1803 commemorates the starting date). The rock was blasted with black powder, and fumes from this mixing with the already poor air gave rise to great concern. Water seeping into the workings was also a problem. Ventilation was improved by the use of a 40 ft water-wheel driving Cornish pumps at the shafts by long rods. During the cutting of the tunnel, large deposits of copper were found, and exploited at Wheal Crebor mine. When the canal emerged from the tunnel, it was 237 ft above the Tamar, so an incline was built down to Morwellham quay. By 1883 this incline was derelict, and in the 1930s the constantly-flowing water supply was turned to operate a hydro-electric plant.

Plate 4(c)

CROWNDALE AQUEDUCT (*175/SX 463727 – about 1½ miles south-west of Tavistock*). This aqueduct on the Tavistock canal is an example of a primitive type, little more than an embankment with a culvert underneath. The aqueduct was ready in 1809, although the canal as a whole was not opened until 1817. On it were floated the first iron barges to use any canal in England. At the level of the canal above, it is not obvious that an aqueduct is being crossed. The embankment remains in excellent condition, and the original baffles and overflow weir are still in situ.

13

When such a navigation weir was opened or 'drawn' it released a fierce torrent of water and boats travelling downstream relied upon this 'flash', as it was called, to carry them through the river reach below. Conversely, craft coming up stream had to be winched through the gap in the weir. Obviously the hazards and delays caused to navigation by such crude devices were very great. Nevertheless they continued in use in England for many centuries. It is believed that flash locks may have been introduced on the Thames as early as 1200, while they survived on the upper river between Oxford and Lechlade until 1898. Two 'watergates' survived in use on the Warwickshire Avon at Pershore and Cropthorne until the navigation of this river was restored in recent years by the Lower Avon Navigation Trust.

The kind of lock we know with its two sets of timber gates enclosing the water in a masonry chamber did not appear in England until 1567 when one was built on the Exeter Canal (a short lateral cut beside the river Exe) by John Trew of Glamorgan. It was properly called a 'pound lock' to distinguish it from the older flash lock, but, because early writers refer enigmatically to 'locks' or 'sluices' without making clear what they mean, it is often impossible to determine with certainty from documentary sources whether a particular river navigation was built with pound locks or flash locks. Only investigation on the site can determine this. In 1968-69 a team of three industrial archaeologists carried out a nationwide survey of flash locks which yielded the surprising total of seventy-three. The report of this survey, 'Flash locks on English Waterways', was published in *Industrial Archaeology* for August, 1969 and is a most valuable contribution to our knowledge of this subject.

With the pound lock a much greater fall could be overcome than was the case with the older flash lock and so by its use fast flowing rivers could be tamed for navigation. The Wey Navigation from the Thames at Weybridge to Guildford of which Sir Richard Weston was the engineer-undertaker was the most notable early example of a waterway of this kind. Built between 1651 and 1653, it included ten pound locks and four navigation weirs to overcome a fall of 86 ft. What is more significant is that out of a total length of fifteen miles, seven miles consisted of artificial cuts, made to straighten the tortuous course of the river. Weston had to build twelve new bridges to carry existing roads over these cuts, an expense which earlier engineers had been concerned to avoid.

The expansion of trade in the eighteenth century with its increasing demand for bulk water transport in a country virtually without metalled roads led to the promotion of a number of increasingly ambitious river navigation works on the model of Sir Richard Weston's Wey Navigation. The most notable of these were the Aire and Calder Navigation (1703), engineer John Hadley, the Kennet Navigation (1723), engineer John Hore, and the Calder and Hebble Navigation (1758), engineer John Smeaton. On the Kennet Navigation (now part of the Kennet and Avon Canal) between Reading and Newbury, John Hore modelled his pound locks on those built by Weston on the Wey. These did not have masonry chambers; instead the 'pounds' had sloping turf sides. Some of these old turf-sided locks still survive [Plate 8(c)] and have subsequently been fitted with guard rails to prevent boats settling on the banks as the lock empties. The turf-sided lock is extremely wasteful of water and it is significant that on the Calder and Hebble Navigation John Smeaton, the first man to describe himself as a civil engineer, built no less than twenty-six masonry-chambered locks to overcome a fall of 178 ft between Salterhebble and Wakefield. Although his work was seriously damaged by an unprecedented flood and was subsequently rebuilt by his protégé, William Jessop,

14

2.3

BRINDLEY'S ABUTMENTS – BRIDGE-WATER CANAL (*101/SJ 767977 — at Barton-upon-Irwell, next to the Barton swing aqueduct*). These masonry abutments are all that now remain of the first aqueduct in the British Isles, justly celebrated in canal history. Brindley's aqueduct over the Mersey and Irwell Navigation's channel and towpath was opened on 17 July 1761, and carried the Bridgewater canal 38 ft above the level of the lower channel on three arches of 63 ft span.

It seems likely that the Duke of Bridgewater's agent, John Gilbert, had some say in its design. The success of this canal, and especially of this aqueduct, was crucial to the development of the canal system. In 1893 the original aqueduct was demolished to make way for the Manchester Ship Canal. The impressive swing aqueduct designed by Sir E. Leader Williams now takes the old canal over the new, a few yards to the east of the original line. The end of this new line can be seen at the extreme right edge of the photograph.

Smeaton's Calder and Hebble Navigation represents the apogee of this form of construction. For the further extension of inland waterways, wholly artificial still-water canals were needed and they were not long in coming.

By bringing the advantage of cheap bulk transport to areas remote from river navigations, the canals had an immense effect on the impetus of Britain's Industrial Revolution. The work which ushered in the canal age was the Bridgewater Canal, opened from Worsley to Manchester in 1761 and subsequently extended to the Mersey at Runcorn. The original section included the first canal aqueduct in Britain, built to carry the canal over the river Irwell at Barton. When the Manchester Ship Canal was built in the 1890s, this original structure was replaced by the Barton swing aqueduct, but its abutments can still be seen [2.3].

The Bridgewater Canal is remarkable not only as a pioneer work but because its construction was financed entirely by one man – Francis Egerton, Duke of Bridgewater. In this the 'Canal Duke' was following in the tradition of earlier 'undertakers' such as Sir Richard Weston but with the difference that a canal was a far more costly work of civil engineering than any river navigation. It is estimated that the Duke expended the colossal sum (for those days) of £3M on his canal. Only a man of immense wealth and great courage could have staked so much on the success of what was, so far as this country was concerned, a completely novel undertaking. All subsequent canal construction was financed by joint stock companies headed by manufacturers like Josiah Wedgwood, the great potter, who stood to benefit from them. But such men were only prepared to put up their money when they were satisfied that the Duke's gamble was going to pay off. Hence, but for the Duke's enterprise, the dawn of the canal era in Britain might have been postponed for many years.

Men travelled from far and wide to see for themselves what the Duke and his engineer, James Brindley, were doing and, as a result, a number of canal companies had not only been formed but had completed their canals by the time the Bridgewater canal reached Runcorn. The first of these new canals were the Grand Trunk or Trent and Mersey from the Duke's canal at Preston Brook to the river Trent at Derwent Mouth, the Staffordshire and Worcestershire Canal [2.5] from the Grand Trunk to the river Severn, and the Birmingham Canal, which, by linking that city with the Staffs and Worcs near Wolverhampton, brought water transport to the heart of the Black Country. These three waterways formed the skeleton around which the present Midlands canal system soon grew – a dense network covering the industrial area round Birmingham with arms radiating from it to our four great rivers: Mersey, Trent, Severn and Thames.

It was natural that the promoters of these canals should seek guidance from the only man they considered qualified to provide it – the Duke's engineer, James Brindley. The idea of linking the four great rivers was Brindley's and the whole system was built by engineers of Brindley's school who, if they had not actually been trained by him, followed his principles and the standards he laid down.

The Bridgewater Canal, however, was not typical of the canals which followed it. Its course lay entirely in the valleys of the rivers Irwell and Mersey and was level throughout. The only locks on it were those at Runcorn which brought the canal down to the level of the tidal Mersey. It did not, like the other canals, link one river valley with another, crossing the high watershed between them. Thus it was not what is usually termed a summit level canal as is the canal from the Trent to the Mersey. The construction of a summit level canal not only involves much heavier civil engineering works in carrying it through upland country, it also creates difficult problems of water supply. Each boat as it crosses a summit level draws two locks full of water away from it, one as it ascends and another as it descends. Consequently the main water supply for such a canal must be fed into its summit level. To maintain an assured supply on a high watershed between two river basins is by no means easy. Large catchment reservoirs have to be constructed and in some cases it is necessary to pump water into the summit levels from underground springs which is a costly expedient.

The larger the lock size, the greater the consumption of water will be. With an assured water supply, the Bridgewater was constructed as a broad canal, its locks at Runcorn accepting barges 14 ft in beam and 70 ft in length. In order to save money in construction and to conserve water in working them, Brindley came to a fateful decision in determining a standard for subsequent canal construction. This was to reduce the size of their lock chambers to half that of the Bridgewater dimensions so that they would

2.4

FOXTON LOCK AND HOUSE (*133/SP 692898 – 3 miles north-west of Market Harborough*). The main line of the Grand Union canal passes through this lock, while the branch to Market Harborough leaves the line behind the camera position. The paddle-operating equipment on the gate is seen to be in order on the far gate, but missing on the near one. The raised bricks give purchase for the feet when pushing against the beam to swing the gate.

2.5

GAILEY TOP LOCK – HOUSE (*119/SJ 920103 – about ½-mile to the east of the Gailey roundabout on A5*). This unusual circular construction marks the top lock of the twelve taking the canal from its summit level down to its junction with the Trent and Mersey at Great Haywood. James Brindley set out the line of the navigation, while the actual engineering was done by his assistants Samuel Simcock and Thomas Dadford; the canal was opened in 1771. The lock is typical of Brindley, having a single top gate and paired bottom gates meeting in a vee.

accept boats 70 ft long but of only 7 ft beam. Thus the famous 'narrow boat' of the Midlands canal system was born. With a maximum payload of 30 tons (less if it is mechanically propelled) it was too small to be economically viable as a commercial transport vehicle. Consequently, despite the inherent advantages of water transport, commercial use of the narrow canal system that Brindley originated has virtually ceased in the last decade and working narrow boats are now only very rarely to be seen [Plate 2(b)].

Brindley's construction policy was to avoid heavy engineering works as far as possible by routing his canals along the natural contours. Consequently a typical

17

Brindley canal is extremely tortuous. Some lengths were subsequently straightened and shortened by a later generation of canal engineers and the best surviving example of a canal of the original type is the summit level of the Oxford Canal between Marston Doles and Claydon in Warwickshire. The straight line distance between these two points is little more than four miles, but the length of the canal is eleven miles. Yet there was method behind even this apparent madness, for Brindley always favoured a long summit level, arguing that it would itself act as a reservoir to conserve precious water.

Sooner or later Brindley would encounter some natural obstacle blocking his line of route which no amount of twisting and turning along the contours could avoid – a river valley to be crossed or a ridge of high ground to be pierced. In the former case he adopted the method used in the Irwell crossing at Barton, carrying the canal over the river in its bed of puddled clay on a series of squat brick arches. Typical Brindley aqueducts of this type are to be found at Great Haywood on the Staffordshire and Worcestershire Canal, at Brindley's Bank near Rugeley on the Trent and Mersey or, on the same canal, the aqueduct over the Dove near Burton-on-Trent.

When high ground was encountered, Brindley and the engineers of his school always preferred to tunnel rather than form deep cuttings, probably because the amount of soil to be excavated and handled was so much less. This is why, in the case of early canal tunnels, there is often comparatively little ground cover. Indeed one such tunnel on the Oxford Canal near Fenny Compton was subsequently opened out into a cutting which was referred to by later generations of working boatmen as 'the tunnel'. But undoubtedly the greatest early canal tunnelling feat was the driving of Harecastle Tunnel [Plate 2(d)] at Kidsgrove to the north of the Potteries. This carries the summit level of the Trent and Mersey Canal beneath the central 'spine' of England that here divides the upper valley of the Trent from the Cheshire plain. It is 2897 yards long and much of it had to be driven through hard rock. It took eleven years to build and Brindley did not live to see it completed. Like all early canal tunnels, its dimensions are extremely restricted, the width of the channel being 8 ft 6 in. and the height only 5 ft 10 in. This meant that boats could not pass each other and it was therefore a serious traffic 'bottle-neck'. Because there was no towing path, the boats had to be 'legged' through by men pushing with their feet against the tunnel walls while the boat horses were led over the top of the tunnel by a horse-path [2.6].

All these early canals of James Brindley and his school are built in the same simple and pleasing functional style and this applies to warehouses, lock cottages and over-bridges no less than to aqueducts and tunnel portals. Because most of them were situated in the English Midlands where good building stone was not locally available, brick was the material most commonly used for all structures. But wherever good local stone was obtainable it was used in the same simple, functional style as, for example, on the southern end of the Oxford canal.

John Smeaton's successor William Jessop was a great canal engineer whose career linked the Brindley generation with the last great canal engineers, John Rennie and Thomas Telford. In comparing the work of the first canal builders with those who followed them it is interesting to observe that a growing mastery of new engineering techniques was accompanied – indeed emphasized – by a conscious architectural style, a classical splendour that is in direct contrast to the functional simplicity that had gone before. Of this classical language John Rennie was a particularly eloquent exponent; his major canal works reveal an awareness of the vital national importance of canals as Britain's Industrial Revolution gathered momentum.

2.6
BOATHORSE LANE (*110/SJ 842532 – 1 mile south of Kidsgrove town centre*). This little road in the fields round Kidsgrove is so named because it is the route by which horses were led over Brindley's Harecastle Tunnel, which lacked a towpath. Such names live on long after their original purpose has been forgotten, and can sometimes provide a valuable clue to a site when all else may have been obliterated.

William Jessop was virtually Smeaton's adopted son and, along with his business as a consulting engineer, he inherited much of the prestige of England's first civil engineer. He was responsible for the construction of the Grand Junction Canal which provided a shorter route between the Midlands and London than that via the Oxford Canal and the Thames. He also built the Cromford Canal in Derbyshire and a number of other waterways in the East Midlands. At the height of his career there was scarcely a waterway project in the country about which he was not consulted. In two respects particularly Jessop was farsighted; he favoured broad waterways and he was always generous in his provision of adequate water supplies on the summit levels of his canals. Unlike many engineers before and since his day, Jessop was always quick to recognize talent and initiative in younger men and to encourage it regardless of his own reputation. In this respect he can be said to have launched both Rennie and Telford on their canal careers. It was on his recommendation that Rennie obtained his first major appointment as engineer to the Lancaster Canal, while as consulting engineer to the Ellesmere Canal Company Jessop gave Telford his wise and experienced guidance when the younger man was appointed 'engineer and agent' to that company. Yet he was content to remain in the background and to concede to Telford all the credit and acclaim which his great works on that canal received.

John Rennie's principal canal works, the Lancaster and the Kennet and Avon Canal, which linked the old Kennet Navigation to the river Avon at Bath, are chiefly remarkable for their magnificent stone aqueducts in the classical style spanning the Lune at Lancaster and the Avon at Limpley Stoke, near Bath – the Dundas Aqueduct [Plate 5(b)].

Plate 5(a)
DUNDAS BASIN (*166/ST 784626 – about 2 miles south-east of Bath*). This was a private basin, and shows several items of interest to the canal archaeologist. The crane and warehouse are typical canal installations, while in front of the wharf are the reed-covered remains of a sunken barge. On the hillside is a tollhouse, for this was the junction of the Kennet and Avon Canal with the Somerset Coal Canal, which locked up out of the basin to the left. Traces of this canal can still be made out in private gardens nearby, together with fragments of lock gates. Dundas aqueduct is behind the camera.

Plate 5(b)
DUNDAS AQUEDUCT (*166/ST 785626 – about 2 miles south-east of Bath*). This aqueduct, on the Kennet and Avon Canal, was designed by Rennie in the Roman Doric style, with twin pilasters flanking the semicircular 64 ft main span. Two 20 ft flood arches of parabolic shape are included. The entablature has a very deep cornice, probably designed to throw off rainwater to protect the masonry below (inferior stone used on sections of the canal at this end had caused concern during its making, and the north face of the aqueduct has suffered badly from weathering). The overall length is 150 ft, and the elegant structure was completed in 1800.

Plate 6(a)

COALPORT INCLINE – TOP BASIN (119/SJ 695028 – about 6 miles south of Wellington). The recently-excavated basins at the top of the 'Hay Incline' have been cleared as part of the development of the Ironbridge Gorge museum. The Shropshire Canal was a tub-boat canal running through very difficult country, and Telford himself regarded it as proof that a canal could be built over almost any ground. Although the craft carried only about five tons, the hilly nature of the line and the shortage of water for lockage made it vital to find an alternative means of transferring the tubs to different levels. As can be seen, instead of a leaky lock gate at the top, Reynolds designed the plane to start with a short reverse slope, over which the tubs were hauled. Special rails at the sides of the docks engaged with wheels on the cradle to keep the tub level over the sill. This system will be restored, so that it will be possible for the visitor to see the plane in action.

Plate 6(b)

ANDERTON LIFT (101/SJ 647753 – immediately north of Northwich). To avoid a flight of locks, with their time-consuming passage and loss of water, the Weaver Navigation was connected with the Trent and Mersey Canal by means of this massive lift – the canal is clearly seen in the trough at top right, and the river is below. Opened in 1875, the lift was originally hydraulically operated, each caisson (of wrought iron, 75 ft × 15 ft 6 in.) being supported by a ram 3 ft diameter, most of the effort required to raise a boat the 50 ft being derived from overfilling the top caisson relative to the bottom one (one was always at the top in those days when the other was at the bottom). Each tank full of water weighed about 252 tons, and the system worked well for twenty years, until scoring of the rams made replacement necessary. In 1907 the lift was reopened using the present electric power (with a 30 h.p. motor), most of the weight being counterbalanced by the cast iron weights working over the pulleys shown. The lift is still in use, and well worth a visit, for it is a good alternative to either the flight of perhaps ten locks, which would have been needed instead, or the troublesome trans-shipment of goods, which had been necessary before it was built.

But many lesser structures on these two waterways reveal that Rennie was a master of stone masonry work. At the Dundas Basin [Plate 5(a)] beside the aqueduct, the now defunct Somerset Coal Canal joined the Kennet and Avon and until its closure supplied the latter with most of its mineral traffic.

Unlike Jessop, if Rennie had a fault it was that he failed to provide adequate water supplies to the summit levels of his canals. The summit pound of the Kennet and Avon at Savernake is perilously short and has to be supplied with water pumped from a single inadequate reservoir at Wilton Water by two beam engines in a house beside the canal at Crofton [Plate 9(b)]. This water had to supply the canal for many miles to the westward including the great flight of twenty-nine wide locks at Devizes [2.7]. It was only supplemented by the unique canal pumping station at Claverton, near Bath [2.8 and 2.9] where a pair of beam pumps is driven through gearing by two large under-shot water-wheels powered by the waters of the Avon.

Rennie was also responsible for surveying the route of the Rochdale Canal, a broad waterway that crosses the Pennines to link Manchester with Smeaton's Calder and Hebble Navigation at Sowerby Bridge. This canal, too, has an extremely short summit level at Warland [2.10] reached by formidable ladders of locks. The Rochdale Canal is also notable for March Barn bridge [2.12], the earliest known example in England of skew bridge construction using winding courses, though the technique was introduced about ten years earlier in Ireland, by William Chapman. Earlier canal engineers had evaded this problem by diverting the course of either the canal or the road to secure a right-angled crossing.

The many forms of canal bridge to be found are alone worthy of detailed study. Where a canal crossed a road on the level, to avoid the expense of building road approach embankments engineers frequently provided wooden bridges of either lifting or swinging type, the latter turning on large ball bearings. Numerous examples of these picturesque types of movable bridge are still to be found [Plates 9(c) and (d)].

2.7

LOCK SILL, DEVIZES FLIGHT (*167/ST 981615 – 2 miles west of Devizes*). The magnificent flight of 29 locks at Caen Hill had large side ponds, and made a most impressive sight; unfortunately all are now derelict. The dereliction does, however, allow details of the locks to be seen, and the sill with the timbers against which the top gates closed is plainly visible. The large masonry blocks of which the base sill is made are the originals. The ground paddle frames are still in place.

2.8

CLAVERTON PUMPING STATION
(*166/ST 792643 – about 3 miles east of Bath*).
This is a most ingenious solution to the need
to supply the Kennet and Avon Navigation
with water, for water is pumped from the
river Avon by its own force. Unusually wide
and powerful undershot water-wheels are
arranged in a pair, and the rotation thus produced caused connecting rods to work two
beams, each attached to a bucket pump. The
two wheels are each 19 ft 4 in. diameter and
11 ft 6 in. wide. In this view the head race is
shown, the wheels being under the roof at the
side of the taller building.

2.9

CLAVERTON PUMPING STATION
INTERIOR (*166/ST 792643*). The wheel with
the double row of slots is the 16 ft diameter
cast-iron pit-wheel, its $12\frac{1}{2}$ in. broad rim
having 204 slots which contained wooden
mortice teeth. Just visible at the far end of the
pit-wheel is the cast-iron follower, 4 ft 10 in.
diameter with 64 teeth. The wheel alongside
the pit-wheel is the 15ft flywheel, with a 6 in.
rim. These wheels were set in motion by the
water-wheel on the other side of the wall on
the left, and connecting rods, from cranks at
each end of the flywheel/follower axle, can be
seen disappearing through the ceiling. Here
they are connected to cast-iron beams, which
in turn operate the pump rods. The sump
which supplies the bucket pumps, and in
which they stand, is fed from the head race.
Water is raised 53 ft to the canal, and the
pumps were first used in 1813. This pumping
station is one of the triumphs of the canal
system, and well worth a visit.

23

Plate 7(a)

BURNLEY EMBANKMENT (*95/SD 843321 – in the middle of Burnley*). Robert Whitworth was the engineer responsible for the impressive embankment which for three-quarters of a mile carries the water of the Leeds and Liverpool Canal 60 ft above the town of Burnley. From this level the industrial landscape is one of the most striking in Britain. Whitworth's original embankment, as opened in 1796, was 46 ft high, spoil from the deep cutting and short tunnel at Gannow beyond having provided most of the 345,000 cubic yards of material needed. Mining subsidences have since required the progressive raising of the embankment to its present height.

Plate 7(b)

CUTTING ON THE SHROPSHIRE UNION CANAL (*119/SJ 694316 – 2 miles south of Market Drayton*). Thomas Telford engineered what was then the Birmingham and Liverpool Junction canal when the menace of the railways was evident to the proprietors of most canals, and it is significant that this waterway cuts right across country, in what is still the most direct line between the two cities. Deep cuttings such as this one were required to maintain the direct line, and the contrast with the contour canals of Brindley is complete. Opened in 1835, the canal was Telford's last work; the bridge high across the steep cutting, its walls protected by lush vegetation, is a fitting monument to the later canal age and its engineers. Undoubtedly, Telford tended to employ too steep an angle of slope for his embankments and cuttings and to this day occasional slips of soil occur on this canal.

Plate 7(c)

COALPORT INCLINED PLANE (*119/SJ 694026 – about 6 miles south of Wellington*). This incline is one of three built on the Shropshire Canal, the engineer being William Reynolds helped by Jessop. The plane drops 207 ft in 350 yd, but terminates above the flood level of the river Severn. Under the bridge, a basin existed which was the start of a canal going rather less than a mile to Coalport through the famous china works. At the Coalport end was a complicated hoist system to trans-ship goods into Severn boats. The plane was opened in 1791, and two sets of rails were in use, with a cradle on each connected by chain. Four men operated the plane, which could pass six tubs in each direction per hour. Power was provided by a steam engine at the top of the incline. The site has now been cleared after lying derelict for many years. It will be restored, as will the canal through the china works, as part of the Ironbridge Gorge museum.

Plate 8(a)
BINGLEY FIVE-RISE LOCKS (*96/SE 108399 – about 3 miles east of Keighley*). The Leeds and Liverpool canal is a broad waterway traversing the Pennines, and so involves heavy lockage. At Bingley the locks are arranged in an unusual way, as a staircase – the top gate of one chamber acting as the bottom gate of the next above. The engineer of the canal was a Mr. Longbotham of Halifax, his route being resurveyed by James Brindley and Robert Whitworth. On the Yorkshire side the canal had to be lifted out of Airedale, and in sixteen miles there are three double locks and four staircases of three locks each, culminating in Bingley Five-rise, or Bingley Great Lock as it was originally called. The chambers at Bingley can take craft 62 ft long by 14 ft 3 in. beam, and when finished in 1777 the Great Lock must have seemed an almost miraculous achievement, for it is still one of the outstanding features of the entire canal system. The trouble with such a staircase is that although a boat going down takes only the water content of one lock chamber with it, an ascending boat must draw enough water from the summit to fill all five locks. This. great consumption of water was most serious when the canal was in intensive use before the coming of the railways.

Plate 8(c)
SHEFFIELD LOCK – KENNET NAVIGATION (*158/SU 649706 – about 3 miles south-west of Reading*). The Kennet Navigation was absorbed by the Kennet and Avon Canal Company. It is a good and accessible example of an improved river navigation, opened to traffic in 1723 with seven miles of river and eleven and a half of canal. Twenty locks raise the navigation a total of 134 ft. Since there was no difficulty about water supply on a river, the lock chambers were built of timber to about two feet above the lower water level, with sloping turf above that. Four locks of this early construction survive. Iron rails fend off passing boats, and the whole lock at Sheffield (called Shenfield by British Waterways) is a first-rate example of early constructional methods.

Plate 8(b)
FOXTON FLIGHT OF LOCKS (*133/SP 692896 – about 3 miles north-west of Market Harborough*). The Grand Union Canal between Nottingham and Norton Junction was originally four separate canals, and progress towards the south was halted at Debdale near Foxton from 1797 until 1810. The difficulty of the country to be passed was daunting, and both James Barnes and Thomas Telford submitted plans to link with the Grand Junction near Braunston. Benjamin Bevan reconciled the various lines which had been suggested, and decided on the present one, designing the greatest lock staircase in England – two staircases each of five locks. The total fall is 75 ft, and each lock has a side pond to minimize water consumption. Between the two staircases is a passing place, for it takes about ninety minutes to negotiate all ten locks. This is another outstanding example of canal engineering of the early nineteenth century.

2.10

SUMMIT, ROCHDALE CANAL (*101/SD 947188 – about 3 miles south of Todmorden*). The summit pound of the canal is only about a mile long and still watered, although much of the rest of this canal has been allowed to fall into decay. The typical shape of the lock house is seen. Beyond stand a brickworks and a quarry, both of which produced goods needing cheap and commodious carriage for their success.

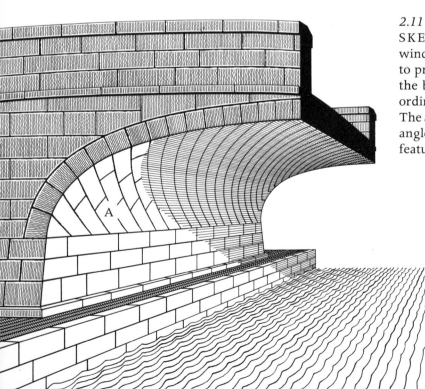

2.11

SKEW ARCH CONSTRUCTION. The winding courses of masonry (A) are designed to prevent lines of weakness occurring across the bridge's width, as would be the case if an ordinary bridge was to be built on the skew. The angle of wind of the courses varies with the angle made by the bridge relative to the feature crossed.

2.12

MARCH BARN BRIDGE (*101/SJ 886111 – ½-mile north-east of Castleton station*). The Rochdale Canal, engineered by William Crossley with William Jessop as consultant, was opened from Sowerby Bridge to Rochdale in 1798. The line south from Rochdale to Manchester was, however, not completed until 1804, although its March Barn bridge was built in 1797. This bridge has an importance which belies its nondescript appearance. It and the neighbouring Gorrel's bridge are both skew, making an angle of about sixty degrees with the canal. There is, however, a difference. Gorrel's bridge achieves the skew effect by the use of large blocks of masonry, while March Barn is probably the first example in England to have a true winding construction in its courses.

It was necessary for fixed bridges to span the towpath as well as the canal, otherwise the towline would have to be detached. On some canals, notably the Stratford, this was obviated by the so-called 'split bridge' consisting of two cast-iron cantilevers leaving a slot in the roadway through which the tow-rope could pass [*2.13*]. Again, where the towpath changed from one bank to the other it was necessary to provide a special 'turnover' bridge so that the horse could cross the canal without detaching the towline [*2.14*].

In order to overcome an unusually steep fall at Botterham, on the Staffordshire and Worcestershire Canal near Wombourne, Brindley designed an unusual form of lock with two successive chambers divided by a single intermediate gate. This type of lock is known as a 'riser'. When subsequently extended to include more than two chambers by later engineers, such a type of multiple lock became known as a 'staircase'. The best examples of this type are the staircase of five broad locks on the Leeds and Liverpool Canal known as Bingley Five Rise and the flight of narrow locks on the Grand Union Canal at Foxton, near Market Harborough, which consists of two five-lock staircases [Plates 8(a) and (b)].

27

Plate 9(a)
GUILLOTINE GATE – SHREWSBURY CANAL (*118/SJ 672133 – about 2 miles north-east of Wellington*). The long abandoned line of the Shrewsbury Canal from Wappenshall to Trench is only about a mile and a half long, but contains unique examples of lock gates of the guillotine type. In these narrow locks, the top gate is a single one of conventional type, but the lower gate is opened by raising it vertically – hence the name guillotine. Two distinct types of such gate survive at present, and this example is of the kind which was counterbalanced by a wooden box filled with stones slung over massive supporting timbers. The original winch (marked 'K A Mansell – Maker – Wellington'), gate, and counterweight box are clearly visible. This is a rare survivor of the early design as described by Telford, most others being converted to the operation shown in *2.21* and *2.22*. It was probably intended that guillotine gates should also be placed within the length of each lock, so as to allow for part only being filled if one tub boat alone was to pass, but there is no evidence that this was ever done. The locks are 71 ft long by 6 ft 7 in. wide, and would have taken three tubs at once, the tubs measuring 19 ft 9 in. by 6 ft 2 in.

Plate 9(b)
CROFTON PUMPING STATION (*167/SU 261623 – about 6 miles south-west of Hungerford*). It is sometimes necessary to pump water to the summit level of a canal to allow for that which leaves it through lockage. The summit level of the Kennet and Avon is short, which means that it acts as only a very small reservoir itself. The natural lake at Wilton Water is eight acres in extent, but 40 ft below summit level. Pumping was the obvious solution. An 1801 Boulton and Watt engine was purchased from the West India Dock Company, in 1802, but did not commence pumping until 1809. A second engine was operational in 1813. The earlier engine had a 36 in. bore and 8 ft stroke, while the later one had a 42 in. bore and the same stroke. Steam at $4\frac{1}{2}$ psi was supplied by two of three wagon-top boilers (the third being in reserve). Later, boilers of more modern design were supplied by the GWR works at Swindon, and are still in use, being preserved, including their engines, by a local society. The site is very well worth a visit.

Plate 9(c)
DRAWBRIDGE ON THE WELSH CANAL (*118/SJ 494354 – about 6 miles east of Ellesmere*). This drawbridge and others in the locality are typical of those which were once very numerous along this canal. They were cheap to erect as accommodation bridges, especially since they are only a few inches above the water level and thus need no approach embankments. Most of the bridge is counterbalanced by the weight high above the roadway, and it needs only a hard pull to lift it out of the way of a boat.

Plate 9(d)
SWING BRIDGE ON THE MACCLESFIELD CANAL (*110/SJ 917694 – 2 miles south of Macclesfield, at Fool's Nook*). This kind of bridge is more common than the drawbridge, and as can be seen, it allows for a crossing without approach embankments. The pivot is of cast iron, and only a relatively light push is needed to swing it out of the way of a boat.

Plates 10(a) and 10(b)

TRACE OF PENYDARREN TRAMWAY (*154/ST 083969 – 6 miles south of Merthyr Tydfil*). The trace of this famous tramway can be followed for almost all its original 9½ miles, from the old canal at Abercynon north along the valley towards Merthyr and the site of the Penydarren ironworks. Along much of the route one need dig only an inch or so under the covering soil and turf to find the stone sleeper blocks to which the track was spiked in characteristic early plateway fashion. The original masonry retaining wall shown in the plate is in remarkably good condition, and the level of the earthworks makes a very easy walk. Opened in 1802, the line had a gauge of 4 ft 2 in. and was engineered by George Overton to carry bar iron from the foundry down to the canal. It has a lasting place in railway history because it was the site for the first full experimental use of steam locomotive traction; on 13 February 1804 Richard Trevithick's second engine was given its initial test on this line. Trevithick had been employed in the foundry to erect a forge engine, and took the opportunity to design a locomotive which was made in the blacksmith's shop of the company's works. The single cylinder had a stroke of 4 ft 6 in. and a diameter of 8¼ in.; connection to the wheels was by a spur gear. The waste steam was put through the chimney, and while this could draw the fire to encourage free steaming, with so simple a boiler this was not necessary. At first trial the locomotive drew ten tons of iron at 5 m.p.h., and generally worked very well. Subsequently, though, she proved far too heavy for the plateway and the couplings, and had only a short life as a locomotive before being converted to a stationary engine for pumping.

Plate 10(c)

COALBROOKDALE TRACK AND WAGON (*119/SJ 668049 – on the museum site 5 miles south of Wellington*). Railways of cast iron were laid down in the factory here as early as 1767, making them among the very earliest in this country and the world. The 1767 track was an edge railway, for flanged-wheel vehicles, of approximately 3 ft 9 in. gauge. The angle-iron tramplate, of gauge about 2 ft 3 in. was introduced about 1793

2.13

KINGSWOOD JUNCTION (*131/SP 187708 – 9 miles north-east of Redditch*). Here, the southern section of the Stratford canal leaves the Warwick and Birmingham canal. An interesting feature of the canal is the use of cantilever bridges. These have a central opening about two inches wide through which the tow line could be passed. This, by avoiding the need to detach the line, made a towpath beneath the bridge unnecessary. Many rope marks in the cast-iron rails testify to heavy usage in years gone by, and strips of iron were added to reinforce some of the edge rails when these had been nearly worn through. The short branch linking the two canals was built by the Stratford, and includes one falling lock so that, under the Act authorising the junction, the Warwick and Birmingham received one lock of water from the Stratford for each boat that passed from one canal to the other.

2.14

TURNOVER BRIDGE, MACCLESFIELD CANAL (*110/SJ 925719 – at Gurnett, $1\frac{1}{2}$ miles south-east of Macclesfield*). Crossover bridges were needed whenever the towpath changed sides, so that the horses also could change sides without being unhitched. This pleasant bridge combines a turnover with an accommodation bridge, and is built of the local stone. The canal was opened in 1831, to the plans of Telford, although the engineer in charge was William Crossley. Another influence was also at work. The monumental nature of the stonework along the canal was no doubt partly due to the presence of excellent stone in nearby quarries, but it also owed something to the time that Crossley had spent as Rennie's assistant on the north end of the Lancaster canal.

2.15

HORSE BRIDGE, CROMFORD CANAL (*111/SK 359523 – 3 miles north of Belper*). This canal was engineered by William Jessop, with Benjamin Outram assisting, and opened in 1801. The need to get horses from one side to the other whenever the towing side was altered was overcome here by use of a swing-bridge just wide enough to take a horse. This bridge still exists; unfortunately, the impressive aqueduct which once stood a few yards away to the south has recently been demolished to make way for a wider road.

2.16

HORSE TUNNEL, MARPLE, PEAK FOREST CANAL (*101/SJ 963891 – in Marple itself*). The magnificent flight of locks going under Marple high street and down to the large aqueduct across the river Goyt has many features of interest. Where the canal passes under the road there is this unusual horse tunnel, just wide enough to allow a horse to pass through and follow the boat as it locked up or down the flight.

Occasionally, boat lifts, which might be either of inclined plane or vertical type, were used in place of locks to overcome abrupt and considerable changes of level. Boats were floated into metal caissons to be raised or lowered, thus saving both time and water. The only such lift of either type still in use today is the vertical lift at Anderton [Plate 6(b)] which transfers boats between Brindley's Trent and Mersey Canal and the river Weaver 50ft below.

In some hilly districts where water was short a special type of waterway known as a tub-boat canal was constructed. Tub boats were simply rectangular floating boxes, each loading about five tons, which were towed along in trains. This meant that the channel of a tub-boat canal could be narrower, shallower and more sharply curved than normal canals. No locks were used; instead, the tub boats were lowered and raised by means of inclined planes or, in some cases, by vertical lifts. A notable west country example of such a waterway is the Tavistock Canal with its 2540 yd tunnel at Morwelldown [Plates 4(b) and (c)]. Opened in 1817, its purpose was to convey ores from the local mines to Morwellham Quay on the Tamar for shipment. Although disused for almost a century, the canal has now become the head-race for a hydro-electric plant.

Although a number of tub-boat canals were built in the west country, the idea originated in Shropshire where the ironmaster William Reynolds built the first short

31

2.17
THE INCLINED PLANE at work in the 1870s. The two tracks are seen, with the cable on the right hand one leading to the cradle in the bottom basin. The covered entrance at the top of the incline is seen next to the engine house. The two walls half way up the incline are those of the railway bridge over the Coalport line below.

2.18, 2.19 and 2.20
WAPPENSHALL JUNCTION WARE-HOUSE (*119/SJ 664146 – 2 miles north of Wellington*). The Shrewsbury canal was an isolated waterway from its opening until 1835, when the Birmingham and Liverpool canal's Newport branch linked Wappenshall with its mainline at Norbury. This connection rapidly reduced the importance of the upper river Severn as a navigation, and trade along the Shrewsbury canal was much increased as the result. The canal was abandoned in 1944 and is at present a happy hunting ground for the

canal of this kind to supply his works at Ketley with coal and ironstone in 1788. It was the forerunner of the extensive tub-boat canal system of Shropshire which included several inclined planes. One of these, the Hay Plane which lowered boats 207 ft down to transhipment wharves beside the Severn at Coalport, has recently been cleared and excavated by industrial archaeologists associated with the Ironbridge Gorge Museum Trust project [Plates 6(a) and 7(c)].

When the Shrewsbury Canal was built to connect that city with the industrial district of Shropshire, a further inclined plane was built at Trench to link the tub-boat system with it. Opened in 1795, this did not finally go out of use until 1921.

32

industrial archaeologist, although it is being rapidly filled in. The canal has a fine half-mile tunnel near Shewsbury, and the very important aqueduct at Longdon-on-Tern, plus the guillotine locks. When the branch was opened a warehouse and a splendid masonry skew bridge were built at the junction [2.18 (above left)]. The warehouse is a good illustration of functional design. A barge could enter a spur of the canal beneath the building, and discharge its cargo directly onto internal wharves or up through the floor to road level above.

The end doors enabled goods to be hoisted from barges lying outside in the main canal basin. 2.19 (above left) shows the road-level floor of the warehouse, with simple hoist and two of the three trap-doors opening above the canal spur below. 2.20 (above) shows the view down through the central trap door to the wharf below, and although the canal is largely de-watered an excellent idea is gained of the very well-organized arrangements for cargo handling.

Although it is now derelict, the Shrewsbury Canal is of particular historic interest in several respects. It was intended to be used either by conventional narrow boats or by trains of tub boats. Its locks are unusual in having counterbalanced guillotine gates reminiscent of the old East Anglian staunches [2.21 and Plate 9(a)]. It also boasts the first considerable iron trough aqueduct in England which carries the canal over the Tern at Longdon [2.23 and Plate 4(a)].

All masonry aqueducts had to be capable of supporting and resisting the great weight of the canal in its puddled clay bed. This meant that they could not be built to any great height and that their side-walls tended to burst outwards. Jessop's aqueduct

33

2.21 and 2.22
GUILLOTINE GATE, SHREWSBURY CANAL (*118/SJ 674131 – ¼-mile south of the gate in Plate 9(a)*). This gate shows the modified operation introduced to almost all the locks on this canal. *2.21* shows the lower gate from below, with the winch on the left and the weight-pit on the right. The winch is marked 'K A Mansell – Wellington – Maker' and was used to wind up the gate, most of the weight being balanced by the counterweight. *2.22* shows the weight-pit in closer view, and large amounts of bramble had to be removed to show the nature of the pit. Until this is done the mechanism is puzzling. Very few of the locks along this canal still have enough of their gear to show how they worked, although one gate is to be re-erected on the Ironbridge Gorge Museum site.

at Lea Wood on the Cromford Canal and that carrying the Grand Junction Canal over the Ouse near Wolverton both failed in this way. Josiah Clowes, the engineer of the Shrewsbury Canal, built a conventional masonry aqueduct over the Tern which was almost immediately swept away by a great flood. Shortly after this, Clowes died and was succeeded by Thomas Telford who, in association with William Reynolds, conceived the idea of replacing it by an iron trough, using Clowes' original abutments.

Longdon aqueduct is a significant prototype, for its success was followed immediately by the design and construction of Telford's two great aqueducts carrying the Ellesmere Canal across the valleys of the Ceiriog and Dee on the Welsh Border. To outward appearance Chirk aqueduct over the Ceiriog is an orthodox masonry structure of unusual size. In fact, Telford used cast-iron plates to form a watertight bed for the canal and at the same time to act as a continuous cross-tie for the masonry side walls.

2.23
LONGDON-ON-TERN AQUEDUCT –
DETAIL (*118/SJ 618156 – 3½ miles north-west of Wellington*). The relative crudity of the ironwork is strikingly seen here from the towpath carried alongside the trough.

2.24
PONT CYSYLLTE AQUEDUCT (*117/SJ 271420 – 3½ miles east of Llangollen*). This view is from the boatman's eye level, and shows the small thickness of cast iron which is all that separates the boat from the waters of the Dee 127 ft below. It is awe-inspiring nowadays to cross this aqueduct; in 1805 when it was first opened, it must have seemed miraculous. The picture also shows clearly how relatively little material is needed to take the canal across this aqueduct. To carry the water in a masonry aqueduct would have been difficult, since the great weight of stone required would have made the high piers impossibly large in section.

35

Plate 11(a)
TEMPLE MEADS STATION, BRISTOL
(*156/ST 597725 – in centre of Bristol*). The
façade of the station faces Temple Gate, and
inside the old station the timber-roofed train
shed remains substantially as built by Isambard Kingdom Brunel; the first train ran to
London on 30 June 1841. At the Temple Gate
end of the building is the office block, then an
engine shed, then the train shed. The tracks
are 15 ft above ground level, and the span is
72 ft over four tracks, flanked by 20 ft aisles
containing the platforms. The roof has the
appearance of a hammerbeam type; in fact it
is of cantilever construction – this avoids the
side-thrust of an arched roof. The timbers are
of oak held together by wrought-iron straps.
This station is the most important surviving
from the early railway era, and the earliest
terminus in anything like its original condition anywhere in the country.

Plate 11(b)
MONKWEARMOUTH STATION (*78/NZ
396577 – in Sunderland*). Built by John Dobson
in 1848, the grand façade is impressive out of
all proportion to the station's very light
traffic; it seems to have been erected to commemorate the election to Parliament of George
Hudson, the 'railway king'. The classic orders
are used here very skilfully and rather more
lightly than in the same architect's Newcastle
Central Station of 1850. At Monkwearmouth,
one of the most handsome early stations still
in existence, the neo-Greek treatment has
tetrastyle unfluted Ionic portico and pediment, coupled pilasters at the outer angles,
and then very pleasing quadrant curves with
Doric columns. The station is now closed, and
it is to be sincerely hoped that it is not
wantonly demolished.

Plate 11(c)
BATTLE STATION (*184/TQ 755156 – on
the south-east outskirts of Battle*). This station,
by William Tress, is a masterpiece, and perhaps the best surviving example of wayside
gothic. Dating from 1852, it was possibly
built in the mediaeval style so beloved of the
Victorians because they associated Battle with
particular mediaeval happenings.

Plate 12(a)

NEWCASTLE BRIDGES (*78/NZ 252633 – linking Newcastle upon Tyne with Gateshead*). This view shows three of the bridges across the Tyne, the one in front being the High Level Bridge of Robert Stephenson, opened in 1849. The upper level carries three rail tracks on a deck laid over the top of six tied-in or bowstring arches, each of 125 ft span; a roadway is slung beneath them. This is the earliest example of the dual-purpose type of structure, and is also remarkable in that cast iron was used extensively in its construction. In 1847 a Stephenson bridge at Chester, built of cast iron, had collapsed, showing that cast iron was not a suitable material for long girders. The bow-and-string design avoids excessive tension in the members, and this, coupled with the short spans of carefully-cast massive beams, makes the bridge, 146 ft above the river, still entirely serviceable today.

Plate 12(b)

THE FORTH BRIDGE (*camera position 62/NT 136784 – 8 miles north-west of Edinburgh*). Preliminary works for a bridge across the Firth of Forth, to the design of Thomas Bouch, were already in progress when his Tay bridge collapsed. Needless to say, operations stopped at once, and Sir John Fowler and Benjamin Baker submitted designs for the present bridge. Fowler was responsible for the masonry approach viaducts and Baker for the main structure. The spans called for here were each 1710 ft – four times longer than those of the Britannia Bridge at Menai. Just as Stephenson had employed wrought iron for Menai on a scale new in its magnitude, so Baker decided to use steel in the grand manner to cross the Forth. Baker, who had been apprenticed at the Neath Abbey Ironworks, had plenty of practical experience in the handling of metal. He measured the wind velocity in the Firth as a maximum of 35 lb/sq ft, and designed the bridge to withstand 56 lb/sq ft. The increased size of the steel ingots available to the improved rolling mills allowed the production of large steel plates and sections of high tensile strength; without such steel, the design would have been impossible. The main towers are 343 ft high, and the cantilevers reach out 680 ft from the piers. The building took eight years, and when the bridge was opened on 4 March 1890 it was the largest bridge in the world. This bridge is an achievement of the first importance, marking the beginning of the age of steel, and demonstrating the full potential of this material.

Plate 12(c)

CORNWALL RAILWAY VIADUCT, LISKEARD (*186/SX 236639 – 1 mile west of Liskeard*). Work on this railway began in 1847 when the GWR stated that the South Devon Railway could not be extended beyond Plymouth, but progress was slow as capital was limited. The line was finally opened in 1859, with the completion of the Royal Albert Bridge over the Tamar. Many viaducts were needed, almost all of them having a wooden superstructure on masonry piers, which terminated 35 ft below rail level. Longitudinal timber beams were supported by a fan of four timbers radiating from the top of each pier. The piers have a constant separation of 66 ft, and the viaducts (although built from the best kyanised yellow pine) were very cheap to erect. Unfortunately, they were expensive to maintain, and replacement by masonry or iron structures started in the 1870s. This viaduct was one of the highest, 150 ft above the valley, and the original piers can still be seen very clearly against the later masonry. Similar piers, from Brunel's design, are to be seen alongside rebuilt viaducts in South Devon, notably at Ivybridge.

But it is the Pont Cysyllte aqueduct (1805) over the Dee, 1000 ft long and 127 ft high, that is undoubtedly Telford's masterpiece and the greatest single engineering work on Britain's waterways [*2.24* and Plate 3]. The waters of the canal are carried across the Vale of Llangollen in a cast-iron trough supported on towering stone piers. Here the full potential of the crude little prototype at Longdon has been magnificently realized. Quite apart from the huge scale of Pont Cysyllte, its workmanship is incomparably finer and there is one significant difference in design. Instead of mounting the towpath *beside* the trough as at Longdon, Telford now cantilevered it *over* the trough so as to allow the ratio between the width of the waterway and the width of the boat to be increased.

Although Pont Cysyllte remains unique in its magnitude, many other iron aqueducts were subsequently built on the canals. An iron trough replaced Jessop's defective masonry aqueduct over the Ouse at Wolverton. On the southern section of the Stratford Canal, completed in 1816, there are three iron aqueducts at Yarningale, Wootton Wawen and Bearley. The last-named, commonly known as the Edstone Aqueduct, although of no great height, is the second longest after Pont Cysyllte. Here, however, the towpath is carried beside the trough as at Longdon [*2.25*].

The Shrewsbury Canal influenced the future of canal construction in yet another respect. Although it has long since disappeared, as originally built, Berwick tunnel had a towpath running through it supported on a wooden framework. It is said to have been provided at the suggestion of William Reynolds, probably owing to the difficulty of 'legging' trains of tub boats through the tunnel. But because Telford felt that 'legging' was work fit only for beasts of burden, he provided towpaths, using a cast-

2.25

EDSTONE AQUEDUCT (*131/SP 674131 – 4 miles north of Stratford-on-Avon*). As can be seen from the detail of the towpath side of this aqueduct, the path is carried alongside the water and not over it – a surprising feature since the canal was opened as late as 1816. Although the aqueduct is not very high, it is in length second only to Pont Cysyllte, and exhibits quite a modern appearance. The Stratford canal had been authorized in 1793, and was started under the direction of Josiah Clowes, the northern section to Kingswood being finished in 1801. The southern section, including the Edstone aqueduct, has been restored and is now owned by the National Trust. William James was responsible for this section, which terminates in a flight of locks into the Avon. When the Alcester branch railway was built under the aqueduct, the canal was owned by the Great Western Railway, which installed a pipe and stop valve in the trough to feed their locomotives.

iron framework in his Ellesmere Canal tunnels at Ellesmere, Chirk and Whitehouses. He adopted the same arrangement when, much later in his career, he was asked to build a new and larger tunnel beside Brindley's old one at Harecastle [Plate 2(d)]. It speaks volumes for the progress of engineering technique during the canal age that this new tunnel was completed in less than three years (1825–27).

The new Harecastle tunnel was a long overdue improvement undertaken by the Trent and Mersey Canal Company in response to the threat of competition from the new railways. Hitherto they had felt too secure in their monopoly. This same threat was the spur behind the construction of England's last canals. The Macclesfield Canal, with its monumental masonry work, was built between 1826 and 1831 by William Crossley, a disciple of Rennie, to provide a shorter route between the Potteries and Manchester [*2.14*]. Similarly, the last of all the main lines of canal, Telford's Birmingham and Liverpool Junction Canal provided a new direct water route from the Black Country to the Mersey.

There are two cast-iron aqueducts on the B. & L. J. C., at Nantwich and over Telford's own Holyhead Road at Stretton [*2.26*], but what chiefly distinguishes this last canal are its earthworks. There are certainly very considerable earthworks on earlier canals. The great southern approach embankment to the Pont Cysyllte aqueduct, for example, or the splendid embankment raised by Robert Whitworth to carry the Leeds and Liverpool Canal high above the town of Burnley to provide, incidentally, one of the finest industrial townscapes in Britain [Plate 7(a)]. But the way in which high embankments alternate with deep cuttings [Plate 7(b)] makes Telford's last canal unique. Nothing

2.26

TELFORD AQUEDUCT (*119/SJ 873107 – 2½ miles west of the Gailey roundabout on A5*). This Aqueduct takes Telford's Birmingham and Liverpool Junction canal (now called the Shropshire Union canal) across the present Holyhead A5 road. This is not the same route as that surveyed by Telford between 1815 and 1817: his Holyhead road runs to the south of the present one. The canal was the last major navigation to be built, receiving its Act in 1826. The iron aqueduct is dated 1832, but the canal as a whole was not opened until 1835, six months after Telford's death. The aqueduct is in its original form, but extra brickwork has been added below the original abutments when the level of the road was lowered to provide greater headroom for road traffic.

could be in greater contrast to Brindley's old contour canals than the way this thin ribbon of water cuts straight and true as a sword blade across the grain of the landscape. Whereas on earlier canals, earthworks had been considered in isolation, here they were part of a sophisticated 'cut and fill' technique, a legacy of accumulated experience which the canal builders handed on to the railway engineers. The Birmingham and Liverpool Junction Canal was built in reply to George Stephenson's unsuccessful scheme for a railway along a similar route. It was the canal engineer's last victory.

FURTHER READING

BRACEGIRDLE, B. AND MILES, P. H. *Thomas Telford* (Newton Abbot: David and Charles, 1973)

EDWARDS, L. A. *The Inland Waterways of Great Britain and Ireland* (London: Imray, 1962)

HADFIELD, C. *British Canals* (Newton Abbott: David and Charles, 2nd ed. 1970)

HADFIELD, C. *The Canal Age* (Newton Abbot: David and Charles, 1968)

ROLT, L. T. C. *Inland Waterways of England* (London: Allen and Unwin, 2nd ed 1970)

ROLT, L. T. C. *Navigable Waterways* (London: Longmans, 1970)

WILLAN, T. S. *River Navigation in England 1600–1750* (London: Cass, reprinted 1964)

3. Railways

Charles E. Lee

For more than three and a half centuries railways have played their part in the industrial development of Great Britain, although it is only 140 years since they began to convey public passenger and goods traffic at a speed substantially greater than that provided by animal traction. As the interest of the industrial archaeologist is in structures rather than any particular type of vehicle, he has with railways a longer period to survey than might at first be realized.

The one common characteristic of the many forms of track which may be regarded as railways is that the combination of track and vehicle is self-steering. Our first certain knowledge of a self-steering road is provided by the rutways of ancient civilizations. In difficult country, grooves were sometimes cut into the native rock or the stone surface of a road to guide the wheels of vehicles along a safe path. Traces may be found in Greece, Malta, Italy, and in other parts of the Roman Empire. Very little is known of Roman rutways in Great Britain and it seems unlikely that their use was widespread. An example was uncovered and examined in 1901, and again in 1908, under the grounds of Abbeydore Railway Station in Hereford, when the ruts were found to be about 4 ft 6 in. apart. The ruts themselves averaged 8 in. in depth and 9 in. in width.

After the fall of the old Empires, there is a gap in our story. Road construction and maintenance were at a low ebb and even the use of the wheeled vehicle seems to have been severely limited. There is no evidence of continuity. The origin of railway track for the exclusive use of vehicles with flanged wheels is to be found in medieval Central European mining practice, where such tracks were confined to the interior workings of mines or to the immediate neighbourhood of an adit. The practical development of the railway as a more extended means of transport took place entirely in Great Britain, where it was associated mainly with the coal-mining industry and originated as a result of the first great boom in the coal trade at the beginning of the seventeenth century. The earliest known example is a coal railway in the neighbourhood of Nottingham built by Huntingdon Beaumont in 1604 but this was short-lived as the pits proved unprofitable. However, Beaumont was also active in Northumberland, where he joined with others in buying the remaining years of a lease at Cowpen and Bebside in 1605, and there built railways leading to the River Blyth.

Similar railways at Broseley, in the Shropshire coalfield, were built at the same period and formed the subject of complex legal proceedings in the Court of Star Chamber in 1606–08. However, the disturbed period in England during the contest between the King and Parliament was not an era of industrial development; nor were the uncertainties of the Protectorate likely to induce private expenditure on capital works. It seems fairly certain that it was the second half of the seventeenth century which witnessed the widespread adoption in the coalfields of railways, or 'wagonways' as they were called. Neither of the composite words 'railroad' nor 'railway' seems to have entered the language until very much later; the earliest known use of 'railway' is in 1756 and of 'railroad' in 1773.

3.1
TRAMWAY TUNNEL PORTAL, CHAPEL MILTON (*111/SK 059815 – in the grounds of the Publicity Department, Ferodo Ltd.; ½-mile north of Chapel-en-le-Frith*). This is the oldest tramway tunnel in the country. Part of the Peak Forest Tramway, it was engineered by Benjamin Outram and opened in 1796. The trace can still be followed for most of its 7-mile length, but the tunnel was blocked by road widening operations some years ago. The gate seen at the entrance was put there when the tunnel was used as a store, and the generally dilapidated appearance is unfortunate given the importance of this monument.

By the first half of the eighteenth century, the use of railways was spreading to other industries and to various parts of the country, including the South. The first such line of which a detailed description has survived is that at Prior Park, Bath, where a wagonway of 3 ft 9 in. gauge was built in 1731 by John Padmore of Bristol for Ralph Allen (1694–1764), to link Allen's Combe Down Quarries with the River Avon. Wagonways were recognized by Parliament as early as 1746 in Acts for repairing roads, which preserved the rights of owners or occupiers of collieries to make, repair, and use wagonways along or across such roads. Then, in 1758, Parliament went further by authorizing Charles Brandling, Lord of the Manor of Middleton, to establish binding voluntary agreements with occupiers of intervening properties for making a wagonway – 'such as is used for and about the Coal-works and Coal-mines in the Counties of Durham and Northumberland' – from Middleton Collieries to Leeds.

A typical description of the Newcastle wagonway is given by Gabriel Jars in *Voyages Metallurgiques* as a result of his visit to County Durham in 1765. He said that cross timbers of 4, 5, 6, and even 8 in. square were laid at 2 or 3 ft from one another and that upon these the two timber running rails were fixed with wooden pegs [*3.2a*]. The running rails were well squared, of about 6 or 7 in. breadth by 5 in. depth, and commonly placed at 4 ft distance from each other. As the cross timbers were described

3.2
TYPES OF TRACK – (a) Wooden track (early form) (b) Improved wooden track (c) Wooden rails from a culvert mine (d) Cast tram rail, Surrey Iron Railway (e) Losh and Stephenson's patent cast rail, 1816 (f) Stephenson's wrought iron rail, Liverpool & Manchester Railway.

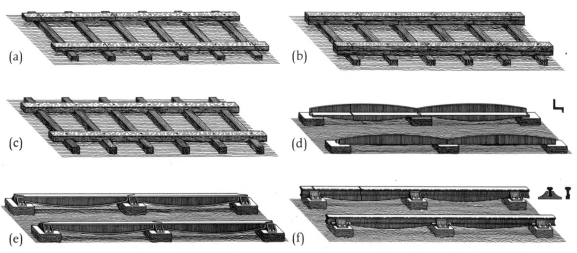

(a)

(b)

(c)

(d)

(e)

(f)

3.3

KEYS OF TWO TYPES (*149/TL 876411 – Sudbury station yard*). The keys which wedge the rails in position in the chairs have their own history of evolution, just as do more noticeable parts of the railway system. Here, side by side, are the earlier timber and the later steel versions. Such details as this are well worth noticing when looking at railways; so are the chairs in which the rails sit, for these often have cast into them their date of manufacture as well as other information.

as 'dormant' timbers they became known as sleepers, a term which was sufficiently well recognized to be used in a Chancery case of 1721. A subsequent development, to facilitate repairs, led to the fixing of an additional and more easily replaced wooden rail on top of the first [*3.2b*]. New construction on this principle enabled fir or pine to be used for the bottom rail, with a hardwood top rail of oak, beech, or sycamore to provide the wearing surface.

On curves and gradients strips of wrought iron (in Germany called *Reibeisen*) were fixed on top of the wooden rails, a practice said to have been introduced into England 'at least as early as 1716', but we have no contemporary evidence for the date. In a few cases, it appears that the whole surface of the rail was covered. The covering of existing oak rails with flat cast-iron plates, 5 ft long, 4 in. broad, and $1\frac{1}{4}$ in. thick, began at Coalbrookdale in 1767 [Plate 10(c)] but the practice was not widely copied. A few years later, an entirely different use of cast iron for rails was introduced by John Curr (1756–

3.4

TRAMWAY BRIDGE, ABERDARE (*154/ SN 997037 – in the middle of Aberdare*). This unremarkable-looking structure is probably the oldest cast-iron railway bridge in the world. The Llwydcoed tramway of 1811 has left sleepers at Aberdare in addition to this bridge across the Afon Cynon. Like the other two lines in the neighbourhood, it was an ironworks tramway associated with the Aber-

dare Canal. The tramway ran from the terminus of the canal to join with the Hirwaun-Abernant Tramroad at Llwydcoed 2 miles away; engineered by George Overton, the gauge was the usual 4 ft 2 in. This is a monument of considerable importance, and, although it seems to be little regarded locally, it deserves preservation.

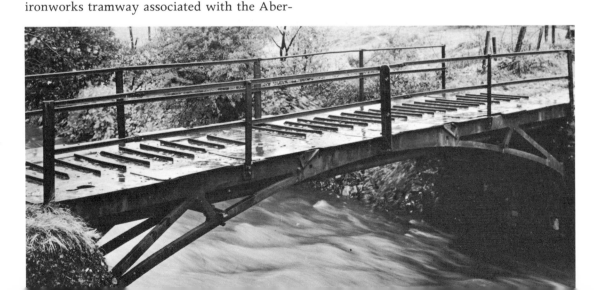

Plate 13(a)
THE TAY BRIDGE (*50/NO 395264 – 2 miles south of Dundee*). This view shows the remains of the piers of Bouch's original ill-fated structure (they are covered at high water) alongside the later bridge, which uses the trusses of the earlier one. Thomas Bouch designed the old bridge for the North British Railway, using wrought-iron lattice girder trusses supported on cast-iron columns with masonry bases. The bridge, opened in 1878, was over 2 miles long and was regarded as a triumph of engineering. Unfortunately, the 'high girders' in the centre (higher to allow ships to pass below), were swept away in a storm on 28 December 1879; bad design, poor construction, and little inspection, all combined with the weight of a train to lose 75 lives. Bouch had consulted Sir George Airey, the Astronomer Royal, as to the allowance to be made for wind pressure, and had been given a ridiculously low figure. Since the then regulations did not allow the use of steel for bridge construction, the replacement bridge (by W. H. Barlow and Son), utilized most of the trusses saved from the Bouch bridge (it was the cast columns which gave way). This viewpoint is a highly evocative one, and the site is well worth a visit.

Plate 13(c)
THE FESTINIOG RAILWAY (*116/SH 656414 – 1 mile north of Maentwrog*) is seen here on a mountainous stretch, showing the superb engineering of this exceptionally well-constructed line. Opened in 1836 to link the quarries of Blaneau Ffestiniog with the quays of Portmadoc, the line was converted to steam locomotion in 1863; passengers were carried from 1865 which was an unusual privilege for a gauge of only 1 ft 11½ in. The railway is now operated by the combined efforts of a voluntary society and the company, and opportunity should be taken to visit the line, for many original features of great interest are used rather than merely preserved – not least being the rolling stock and locomotives. The section shown in the picture is above the station at Tan-y-Bwlch, with the camera positioned on the west end of Garnedd Tunnel.

Plate 13(b)
MIDDLETON INCLINE ENGINE HOUSE (*111/SK 275552 – 3 miles south-west of Matlock*). Josias Jessop (1781–1826), who engineered the remarkable Cromford & High Peak Railway, did not live to see its completion in 1831. The 4 ft 8½ in. gauge fish-bellied edgeway, which spanned 34 miles of Derbyshire and rose to a summit height of 1226 ft, was designed not only to link the Cromford Canal in the east with the canal at Whaley Bridge in the west, but also to create a through route from Manchester to London. Steam locomotives were used as early as 1834, and passengers were carried until 1899. All the route is now closed, but the track, which can be followed without difficulty, provides a most impressive walk across the high plateau. There are many engineering features of interest, the most prominent being the great incline at Middleton. This is about three-quarters of a mile long and 400 ft high. The winding house shown in the picture is fortunately scheduled for preservation, and contains within its curiously polygonal exterior (reminiscent of the lock houses on the canal) the original 5 psi steam engine. Also still in place are the unusual signalling arrangements, like a ship's telegraph, by which the movement of the locomotive up the 1 in 9 gradient was controlled. This is a line which shows the great development of railway engineering by the beginning of the 1830s, and is strongly recommended for a visit. It is hoped that restoration may be attempted, possibly by a blend of official and voluntary work, for the way is unique in railway engineering.

Plate 13(d)
BARMOUTH VIADUCT (*116/SH 624149 – 1 mile south-east of Barmouth*). The coastal stretch of the Cambrian Railways was opened in 1867, and this massively-constructed timber viaduct spanning the estuary of the Mawddach is still in use. It is 800 ft long with an iron swing-opening span (replaced in 1899); this viaduct, designed by Thomas Savin, is a rarity, most other timber bridges having been replaced years ago. How long this particular example will survive is in doubt, for the line it carries is in danger of closure.

44

Plate 14(a)

WATER-TANK AND SEMAPHORE SIGNALS (*82/NX 974191 – ½-mile north of Whitehaven*). With the electrification of both locomotives and signalling, it is becoming rare to find semaphore signals and water tanks still existing in good order, such as these specimens at Whitehaven. Details of the arrangement of the signals and watering facilities are clear from this view.

Plate 14(b)

TABLET-CHANGING APPARATUS (*116/SH 629142 – at Morfa Mawddach Station, south of Barmouth*). Easily confused with mail-bag exchanging apparatus, this line-side equipment is actually for the exchange of the block tablet carried between signalling sections on single-line working. This apparatus is of standard GWR pattern.

Plate 14(c)

SIGNAL BOX INTERIOR (*111/SK 384556 – at South Wingfield Station, 6 miles south-east of Matlock*). Although the small station at South Wingfield is exquisitely built in lovely stone, it may not be long preserved. Its signal box was rendered superfluous by the electrification of the signalling out of Derby, and this photograph was made just after the box was superseded but before it was destroyed. All the instruments were in working order, and such a group will shortly be seen only within a museum.

Plate 14(d)

BOSTON LODGE LOCOMOTIVE WORKS (*116/SH 585379 – 1 mile east of Portmadoc*). This depot on the Festiniog Railway is substantially as it was in the 1860s, and is one of the few places where it is still possible to see steam locomotives being manufactured and serviced. Many pieces of early machinery are retained, making this an important location for those seeking an understanding of steam railway working. Members of the Festiniog Railway Society may get permission to visit the works.

Plate 14(e)

CRANE, SUDBURY STATION YARD (*149/TL 876411 – at Sudbury*). Typical of a great many small hand-operated cranes which existed in station yards in the days when a heavy goods traffic was still carried by the railways. This example is in good order, and unusual in that the jib is of timber.

Plate 14(f)

SLOTTED SIGNAL, BOSTON LODGE (*116/SH 583379 – 1 mile east of Portmadoc*). In some very early signals the arm slotted completely into the post to show 'clear'; in cold weather the arm sometimes froze into this position. The signal pictured is of slotted arm construction, and very unusual in that respect, but 'clear' is shown in the more modern way by lowering the arm rather than slotting it fully into the post.

3.5

THE CAUSEY (OR TANFIELD) ARCH of 103 ft span across the Houghwell Burn in County Durham. Built by Ralph Wood, a local master mason and completed in 1727, it is probably the oldest surviving railway bridge in the world. This contemporary print was made by Thomas Jameson, and appears to show the railway at work.

1823), in which angle-iron plates without longitudinal timber supports were laid on transverse wooden sleepers. The angle-iron provided a flange on the rail which guided flat-tyred vehicles that were capable of being used apart from the railway. Curr stated that he introduced such rails at the Sheffield Colliery in 1776 but that twelve years passed before they were much imitated. These were initially used underground and the first surface line on this principle was built in 1788.

During the last decade of the eighteenth century, stone began to be used for railway sleepers, possibly because the price of timber rose steeply as a result of the demands of the Napoleonic Wars. Also, independent edge-rails of cast iron were introduced at the same period; the most popular form of rail was about 3 ft long, shaped elliptically on the underside to reduce the risk of fracture, and known as the fish-bellied rail.

Both types of track had their advocates, but the angled plateway (or tramroad) made little progress in the North, with its long experience and extensive mileage of wagon-ways for flanged-wheeled vehicles. Tramroads were adopted more widely in the Midlands and the South, usually with stone sleeper blocks, although it would seem that very limited use was made of the road-rail facility. By far the most extensive adoption of flanged plates was in the South Wales area [*3.2d*]. Between 1800 and 1812 some 150 miles of line were built and the total was stated in 1824 to have exceeded 400 miles. Much of this was due to the successful advocacy of Benjamin Outram (1764–1805), the engineer who was the great proponent of flanged plateways.

Until the development of the railway as a public carrier by mechanical traction which, for practical purposes, began with the opening on 15 September 1830 of George

46

Stephenson's Liverpool & Manchester Railway, surviving traces are confined to the track, earthworks, bridges, tunnels, and wharves or staiths. In a few cases, also, remains may be found of winding engines and cranes. One of the most remarkable early wagonway bridges, and probably the oldest surviving 'railway' bridge in the world, is that known as the Causey Arch in County Durham [3.5], which spans the Houghwell Burn one mile north-east of Tanfield village. It is therefore sometimes called the Tanfield Arch, although an agreement in connection with its construction referred to it as Dawson's Bridge (after Thomas Dawson, a local freeholder). It was built by Ralph Wood, a local master mason, and the date 1727 (presumably that of completion) formed part of the inscription 'Ra. Wood, Mason, 1727' on a sundial built into one of the piers. Despite this date, it must have been in use somewhat earlier, as it was seen by Dr. William Stukeley in September 1725. The Causey Arch is a slightly flattened arch of 103 ft span built of freestone. It is 35 ft high from a baseline through the springing points to the underside of the arch and about 10 ft thence to the road surface. The road is about $22\frac{1}{2}$ ft wide and formerly accommodated a double-track timber railway of 4 ft gauge.

Although the Liverpool & Manchester Railway was the first to convey public passenger and goods traffic at a speed substantially greater than that provided by animal traction, it was the building of a link first to Birmingham and then on to London that provided the country with the earliest of its great trunk railways and established practices which influenced subsequent development throughout the remainder of the nineteenth century. This great trunk route was authorized by Parliament on 6 May 1833 in two portions, granted to separate companies. The Grand Junction Railway was to build the seventy-eight mile link between Warrington and Birmingham, which was viewed by the Manchester press as 'not merely a prudent and beneficial speculation to the parties engaged on it but as a great work of national importance'. This line was opened throughout on Tuesday, 4 July 1837. Important engineering works were comparatively few, with the one notable exception of the River Weaver viaduct, completed with ceremony on 9 December 1836 when it was announced that 'no life or limb had

3.6
BRITANNIA BRIDGE MEMORIAL AND BRIDGE (*106/SH 537712 – $\frac{1}{2}$-mile south-east of Llanfairpwllgwyngyll, Anglesey*). As with many of the major engineering schemes of the nineteenth century, the building of the Britannia Bridge brought its share of fatal accidents, partly the result of extending the techniques available into new advanced areas, and partly, no doubt, the result of human failings. This quiet church and graveyard just below the A5 on Anglesey has a memorial column to the victims, giving all their names and occupations. It stands as a fitting tribute to the men who used their hands to build the many railway and other engineering structures we take so much for granted nowadays.

3.7

ST PANCRAS STATION (*160/TQ 300832 – in London*). This station is remembered by most people for the impressive façade of what was the Midland Grand Hotel, designed in the Gothic style by Sir George Gilbert Scott in 1865, and fully opened in 1876. While the 565 ft frontage with the 270 ft clock tower was and is most impressive, the interior of the hotel (before it became mere office accommodation) was even more notable, having a dining room 100 ft long by 30 wide and 24 high and 400 sitting- and bedrooms. The grand staircase and the interminable dead-straight corridors stretching out from each landing still survive, although everything has been redecorated. This, however, is only part of the story, and not the most important. Behind the hotel lies the train shed, 689 ft long, 245 ft wide, and 100 ft high, a tribute to the design genius of William Henry Barlow. The platforms are 20 ft above the level of Euston Road, carried on cast-iron columns and girders strong enough to support a locomotive at any point, thus giving complete flexibility for track layout. The basement beneath, clearly seen in the photograph, was designed to house beer barrels from Burton, which were shipped in great quantities until the 1930s. After this traffic ceased in the early 1960s, the vaults were let for other purposes. The important point about the train shed is that the single span was erected with this platform floor as the ready-made tie for the roof, which does not require support from the side walls. Under Barlow's supervision R. M. Ordish arranged that each of the 25 ribs, of 55 ton weight, should be secured to its brock pier by anchor plates and 3 in. diameter tie rods below. This roof remains as an outstanding piece of engineering, and is certainly worth close inspection, as an impressive example of roofing a very large area without the use of columns.

been sacrificed'. Nevertheless, the actual construction of the line, carried out under Joseph Locke, was a task of considerable magnitude. It involved 100 excavations and embankments, in the formation of which 5 500 000 cubic yards of earth and stone had been cut and removed, 3 000 000 cubic yards of which had been employed in the embankments. The railway passed under a hundred bridges, two aqueducts, and through two tunnels. It passed over fifty bridges and five viaducts. The Post Office used the railway for mail carrying from the outset and the first Travelling Post Office was run between Birmingham and Liverpool on 6 January 1838. The T.P.O. was adopted as a permanent institution and in 1839 was equipped with apparatus for exchanging mail bags at speed.

As the first main line to serve the Metropolis, the London & Birmingham Railway attracted even greater eulogy. It was built by Robert Stephenson (1803–59) and completed in September 1838. Thomas Roscoe described it as 'unquestionably the greatest public work ever executed, either in ancient or modern times', and Arthur Freeling (in 1838) said: 'This is a Roman Work, conceived in a Roman spirit, and accomplished with Roman perseverance and determination'. In keeping with such exalted sentiment, the main stations were planned on the grand scale, and even tunnel portals received architectural treatment. The London terminus at Euston Grove, designed as 'The Gateway to the North', was placed in the hands of Philip Hardwick (1792–1870), one of the noted architects of the period and was approached through his massive and impressive portico or propylaeum, widely known as the 'Doric Arch'. This was demolished in November 1961. He was also responsible for the Euston Hotel, the first railway hotel in the world, which was opened in November 1839 and closed for demolition in May 1963. His son, Philip Charles Hardwick (1822–92), was responsible for the Great Hall, 'the largest railway waiting room in the British Isles', which was brought into public use on 27 May 1849. Of these impressive structures nothing remains, but the company's other terminus at Curzon Street, Birmingham, which was provided by Philip Hardwick with a three-storey building having massive pillars with Ionic capitals, survives.

Railway building has been claimed to contain a complete epitome of the architectural movements of nineteenth century England and, despite extensive demolition in recent years, remaining structures still justify the description. If we except the monumental gesture of the Euston portico, railway buildings of the nineteenth century were

3.8

WEST PORTAL, BOX TUNNEL (*156/ST 830689 – 5 miles north-east of Bath*). This tunnel, which is 308 yards short of two miles, was the longest of its time (1841), and was made on an incline of 1:100. At one period during its construction 4000 men and 300 horses laboured day and night, consuming an average of a ton of gunpowder and a ton of candles per week. The impressive façade owes its appearance to two factors. First, the bore was cut for broad-gauge working, and so, in any case, is larger than most tunnels. Second, this portal was clearly visible from the turnpike road, and the railway was anxious to impress the public with the good taste and grandeur of its construction (in spite of this, for some years nervous passengers posted over the hill rather than brave its depths). At present the sherry coloured Bath stone is badly weathered; it is to be hoped that means will be found to preserve this façade.

3.9

GREEN PARK STATION, BATH (*166/ST 746648 – in the centre of Bath*). Originally called Queen Square, this Midland Railway station was in use in 1870. It is now a car park, but enough is left to allow the full flavour of the nineteenth century to come through. Of Bath stone and with a single-span glass roof covering the tracks and timber platforms, the station still has the original booking-office fittings and superb public lavatories.

designed primarily to meet the basic requirements of firmness, utility, and pleasant appearance laid down by Vitruvius in *De Architectura* but the third desideratum was the one most easily ignored, particularly during the 1859–65 period of 'contractor's lines' when financial and economic considerations were paramount. Nevertheless, in a keenly competitive era, considerable importance was attached to the ability of a building to express the power and prestige of its owners. In urban areas it was often highly desirable, even when not essential, to exemplify the civic pride of the cities and towns in which stations were situated. An excellent extension of the last-named idea is to be found in the Ionic portico of Monkwearmouth Station [Plate 11(b)], built in 1848 to commemorate the election of George Hudson, the 'Railway King', as M.P. for Sunderland. It was designed by John Dobson (1785–1865) who was outstanding among railway architects. He did some of his best work in his own city of Newcastle upon Tyne where he was the architect, and Robert Stephenson the engineer, of the two-tier High Level Bridge over the River Tyne [Plate 12(a)] which was opened in 1849; also the year in which it was visited by Queen Victoria. Dobson was also the architect for Newcastle Central Station. This, however, although an outstanding achievement as built, is a modification of the architect's original conception.

Closely following the completion of the main line between London and Liverpool, trunk lines were developed between the Metropolis and the principal ports. The railway to Southampton was completed in May 1840; that to Brighton in September 1841;

50

and what became the main route to the European continent, the South Eastern Railway to Dover, in February 1844. Isambard Kingdom Brunel's 7-ft gauge line to the West reached Bristol in June 1841, was extended to Exeter in May 1844, and completed to Plymouth in May 1848. The last-named section introduced the first of Brunel's famous timber viaducts, of which eventually there were sixty-seven in the West of England, mostly in Cornwall, when that county had become readily accessible by means of another Brunel masterpiece, the famous Saltash Bridge across the River Tamar, formally inaugurated in May 1859 by the Prince Consort in whose honour it was named the Royal Albert Bridge [*3.10*]. Brunel's mastery of his material and gift of design enabled his timber viaducts to enrich the scenery of the many valleys bridged by his slender and graceful spans, whereas a less sensitive engineer, faced with the task of building railways across the undulating country of Devon and Cornwall, might have been remembered only as a despoiler of the landscape. The last of these viaducts carried traffic until July 1934 but some of their brick piers may still be seen alongside the replacing structures [*3.11* and Plate 12(c)]. Two such timber viaducts, built in 1855, survived in use over deep valleys near Aberdare, in South Wales, until September 1939, and were not dismantled until 1947.

3.10

ROYAL ALBERT BRIDGE (*187/SX 437585 – 3 miles north of Plymouth*). Brunel's extension of the broad gauge westwards into Cornwall was barred by the estuary of the River Tamar. Admiralty requirements made it necessary to build the bridge in wrought iron, to span 1100 ft at a height of 100 ft. Two main spans of 465 ft each were planned, requiring one pier in the water, which is 70 ft deep at high tide. Many difficulties were encountered, not least the lack of capital of the Cornwall Railway Company, which resulted in the bridge being made single-track only. The girders, in the form of tubes 12 ft 3 in. high by 16 ft 9 in. wide, were prefabricated ashore and floated into position when ready for hoisting. As each

weighs about 1000 tons, this was an undertaking of considerable significance in the history of civil engineering. The first was positioned in 1857, the second in 1858. As the width of the girders is the same as that of the bridge platform below, the chains hang vertically. They were made up from those originally manufactured for the Clifton suspension bridge, designed by Brunel in 1830 but, for lack of funds, not built until after his death. By the time the Saltash Bridge was opened in 1859, Brunel was so ill that he could not be present to superintend events. Broken by the difficulties engendered by his ship the *Great Eastern*, he died four months after Prince Albert opened the bridge in May.

Plate 15(a)
CLAPPER BRIDGE (*175/SX 648788 — at Postbridge, 8 miles south-west of Moreton-hampstead*). This (restored) bridge represents an early form of construction, in some cases dating from the thirteenth century. Such bridges usually indicate pack-horse crossing places, and the bridge in the picture carried the Plymouth to Moretonhampstead route over the East Dart. When wheeled traffic grew in importance and proper roads were made, wider bridges were needed; such a later bridge, built at the end of the eighteenth century, is seen in the background. There was a toll-gate nearby.

Plate 15(b)
PACK-HORSE BRIDGE (*91/SE 435806 — 1 mile south of Thirsk*). Pack-horse bridges were also made in more usual form, where large pieces of stone were not available for the clapper construction. This excellent example is typical of these bridges, recognized by their being narrow — too narrow for a cart but wide enough for a horse with panniers.

Plate 16(a)

TURNPIKE BRIDGE (*147/TL 236157 – 2 miles north of Welwyn Garden City*). The various turnpike trusts made bridges which have sometimes outlasted the line of their roads. This one, Lockleys old bridge built about 1834, carried the Hertford road from Welwyn some 200 yd north of the present line. The alignment of the old turnpike can easily be checked from the location of the bridge and the position of the nearby lodge, now marooned in the middle of a field well away from the modern road.

Plate 16(b)

METCALF BRIDGE (*101/SJ 982793 – 6 miles north-west of Macclesfield*). This bridge is on the present road, which still follows the earlier line of the turnpike from Macclesfield to Chapel-en-le-Frith for most of its route. Turnpike mileposts are still present here and there, and the bridge appears little altered from its original state. Bridges built by Metcalf tended to be of this small size, and few still survive.

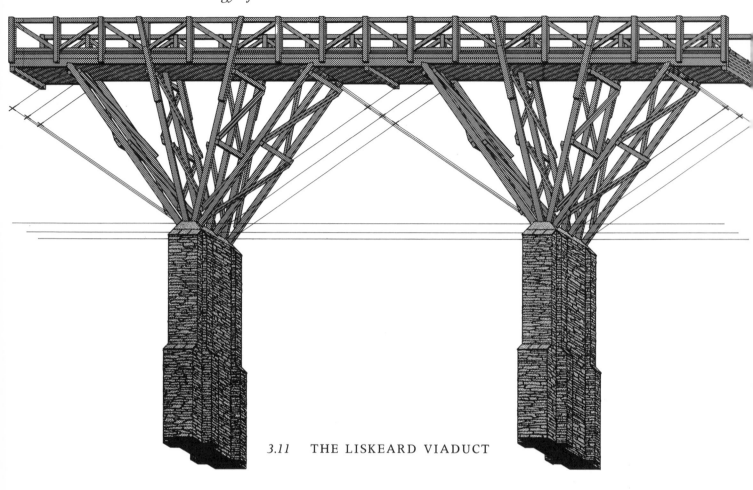

3.11   THE LISKEARD VIADUCT

Edinburgh and Glasgow were reached in February 1848, completing the West Coast route to these cities and both Perth and Dundee were linked with the main railway system later in the same year. The through Royal Mail rail route to Holyhead was opened in May 1848, with the exception of the Britannia Tubular Bridge over the Menai Straits [*3.13*], which Robert Stephenson completed in March 1850. Two other Stephenson achievements were the High Level Bridge at Newcastle (already mentioned) and the Royal Border Bridge, carrying the North Eastern Railway across the River Tweed at Berwick. The latter was opened by Queen Victoria in August 1850 and formed the last permanent link in the continuous line of East Coast railway between London and Edinburgh. By the end of 1850, when the country was preparing for the first Great Exhibition, the total route-mileage of public railway in Great Britain was 6084 miles (5133 miles in England and Wales, 951 miles in Scotland). In a speech at Newcastle, Robert Stephenson observed: 'It seems to me but as yesterday that I was engaged as an assistant in laying out the Stockton & Darlington Railway. Since then, the Liverpool & Manchester and a hundred other great works have sprung into existence. As I look back upon these stupendous undertakings, accomplished in so short a

3.12

SMALL TURNTABLE (*149/TL 876411 – Sudbury station yard*). Such small wagon-turntables were designed to allow maximum flexibility in movement of goods trucks, without need for a locomotive. In this yard, a whole series of such turntables is still to be found; originally they allowed access to the maltings across the public road. Provided the wagon was centrally placed, the turntable could be turned by hand on its large central bearing with surprisingly little effort. The wagon could then be barred along as required. In this age of large electric locomotives, such leisurely means of progress are almost only a memory, but many such small devices can be found abandoned on station yard sites throughout the country, helping to tell the story of the system at its height.

3.13

BRITANNIA BRIDGE (*106/SH 543707 – 2 miles west of Bangor*). Robert Stephenson had taken his railway along the coast of North Wales at the same time that he was designing his High Level Bridge across the Tyne, but when confronted with the estuary of the Conway and the Menai Strait he decided on a different technique from that used at Newcastle. For his Welsh bridges he employed a simple girder structure of wrought iron to form the rectangular tubes through which the tracks were run. This provided a means of spanning a wide distance at constant level. Pure suspension bridges are not suitable for heavy trains, and so his two designs (the tied arch and the plate girder) remained standard practice until the introduction of steel forty years later. Stephenson's faith in the solution tried at Conway led him to use the same arrangement, on a much larger scale, at Menai; the latter was opened in 1850. At Menai, the two approach spans of 230 ft each and the two main spans of 460 ft each represented a considerable advance, as earlier girders had not exceeded 35 ft. The three towers were built unnecessarily high because it was first mooted that suspension cables would be needed as well as the girders. The photograph was made in 1970, after the disastrous fire – the sag in the middle is not part of the original design.

3.14

LEVEL CROSSING, VALLEY, ANGLE-
SEY (*106/SH 293791 – 3 miles south-east
of Holyhead*). This level crossing, with the
wide gates, signal box of characteristic construction, timber filling between the metals,
semaphore signals, and station platforms just
in the background, is typical of those which
were once commonplace. With the closing of
many branch lines (which often had level
crossings on their lightly-used routes), and the
conversion of still-used level crossings to the
automatic type, such crossings as this will
become objects of pilgrimage for railway
historians in the future.

3.15

BUFFER LIGHTS, HERTFORD EAST
STATION (*147/TL 330129 – in Hertford*).
The original station here was built in 1843,
the present station replacing it in 1888. These
buffer stop lamps are electric, but the graceful
fluted iron columns on which they stand were
taken from the earlier station. Such small
items may often be found, even on busy
stations, and provide interesting information
about earlier details of design.

time, it seems as if we have realized in our generation the fabled powers of the magician's wand. Hills have been cut down and valleys filled up; and when these simple expedients have not sufficed high and magnificent viaducts have been raised and, if mountains stood in the way, tunnels of unexampled magnitude have pierced them through, bearing their triumphant attestation to the indomitable energy of the nation and the unrivalled skill of our artisans.' In these words Stephenson ably summarized the activities of the first twenty years of the Railway Era.

Railway mileage in Great Britain reached its peak in 1927 with 20 443 route-miles of which a total length of about 310 miles was in 1085 tunnels (excluding the London Underground). The longest was the Severn Tunnel (4 miles 628 yd) and in addition

3.16

FORTH BRIDGE DETAIL (*62/NT 135795 – in the middle of the Firth of Forth, 8 miles north-west of Edinburgh*). This photograph shows a detailed view of the base of the 343 ft high main tower. The great steel tubes were fabricated at Queensferry, where the contractors, Messrs Tancred Arrol, installed special equipment for rolling, planing, and multiple drilling. 54 160 tons of steel were used, including 4200 tons of rivets ($6\frac{1}{2}$ million), and the surface area of steel exposed for painting is 135 acres.

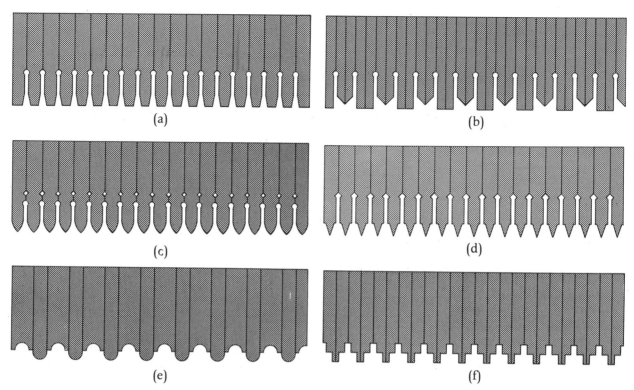

3.17
WOODEN EDGINGS TO PLATFORM AWNINGS (a) West Dulwich (b) Westbourne Park (c) Ipswich (d) Clapham (e) Lowestoft (f) South Kensington.

there were eleven tunnels over two miles long and a further forty-five over one mile long. Bridges totalled 62 244, of which 38 572 were underline bridges carrying the railway and 23 672 overline bridges. Extensive abandonment in recent years has reduced the total to about 13 000 miles, or some 500 miles less than the figure of 1871. The industrial archaeologist, therefore, has an extensive field for research among the abandoned traces of our heritage and its equipment, with lineside furniture such as water tanks, water troughs, gradient posts, mileposts, and signals [Plates 14(a) and 14(f)]. Abandoned stations include distinctive features in the varieties of wooden edgings to platform awnings [*3.17*], lamps, cast- and wrought-iron brackets (sometimes containing crests or company initials), and carved stone corbels [*3.15*]. Similar features of course abound in the older structures that are still in active service.

FURTHER READING

LEWIS, M. *Early Wooden Railways* (London: Routledge and Kegan Paul, 1970)

LLOYD, DAVID AND INSALL DONALD, *Railway Station Architecture* (Newton Abbot: David and Charles, 1968)

MARSHALL, C. F. DENDY, *A History of British Railways down to the Year 1830* (Oxford: Oxford University Press, New ed 1971)

MORGAN, B. *Railway Relics* (London: Ian Allen, 1969)

MORGAN, B. *Civil Engineering: Railways* (London: Longmans, 1971)

ROBBINS, MICHAEL, *Points and Signals: A Railway Historian at Work* (London: George Allen and Unwin, 1967)

SIMMONS, J. *The Railways of Britain* (London: Macmillan, 2nd ed 1968)

SNELL, J. B. *Mechanical Engineering: Railways* (London: Longmans, 1971)

4. Other Means of Communication

Anthony Ridley

ROADS

During the crucial middle years of the eighteenth century when British industrialization began to gather strength, the state of the nation's roads was a positive hindrance to progress. Many highways were little more than dirt tracks and even along major routes the surface was frequently unmade except for a narrow, raised causeway for horsemen. Mud, in which horses floundered and carts stuck fast, was a great impediment to the use of wheeled vehicles. Much of the kingdom's expanding trade continued to be carried by trains of pack-horses following immemorial trails and crossing rivers by bridges of such narrow proportions that surviving examples, like that at Thirsk near York, can easily be recognized [Plate 15(b)].

Roads were bad partly through lack of engineering skill and partly because of the archaic way in which their maintenance was organized. Until 1835 most roads were mended by forced labour exacted under a statute of 1555 that required each parish to muster its men once a year for six days' unpaid work on the highways. Little was achieved by the unwilling and often misdirected efforts of citizens resentful of a system which expected them to maintain roads for through traffic as well as local needs. Carriers paid not a penny for the damage their heavy carts caused to parish highways.

Tolls were introduced in an effort to find a fairer and more effective means for the upkeep of important roads. The first Turnpike Act, 'An Act for repairing the highways within the Counties of Hertford, Cambridge, and Huntingdon', was passed as early as 1663, but such fierce hostility was aroused that toll roads remained a rarity until the eighteenth century. In 1706, however, a new idea was tried for the management of the road between Fornhill in Bedfordshire and Stony Stratford in Buckinghamshire. Previous turnpikes had come under the jurisdiction of county justices, but now a trust of local landowners was set up to administer the tolls. The very people who might have been most influential in their opposition were included in the system. This was the break-through from which the turnpike era proper may be dated.

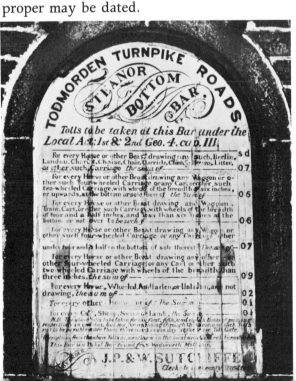

4.1
TOLL-BOARD, TODMORDEN (95/SD 945197 – 3 miles south Todmorden). Toll-houses with still-legible toll-boards are very rare nowadays. The board shown is on the two-storey toll-house at Steanor Bottom Bar. The toll-house itself is of unusual hexagonal shape, with semi-circular headed windows.

Plate 17(a)

CONWAY SUSPENSION BRIDGE (*107/ SH 785775 – by the side of Conway castle*). Telford designed this suspension bridge (which still has the original wrought-iron links in the chains) to carry his Holyhead road to Chester. The chains were hung immediately after the Menai chains had been put in place, by the same men and tackle. The span between towers is 327 ft, but the approach embankment across the sands is 2015 ft long and 300 ft broad at the base – a considerable engineering work. Since the tide runs strongly through the channel, a raft could not be used to float out the chains, so twelve 6½ in. ropes were used to support a timber platform on which the links were assembled in situ. The bridge was decorated in deference to its proximity to Conway castle; the toll house at the far end is particularly ornate. The bridge was opened on 1 July 1826. Alongside the suspension bridge, to the right of the picture, is Robert Stephenson's tubular railway bridge of 1848. Its two wrought-iron tubes were lifted into position as a trial run for the larger Britannia bridge. Each tube weighs more than 1000 tons, the spans being 400 ft. The roof and floor are of cellular construction, while the walls are of single plates with stiffening ribs.

Plate 17(b)

SMEATON'S BRIDGE, PERTH (*55/NO 121238 – across the Tay in Perth burgh*). John Smeaton's bridge was built 1766–71 and remains as a fine monument to this engineer, better remembered for his Eddystone lighthouse off Plymouth. The river is subject to sudden floods, and careful precautions were taken in making the foundations inside coffer dams.

Plate 18(a)
MENAI BRIDGE (*107/SH 557713 – 1 mile south-west of Bangor*). Surprisingly, the chains for this bridge were hung before those of the smaller Conway bridge. The original wrought-iron chains (which were treated in boiling linseed oil and stove-dried to resist moisture) have now all been replaced by steel links to the same pattern. The links were drilled by what we would now call a jig-drilling procedure to ensure accuracy in assembly. The masonry arches are themselves impressive, and would count as major works were they not overshadowed by the greater magnitude of the suspended span. The original railings still survive at the mainland side, as do two toll-gates [see *4.3*]. Inside the building covering the ends of the chains are some of the original blocks which were used to hoist the chains into position [see *4.12*]. The suspended span is 579 ft long, with a headway above high water mark of 100 ft. Chains of composite links were hung from the towers 50 ft above, and buried deep in rock at each end. The sixteen chains were hauled into position one at a time in 1825, and the bridge was opened on 30 January 1826, by the passage across it of the Mail coach.

Plate 18(c)
ATCHAM BRIDGE (*118/SJ 541093 – 3½ miles south-east of Shrewsbury*). The Holyhead road made use of some existing bridges where they were suitable, and this graceful bridge at Atcham was only superseded in 1929. Designed by John Gwynn of Shrewsbury the bridge was built 1769–71. John Gwynn also built Magdalen Bridge in Oxford.

Plate 18(b)
TELFORD TOLL-HOUSE (*106/SH 531715 – Llanfairpwllgwyngyll, on A5*). Telford designed standard toll-houses, mileposts, gates, and fencing for his road to Holyhead, and this toll-house is one of the relatively rare two-storey kind.

61

4.2

TELFORD TOLL-HOUSE (*61/NS 805596 –
3 miles north of Wishaw*). In 1801 Telford was
appointed to examine the communications of
the Highlands, and this led to the celebrated
reports and his work for the Commissioners
for Highland Roads and Bridges. Between
1803 and 1820 Telford designed 1117 bridges
and built over 920 miles of road, at a cost of
between £400 and £450 per mile. All Highland
and many Lowland counties have memorials
to his greatness, especially in his bridges. The
toll-house illustrated is to his standard pattern,
strongly reminiscent of his Holyhead road
design. The overhanging eaves, the bay with
central door, and the very thick walls are well
preserved in this house on the old Carlisle road.

Expanding industry will demand easier access to its markets. Since each new turnpike trust needed an authorizing Act of Parliament, it is possible to infer the onset of
industrialization from the steep rise in road legislation during the latter half of the
eighteenth century. Between 1750 and 1770 there were more than twice as many
Turnpike Acts as in the whole preceding fifty years and significantly the increased
rate of road building was most noticeable in the new manufacturing districts of the
Midlands.

Turnpikes proliferated because they showed results. The reduction in travelling
time between major cities as the toll network expanded tells its own story. In the 1750s
a stage-coach took ten days to reach Edinburgh from London; by the second decade of
the nineteenth century the same journey took under three. Eventually most major
highways were turnpiked, although minor roads continued under parish management.
By the late 1830s there were eleven hundred trusts controlling 22 000 miles of highway
– something like a sixth of all roads in the country.

Many relics of this vast system survive. Road-side toll-houses still reward observant
modern motorists with a glance into the past. There is, for instance, a pleasant two-
storey pike keeper's cottage beside the A5 in Anglesey and many others could be
instanced [Plate 18(b)]. Even toll-gates, though removed, were not always destroyed.
Some of Telford's original iron gates from the Holyhead road can still be seen in Wales.
Two are at Menai [*4.3*]; another is across a farm lane near Corwen. Further survivors
from the turnpike era are numerous milestones and even the occasional toll-board with
its list of tariffs intact [*4.1* and *4.5*]. As for the roads themselves, most lie beneath the

modern highways which replaced them. Despite widening and the adjustment of corners to suit motor traffic, the old routes are generally followed.

Turnpikes brought undoubted road improvements but there was another side to the story – especially in their ealier days they were plagued by inadequate management and poor engineering. Too many small trusts, each administering what was seldom more than a few miles of highway, maintained their own treasurers and surveyors out of incomes already much reduced by the systematic pilfering of their pike keepers. Once interest had been paid on money borrowed to inaugurate a trust, there was often little left for road maintenance. Road-users sometimes found themselves supporting a top-heavy administrative machine, seemingly unmindful of its primary function.

Even the money actually applied to road mending was too often wasted through technical ignorance. Until the nineteenth century most of the surveyors employed by turnpike trusts were men of little ability. Road drainage was scarcely considered, and the usual method of repair was to tip gravel onto the existing mud. The seemingly inexplicable meandering of many present day roads is at least partially due to the incompetence of surveyors with no knowledge of how to lay out a proper line. Highways were for long beneath the notice of trained engineers.

The first scientifically planned roads in Britain since the Roman occupation were the military highways of General George Wade. As part of his scheme for the pacification of the Highlands the General built, between 1726 and 1737, several hundred miles of what were at the time the only metalled roads in Scotland. Forty stone bridges were constructed, the best known being the splendid Aberfeldy Bridge in Perthshire [4.7].

4.3
TOLL-GATE, HOLYHEAD ROAD (*107/SH 557713 – at the mainland side of the Menai bridge*). Although Telford's standard toll-gate was made in relatively large numbers, few have survived. Apart from one at the entrance to a farm near Corwen, there are two at the mainland side of the Menai bridge. Their design is unique to this road, and the locking mechanism, which is very well designed, still functions perfectly. The substantial posts on which the gate is carried are an object lesson in such construction. The railings alongside the gate are also Telford's original pattern and construction.

KEEP CLEAR
NO PARKING

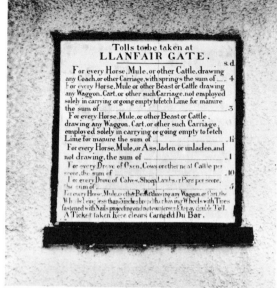

4.4

MILEPOST, HOLYHEAD ROAD (*118/SJ 466133 – on A5, 2 miles west of Shrewsbury*). Another design for the Holyhead road by Telford. Along the length of the road from St Albans to Holyhead many such mileposts are still to be found, despite the various road schemes which have been carried out. The specially-cast iron plates fixed into granite blocks have proved very long-lasting.

4.5

TOLL-BOARD, HOLYHEAD ROAD (*106/ SH 531715 – on A5 on the outskirts of Llanfairpwllgwyngyll*). On a Telford-designed two-storey toll-house, this board has been maintained in good condition. [See also *4.1*].

4.6

BATH ROADS MILEPOST (*156/ST 814671 – 1 mile south-west of Box*). The Bath Turnpike Trust had this typical pattern at its boundaries. John McAdam was surveyor to the Bristol Trust until his resignation in 1825, and was appointed to the Bath Trust the following year. A number of his sons and grandsons were involved in many of the Trusts in Somerset and the West Country. In the area around Bristol, within a radius of thirty miles, there are over 300 mileposts and 50 toll-houses; this large number is not typical of the country as a whole but mileposts and toll-houses are much more common than is usually supposed.

For the most part the routes followed were admirably direct, but the roads, running as they did through sparsely populated country, had little commercial value. Once their military function had been achieved, they stood virtually deserted for half a century.

One of the few civilian road builders of ability active in the eighteenth century was the remarkable Yorkshireman, 'Blind Jack of Knaresborough', John Metcalf. Metcalf was born in 1717 and blinded by smallpox at the age of six. Despite this disability he grew up strong and active. He rode, fished, swam, boxed and wrestled, besides knowing the country so well around his native town that he could act as guide to sighted people. During the rebellion of 1745 he even joined the army – fighting at the decisive battle of Culloden. Metcalf's road making career began in 1765, when he succeeded in winning a contract to construct three miles of the new turnpike from Harrogate to

4.7

GENERAL WADE'S BRIDGE, ABER-FELDY (*48/NN 851493 – in Aberfeldy*). The roads engineered by General Wade between 1726–37 totalled about 250 miles in length, and included forty bridges. As part of a scheme for the pacification of the Highlands, five hundred soldiers built the great road from Crieff to Aberfeldy and on to Fort Augustus, and another from Dunkeld to Inverness and on to Fort William. Of the many bridges which remain from this activity, the bridge of five arches at Aberfeldy, completed in 1733, is Wade's greatest monument. 300 ft long and still in use, this fine-looking structure was almost certainly designed at least partly by William Adam. Wade himself recorded that 'the best architect in Scotland was employed and master masons and carpenters sent from ye northern Countys of England'. The plans of the bridge are to be found in Adam's *Vitruvius Scoticus*, so that the usual attribution to Wade alone is not correct.

4.8

RENNIE'S THAMES STREET ARCH, LONDON BRIDGE (*160/TQ 328807 – Upper Thames Street, London E.C.4*). The main span of London Bridge, recently removed to make way for a wider version, had five main arches plus another crossing Thames Street, and a number of concealed approach spans. The bridge was designed by John Rennie in 1820, but construction was carried out after his death by his son, and completed in 1830. Rennie's design for the bridge can be seen embodied in the Thames Street arch, where the entablature is in its original form. On the bridge proper overhanging granite corbels were added at the beginning of this century to increase the width. Rennie was overshadowed by such giants as Telford, but was responsible for a large number of first-rate works, and deserves to be better remembered than he usually is.

Boroughbridge. So superior was his stretch of road that fresh work came pouring in. Altogether he built about 180 miles of road, mostly in Yorkshire and Lancashire but also extending into Derbyshire and Cheshire. An existing Metcalf road-bridge is illustrated [Plate 16(b)].

John Metcalf, though of outstanding talent, was of humble origin. He could take on work which would have demeaned a more highly qualified individual. Until Telford and McAdam made road building respectable, bridges were the engineering fraternity's almost only contribution to the turnpike system. The great John Rennie (1761–1821) was typical of his profession. His canal work extended internal communications considerably, but his interest in roads was limited to carrying them over rivers. Rennie was the first modern designer to contrive a single-arch bridge without resorting to the then traditional 'hump back'. Vehicles were able to cross his minor bridges without a sickening rise and fall. However, Rennie's chief fame lies in the beauty of his major creations. Although his masterpiece, London's old Waterloo Bridge, was demolished during the 1930s, the architecturally similar bridge at Kelso can still be seen in all its elegance. Another of Rennie's designs, London Bridge, has recently been dismantled and reassembled in the U.S.A. but the Thames Street approach arch survives in its original position [4.8].

The dominant figures in the history of British roads are undoubtedly those of the Scots, Thomas Telford (1757–1834) and John Loudon McAdam (1756–1836). Between them these two men of very different type transformed the turnpike system to such an extent that by the 1840s the United Kingdom's highways were the envy of Europe.

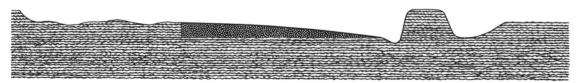

4.9 UNIMPROVED OLD ROAD

4.10

DUNKELD BRIDGE (*49/NO 027425 – in the centre of Dunkeld*). This bridge is one of Telford's outstanding monuments, and although different from his other major bridges at Spean-bridge, Bonar, and Tongland, with them it forms part of a coherent pattern of great attraction. Telford's early work as a mason shows to great advantage in this series of bridges. The Dunkeld bridge dates from 1809.

Telford was an engineer of genius. Before him others had begun to build in iron but he was the first to exploit its potential to the full. His superb road-bridge at Menai in North Wales used the metal to an unprecedented extent. Bridges, however, depend for their value on a good system of linking roads. Alone amongst his professional colleagues Telford saw highways and bridges as of equal value. He was the first great engineer to undertake road building on a massive scale, and well deserves the punning title of 'Colossus of Roads' awarded him by his friend the poet Robert Southey.

After working for some years as a stonemason, the young Telford won his first significant position in 1786 when he was chosen as County Surveyor for Shropshire. While in this post he drew up plans for several buildings but more important he designed his first bridge, a red, sandstone structure which, though much modified for motor traffic, still carries the Holyhead road over the Severn near the village of Montford. Telford's road building career may be dated, however, from 1803 when he was appointed surveyor and engineer to the newly created Commission for Highland Roads and Bridges. During the next eighteen years his workmen created 920 miles of new road for Scotland and, despite the difficulties of isolation and terrain, set a new standard of perfection in surfacing. As part of this great work Telford built the amazing total of over a thousand bridges – some mere culverts, but others huge spans of iron or masonry. Many of these bridges survive to this day as visible evidence of Telford's skill and activity as the pioneer road engineer. The Tay crossing at Dunkeld is thought by many to be the most imposing of his Scottish bridges [*4.10*].

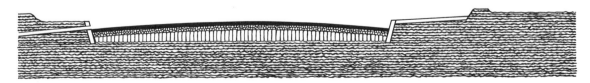

4.11   IMPROVED ROAD BY TELFORD

Plate 19(a)

BUSH'S WAREHOUSE, BRISTOL (*155/ST 586724 – Prince Street, Bristol*). Although the details are not certainly known, it seems likely that the warehouse dates from about 1838 and was designed by R. S. Pope. Originally a tea warehouse, the building became a granary and then a tobacco bond, but it is now empty and in some danger of demolition. The basement is vaulted and supports cast-iron columns and timber beams. This building is the most impressive of all Bristol's warehouses, and is seen in the picture across the dock from Prince's wharf.

Plate 19(b)

ST KATHARINE'S DOCK, LONDON (*160/ TQ 340805 – by the Tower of London*). The old hospital of St Katharine and 1250 houses were demolished to make way for this dock, which covers an area of 27 acres. Thomas Telford was appointed engineer and the site became available in May 1826 – just after the Menai bridge was finished. Only 10 acres could be used for water, and this forced the abandonment of the rectangular shape which Jessop and Rennie had used nearby. Two Boulton and Watt engines were installed to recover water lost in lockage, and with the two basins arranged as they were, either could be scoured without affecting the other. In the design of the warehouses Telford was assisted by Philip Hardwick, later to achieve fame as the designer of the Euston portico. The docks were completed in October 1828, after only two and a half years of work. [See also *4.21* and *4.22* and Plate 21(d)].

Plate 20(a)
HEAVY DUTY CRANE, BRISTOL (*155/ST 584722 – Prince's wharf, Bristol*). This 'Fairbairn' steam crane was built by Stothert and Pitt in about 1875, and is still in occasional use. The special build of the jib enabled heavy loads to be lifted from large-sided vessels. The radius is 35 ft, the height is 40 ft, and the lift is 35 tons.

Plate 20(b)
NAVIGATION LIGHTS, HARWICH (*150/TM 308253 – just offshore at Dovercourt*). The provision of navigation lights for docks was as important as the completion of the other harbour works, but few have survived in unchanged form. The lights shown marked the approach by the old channel, which has now been superseded. With the extension of the Great Eastern Railway's powers to include operation of its own steamers from the Town Quay in Harwich in 1863, the town recovered from its torpor. Frequent services to Antwerp and the Hook of Holland with luxurious vessels and fast rail connections attracted heavy traffic; vast amounts of freight are still carried. Train ferries to Zeebrugge were introduced in 1924, while Parkestone Quay was developed from 1874 to provide excellent deep-water facilities.

Plate 20(c)
HEAVY DUTY CRANE, DUNDEE (*50/NO 410303 – Dundee dock*). A detail of the steam crane shown on the left of *4.27*. This massive piece of equipment, which is still in occasional use, was designed to lift 90 tons. Built by Taylor and Co of Birkenhead in 1874, it is a very impressive example of dockside engineering.

Plate 20(d)
ALBERT DOCK CRANE (*100/SJ 341989 – in the centre of Liverpool docks*). The small cast-iron wall cranes which were widely installed in Victorian times were almost invariably manually operated. Mounted on swivels, and often in recesses on a wall, they could handle relatively light loads only; this was no great disadvantage in the days of small ships, but with the advent of larger iron vessels came the need for the tall dockside cranes with which we are now more familiar.

4.12
PULLEY BLOCKS USED IN THE BUILD-
ING OF THE MENAI BRIDGE (*107/SH
557712 – in the building beneath the cables at
the mainland side of the bridge*). The chains of
the bridge are supported by a wall, against
which stand some of the original pulley blocks
used in the erection of both this bridge and
the Conway suspension bridge.

Telford's other great road building enterprise was the opening up of the Holyhead
road, which despite its strategic importance as the link between London and Ireland
was almost impassable in the Welsh mountains. Knowing the road as he did from his
days as Shropshire Surveyor, Telford was the natural choice as engineer, when in 1815
the Irish M.P.s secured the formation of a Board of Parliamentary Commissioners to
take charge of the highway's improvement.

The 150-mile London to Shrewsbury stretch, administered with reasonable efficiency
by seventeen trusts, was left in the hands of the existing authorities under the supervision of one of Telford's deputies. Within a few years an already generally acceptable
road was transformed into a super-highway by a judicious blend of re-surfacing,
gradient smoothing, corner rounding, and bridge modification. One of the most wel-
comed improvements near the London end was at the Archway cutting in Highgate,
where a slippery nightmare of a hill, which had claimed more horses killed than any
comparable length of road in the country, was tamed by re-surfacing.

The Welsh section presented a far greater challenge. Toll revenues had never been
sufficient for the seven trusts controlling the highway between Shrewsbury and Holyhead to make more than nominal repairs. The road was so bad that complete re-building
rather than mere improvement was required. On Telford's request the Commission
bought out all the local trusts and assumed direct control. Unencumbered by petty
officialdom Telford set himself high standards. Nowhere in that mountainous country
was the gradient of the road to exceed 1 in 20. One hundred and fifty years later the
modern motorist sweeping effortlessly along what is now called the A5 can still testify
to the engineer's success.

The Holyhead road and the related road from Chester to Bangor built at the same
time have bequeathed more than well planned routes to posterity. At Menai and at
Conway formidable natural obstacles were conquered by two of Britain's earliest
sizeable suspension bridges. The Menai Bridge [Plate 18(a)] with a suspended central
span of 579 ft was far longer than anything previously attempted, while the 327 ft span at
Conway was a great achievement in its own right [Plate 17(a)]. Both bridges were opened
to traffic in 1826 and have survived to the present day.

One reason for Telford's success as a highway engineer was his skill in surveying a
route. Another was the attention he paid to the actual fabric of his roads [*4.11*]. A
foundation was formed on the levelled earth by setting in a course of large stones which
were graduated in height to impart a camber to the finished way. Next came a 7 in.

70

layer of stones broken to about the size of walnuts. A top dressing of gravel finished the construction, but the road was actually perfected by the passage of traffic. Iron-bound wheels ground the top stones together, breaking off tiny fragments. This dust mixed with rainwater and worked its way into the spaces between stones, so that the road surface became cemented into a virtually waterproof mass. The camber was now sufficient to cause further rain to run off into the side ditches, leaving the soil beneath the highway dry and firm.

Telford's contemporary, McAdam, had no pretensions to engineering greatness. He was more a mender of existing roads than a builder of new highways. His fame rested on the championship of the cheap but highly effective method of surfacing which was called after him. Macadamized roads have now passed into history but his memory is still enshrined in the abbreviated word 'tarmac'.

4.13
CLIFTON SUSPENSION BRIDGE (*155/ ST 565731 – across the Avon gorge to the west of the city centre*). This famous road bridge was designed by I. K. Brunel in 1829–31, in response to open competition. Work was started in 1836 but ceased in 1840 for lack of funds. In 1861, after Brunel's death, work was restarted, and the bridge was opened in 1864.

McAdam's chance to translate his theories into reality came in 1816, when after years of propaganda he was appointed surveyor to the large turnpike trust around Bristol. Within three years he produced a dramatic improvement in the roads under his direction, while at the same time actually reducing the cost of repair. His methods began to attract general attention and his services were eagerly sought by many trusts. It was the application of McAdam's system to the main roads of Britain which for the first time gave the country an adequate network of reliable highways.

The magic which made McAdam's method of construction more acceptable than Telford's was the far lower cost. Both men agreed on the necessity of a properly cambered surface and good drainage; they differed on the need for foundations. McAdam saved money by completely omitting the footing of large stones. Instead, three courses of broken rock were spread one on top of the other with the bottom layer resting directly on the unaided earth. The road was soon compacted by traffic into a waterproof mass some ten inches thick, below which the soil remained dry and unyielding [*4.14*].

4.14
ROAD SECTIONS – McADAM, TEL-FORD, and M1 (*in the Science Museum*). When a road made by an early engineer such as Telford or McAdam is dug up, an opportunity may occur for an inspection of their method of construction. Much of the length of the A5 Holyhead road, for example, has the original construction underneath later surfaces. On the left McAdam's method of building of about 1816 is shown; the whole foundations were cambered and not flat as with Telford. Two 4 in. layers of broken stone were laid on the camber, each stone passing a 3 in. ring. On top of this a 2 in. layer of 1 in. stones was consolidated first by ramming, and later by traffic. Attrition of the stones provided filling for the interstices.

In the middle Telford's method of 1806 is shown. He started with a level bed, and made drains every 100 yd [see *4.11*]. A 7 in. layer of large stones was packed by hand on the subsoil, and fine chippings were used to fill the interstices. This foundation was covered with stones small enough to pass through a $2\frac{1}{2}$ in. ring; first a 4 in. layer was built up, then a 2 in. layer. All the layers were cambered, and the sides of the road were filled with gravel and broken stones. A binding layer of gravel $1\frac{1}{2}$ in. thick was then added, and the road was left for consolidation by the iron wheels of the traffic.

The M1 construction is shown on the right. Where necessary the subsoil was stabilised, then a 6 in. stratum of lean dry concrete was laid, followed by a 7 in. deep layer of rolled concrete. On top of this a 3 in. thickness of asphalt mixture was covered with a rolled depth of $2\frac{1}{2}$ in. of asphalt/65% stone. The final wearing course was $1\frac{1}{2}$ in. of asphalt containing 30% of stone. Modern rubber tyres require such a surface, since the suction effect produced would rapidly remove the infilling from roads such as those made by Telford and McAdam.

Provided at last with good roads the coaching industry prospered and journey times were slashed. In 1837 turnpike revenues rose to the record £1 500 000 but the moment of triumph was short-lived. Already what McAdam's son, James, described as the 'calamity of railways' had begun. As lines spread, trains with their superior speed and lower fares pushed the stage-coaches out of business. By 1850 only local traffic used the roads. Toll receipts fell sharply and most trusts found themselves in financial difficulties. The turnpike system was in its death-throes but government was slow to end its sufferings. It was not until 1874 that an annually appointed Parliamentary Committee on Turnpike Trust Bills set itself the task of terminating each trust as its Act lapsed. The end of the era was reached in 1895 with the closure of the last remaining trust.

Perhaps because of the current obsession with railways the central government was equally slow in bringing the roads outside the turnpike system under proper management. The General Highways Act of 1835 had swept away the outmoded practice of statute labour and replaced it by a road-rate but it had left the administration of the unturnpiked lesser roads in the hands of some 15 000 parishes. This inefficient multiplicity of authorities persisted for many years, despite various attempts at forcible amalgamation. As late as 1894 there were still over 5000 highway parishes in existence. All had been stripped of their power, however, by the end of the century. The Local Government Act of 1888 introduced a more rational note into highway management. Each of the newly constituted County Councils was given jurisdiction over the main roads in its area and control of the secondary roads was soon vested in the Rural District Councils.

It was as well that the administration of the highway system had been put on a sounder basis for the new century had ushered in the age of motoring. Power-driven car-wheels quickly loosened surfaces intended for free-rolling horse-drawn traffic and the roads were cut to ribbons. New techniques of construction were required. Tarmac roads were the first step. Later came concrete highways, and finally, after much delay, specially designed motorways.

Already the era of mechanical transport is of sufficient age to have left some interesting relics. One or two AA signs are old enough to repay a second glance [4.15], while petrol pumps at some of the remoter garages are of surprising antiquity [4.16]. In towns traces can often be found of older public transport systems, which have succumbed to competition from the motorbus. The illustration shows a long-deserted tram terminus [4.19].

Roads are a digest of history. No journey along them need be without interest.

4.15
AA VILLAGE SIGN (*61/NS 869439 – 1 mile west of Lanark*). The Automobile Association was early concerned with erecting name and direction signs, for when the road system was being developed at the beginning of the century such signs were few, and a motorist could very easily become lost. The circular sign shown here was set up in co-operation with the Royal Scottish Automobile Club, and is of a type now quite uncommon.

4.16

PETROL PUMPS (*135/TL 696646 – 3½ miles east of Newmarket*). Many old petrol pumps can still be found, to help piece together a history of such machines. Usually they have survived only in private yards where they were installed to supply a firm's own transport. These examples are still in use in a public garage, and unusual in that respect. The left hand pump is of 1920s type, the central handle being rocked to and fro to fill the glass vessels, each holding a half gallon. When full, the stop cock on the nozzle is opened to allow the measured amount to flow to the vehicle. The pump on the right dates from the late thirties, and has the now familiar electric pump for a greatly increased rate of delivery.

4.17

OIL CAN (*in the boiler room of Stretham Old Engine at 135/TL 516730*). An eye for details when visiting a site can be very rewarding. This 1930s oil can, still in use for paraffin storage, carries on its side a list of cars whose names are now most evocative – Delage, Hispano Suiza, Lanchester etc.

4.18

TROLLEY BUS (*96/SE 149378 – in Shipley*). Such transport was once a familiar sight in larger towns and cities, but is now rare. When the buses themselves have ceased to run, the tall posts which supported the overhead cables may still remain for a long time, possibly serving as street lighting columns. Similar posts left behind after the removal of tram wires can also be found in many cities.

4.19

BERESFORD SQUARE, WOOLWICH (*171/TQ 438790 – London S.E.18*). In the background is the Royal Arsenal entrance gate, whose severity of style contrasts strangely with its George IV motifs, coat-of-arms, and decorative mortars. The gate, which dates mainly from 1829 though the upper storey was added later, is soon to be demolished. But the main feature of the photograph is the square itself. The stone setts show through where the covering of tarmac has worn away, and tram lines of the old terminus are also beginning to reappear. In places the tall posts that carried the overhead wires remain as apparently functionless features; the island refuge was at one time a tram stop.

HARBOURS AND AIRPORTS

The need for safe harbourage is as old as seafaring itself but while boats remained small enough to be beached any sheltered bay or estuary could be used. Man-made improvement became necessary as the advance of civilization produced larger vessels. The river and canal harbours of the Mesopotamian cities of 5000 years ago already had quays alongside which ships could be moored for unloading, while by late in the second millennium B.C. the sea-towns of Phoenicia had many of the features of modern ports. Both Sidon and Tyre had numerous warehouses and jetties and were protected from the fury of the sea by artificial moles.

Britain's ports are far later in origin. The Romans developed several but when the legions marched out early in the fifth century, never to return, the jetties quickly fell into disuse. European trade took 700 years to recover from the collapse of Roman power and it was not until the twelfth and thirteenth centuries that cities like London, Liverpool, Southampton, and Bristol began to emerge as important merchantile centres.

Plate 21(a)
IPSWICH CUSTOMS HOUSE (*150/TM 168441 – King Street, Ipswich*). Some of the most beautiful port buildings are the Customs houses, and this one is no exception. Remarkably original, in red and yellow brick, the house was built in 1844 to the design of J. M. Clark. The classical river frontage is monumental, with its symmetry broken only by the tower. When the dock was completed in 1842 (by H. R. Palmer) it was the largest in England, and it is still an excellent site to visit.

Plate 21(b)
CAPSTAN, BRIDGWATER DOCK (*165/ST 298376 – in the middle of Bridgwater*). Both the capstan and the sluice date back to the time, at the end of the eighteenth century and the beginning of the nineteenth, when the dock was being developed to make Bridgwater an important port. Trade has now declined partly as the result of silting in the river Parrett, and these docks are at present in their unspoiled nineteenth-century condition.

Plate 21(c)
ALBERT DOCK WINDLASS (*100/SJ 340898 – near the dock offices*). Many interesting details have survived relatively unchanged in this dock. Various small machines, such as the windlass shown, appear to be of the original pattern, and well repay examination during any study of the working of the dock.

Plate 21(d)
BOWHOLE, ST KATHARINE'S DOCK (*160/TQ 340804 – next to the Tower of London*). This dock area is now being partially redeveloped, and many of Telford's warehouses have been demolished [see *4.21*]. The rest may be preserved, and perhaps this unusual bowhole in the quay wall may survive. The indentation enabled a large vessel to be moored next to the warehouse behind the camera position, and for the cranes to reach the hold; this was necessitated by the unusual shape of the dock.

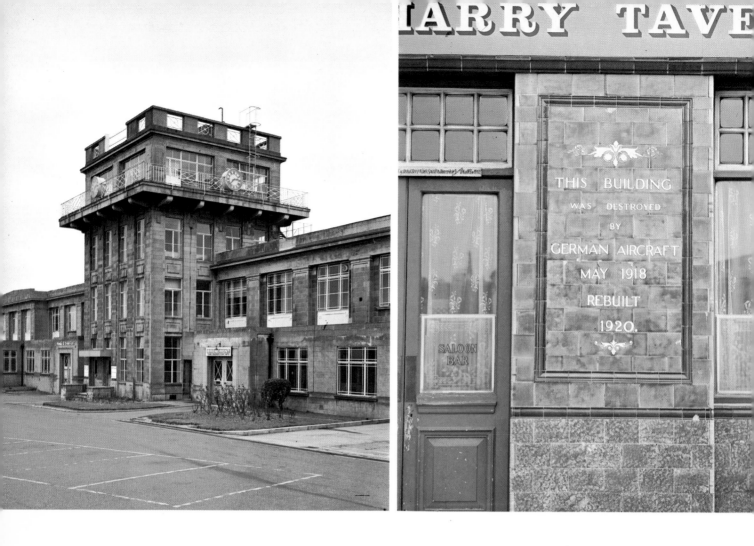

Plate 22(a)

CONTROL TOWER, CROYDON AERO-
DROME (*170/TQ 311635 – Purley Way,
Croydon*). Croydon aerodrome was established
by the Royal Flying Corps in 1915, and in
1920 became London's main civil airport. The
terminal buildings were reconstructed in
1927–28, and officially opened on 2 May
1928. For some years the buildings were the
largest of their sort in the world, incorporating
the control tower, various offices, passenger
and freight handling facilities, and customs
control. The nearby Aerodrome Hotel con-
tinues to function, although the airport itself
is closed and its site redeveloped (the control
tower is used for commercial offices). Control
towers throughout the world still have the
same functional shape of this original one.

Plate 22(b)

WALL INSCRIPTION (*161/TQ 383816 –
Joshua Street, London E.14*). Wall inscriptions
can be a valuable source of information for the
archaeologist, if they are treated with some
reserve until verified. This example, com-
memorating a bombing attack, appears to be
not unusual at first sight – until one reads
more carefully and sees that it was the *first*
world war in which the raid occurred.

Plate 22(c)

WARTIME AIRFIELD (*118/SJ 573107 –
Uckington, 5 miles west of Wellington*). In the
sudden emergency of war, many airfields were
created, with concrete runways (short by
modern standards, but difficult to plough up),
hangars, and other typical buildings. All must
have been built to one standard pattern, and
many have survived remarkably well. Some,
such as this one, have been converted into
extensive storage depots and will probably
still be recognizable in *another* 25 years.

4.20
ALBERT DOCK, LIVERPOOL (*100/SJ 342897 – in central Liverpool*). The first dock in Liverpool was started in 1709 by Thomas Steers, and by 1824 the area of docks had risen to 51 acres. At that date Jesse Hartley was appointed dock engineer, and by 1860 the acreage had risen to 212. During those 36 years he guided some of the mightiest works of their kind ever executed – grand ideas carried through with a strength and skill seldom exceeded. In the 1830s private people built warehouses near to the docks but not in them. Hartley pleaded for public enclosed warehouses, but did not finally win until 1841. The result of his efforts is the Albert Dock, opened in 1845. This dock is the climax of Liverpool's dock architecture, and Philip Hardwick was consulted about the design; in particular the Dock Traffic Office, with its strong reminiscence of the old Euston Arch, was designed by him. Hardwick was architect of St Katharine's docks in London, and the Albert Dock owes much to the earlier work. Five-storey warehouses with open ground floors are on all four sides of the dock. No timber is used in the warehouses, for not only is the main structure of cast-iron pillars and beams with brick arches, but the roof truss is wrought iron and the roof itself is covered with iron slates bolted together. Without doubt, the Albert Dock is one of the most impressive monuments of the nineteenth century.

4.21

TELFORD'S WAREHOUSE, ST KATH-ARINE'S DOCK (*160/TQ 338804 – by the side of the Tower of London*). The warehouses which fronted the river were demolished in 1970, although those facing the Tower still remain and it is hoped that they will be preserved. During demolition many unusual opportunities for understanding methods of construction are presented, and this picture of the partly demolished building shows clearly the original design. Brick walls and timber columns and beams are perhaps a little old-fashioned for the 1820s, as cast iron had been introduced for such buildings more than twenty years earlier. An original winch is still in position near the topmost door, and the original shape of the windows is plain.

The voyages of exploration of the fifteenth century, culminating in the discovery of the New World, opened the way for a vast increase in trade. After lagging behind the other European countries Britain began to make use of its favourable location and by the end of the seventeenth century London had become the focus of world commerce. There followed a period of unprecedented harbour construction reaching a zenith in the nineteenth century after the Industrial Revolution had made England the 'workshop of the world'.

Each port has its own individual and varied history but in such a short article it is impossible to do more than indicate general trends. London and Liverpool must serve to show how rising industrial output was matched by a mounting tempo of harbour building.

Before the nineteenth century London's only docks, with gates to hold the water-level constant, were the small enclosure at Blackwall dating from about 1660 and the twelve acre Howland Great Wet Dock built in 1703 on the site now occupied by the Surrey Commercial System. Both these docks were used only for fitting-out and repairs, so the city's trade was concentrated on wharves and quays subject to the inconvenience of tidal fluctuations. There was also such a shortage of berths that the Thames was often choked with vessels lying at anchor, waiting a chance to unload.

Early in the nineteenth century came a spate of building which did much to relieve the river of congestion. In 1802 the West India Docks on the Isle of Dogs were opened; Rennie's London Docks followed in 1805; the East India Docks came into use in 1806; the old Howland Dock was extended in 1808, and between 1825 and 1829, a little later than the rest, Telford built his St Katharine Dock [*4.21* and Plate 21(d)].

During the second half of the nineteenth century further docks were opened, Victoria (1855), Millwall (1868), South West India (1870), Albert (1880), and Tilbury (1886), nearly doubling the area of impounded water. By 1900 the Port of London extended from London Bridge twenty-six miles downstream to Gravesend.

The expansion of Liverpool during the nineteenth century was equally dramatic. Granted a charter by King John in 1207, it opened its first dock in 1715, but as late as the second decade of the 1800s possessed only thirty-four acres of enclosed water. By

4.22

ST KATHARINE'S DOCK WINCH (*160/ TQ 338804 – by the side of the Tower of London*). This site was, until very recently, probably less changed than most of the major docks, and much furniture was the original. It is known that Joseph Bramah received a contract from the Company for sixteen gate winches, and one at least of these has survived, continuing in use until 1957. It is likely that the winch shown in the plate is of the same early date; it is typical of the rest of the machinery of the dock dating from the 1820s.

4.23

ALBERT DOCK – DOUBLE HASP (*100/SJ 342897 – in central Liverpool*). Details such as this bring alive the working of a dock, for a bonded warehouse was quite a new concept in the 1840s. Goods were stored in these warehouses directly from the ship, under bond of payment when they were withdrawn. Obviously, it was imperative that the Customs man should be able to control such withdrawal of goods so that duty could be levied. The solution lay in having two locks on each door, one controlled by the warehouseman and the other by the customs officer. In this way both had to be present whenever goods were entered or withdrawn.

1846 the total had risen to 108 acres and by the close of the century the area of dock was five times greater still. Although they are often ancient in origin, the major ports as we know them today are very much products of the Industrial Revolution.

Most of the famous early civil engineers have left harbour works as memorials of their intensely active lives. John Smeaton, the father of the profession, made an early contribution to the harbour at Ramsgate as well as building the Eddystone lighthouse now preserved on Plymouth Hoe, while his pupil, William Jessop, constructed London's West India Docks. Those great contemporaries, Telford and Rennie, were connected with so many schemes that it is difficult to decide which to mention. Rennie added to Ramsgate [4.26], but perhaps his most impressive harbour work was the great breakwater at Plymouth, started in 1812 but not finished until 1848, many years after his death. Telford's name is indelibly linked with the Scottish ports. Starting in 1796 and continuing to near the close of his life in 1834, he undertook harbour building and

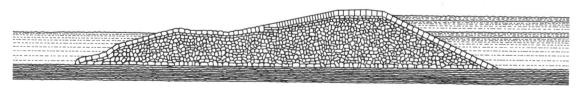

4.24 SECTION THROUGH RENNIE'S PLYMOUTH BREAKWATER.

4.25

DOCK INFILLING AT GOOLE (*97/SE 749232 – near the dock entrance in Goole*). Goole was very well placed as a port of the canal age, but it could easily have faded into obscurity during the railway era. As it was, the Aire & Calder Navigation Co fought a successful battle against a rail crossing of the Humber, and the port has continued to thrive to this day. Inevitably, success has meant increasing pressure on the older parts of this most interesting town, and filling in of the old dock is now almost complete, as seen in the plate. This process is being paralleled in many places throughout the country, and many sites with special claim to a niche in history are being lost.

improvement in over forty separate places in his native country. Even Isambard Kingdom Brunel, although better remembered for other accomplishments, took an active hand in dock construction. His relatively minor docks at Millbay in Plymouth and Briton Ferry in South Wales are significant because of the semi-buoyant gates which they pioneered. Brunel also made improvements at Bristol, Sunderland, Cardiff, and Milford Haven.

Harbours great and small possess a wealth of detail of interest to industrial archaeologists. Installations built to withstand the sea are too massive to be easily removed, and often survive long after they have fallen into disuse. Even ageing machinery is frequently left in position until it becomes a positive nuisance [*4.22*]. Breakwaters [*4.24*], harbour walls, dock gates, and even warehouses [*4.20, 4.21* and Plate 19(a)] can possess their own kind of functional beauty, while Customs houses [Plate 21(a)] in some old-established ports have great architectural appeal. Lighthouses and harbour lights [Plate 20(b)] have a fascination which it is hard to define. Few can resist the magic of the play of sea and sunlight on weathered stone and timber.

In contrast to harbours, airports seem almost startlingly new. All today's immense concrete runways are descendants of a puny 60-ft length of wooden rail laid out by the Wright brothers on the desolate sand hills of North Carolina less than seventy years ago. The Wright's mounted their aircraft on a yoke which ran along this launching rail on two tandem wheels. Once flying speed was achieved the machine rose clear and after completing its flight landed on skids.

Subsequent inventors found this technique too restricting, and by 1906 wheeled machines were being tested. These early aircraft were so slow and light that any large meadow could be used for take off and landing. As flying developed, however, enthusiasts began to congregate together, so that certain sites became recognized landing grounds. Fields were purchased and improved by filling in ditches, levelling hollows, and cutting down trees. Aircraft manufacturers and flying schools began to add sheds, workshops, and offices. By 1910, only a year after the Aero Club had established the country's first field near Leysdown on the Isle of Sheppey, Britain possessed several real aerodromes – the most notable of which were at Hendon, Brooklands, and Eastchurch.

4.26

RAMSGATE HARBOUR (*173/TR 380644 for the camera position*). This was originally designed by Smeaton, and in 1806 John Rennie succeeded Samual Wyatt as architect and engineer. Rennie revised and improved his predecessor's plans, and it was under his direction that the works were carried out. The picture shows the outer harbour and the massive canted masonry walls, designed to resist violent storms.

4.27

DRY DOCK, DUNDEE (*50/NO 412304 – on Dundee waterfront*). Dundee harbour was built largely in the 1860s, although constant modification and improvement took place from 1815–75. The dry dock, with its keel blocks and stepped sides, is typical of such installations, and was designed by Telford. On the left, its jib pointing away from the camera, is the steam crane shown in detail in Plate 20(c).

4.28

BRIDGWATER DOCK – BRUNEL'S SCRAPER (*165/ST 298375 – in the dock*). One of the problems of maintaining a dock was that of dredging the silt carried into it from its river. For Bristol a special scraping boat was designed by Brunel, and until recently, a smaller version still existed in the dock at Bridgwater – indeed, it was occasionally put into steam. The large square-section post carried a blade which could be lowered to the level of the dock bottom. The engine of the boat then winched the craft across the dock, to and fro between the bollards, scraping the silt towards the side of the dock. The water was then let out from the dock through the series of sluices whose controls are seen by the dockside, this flushed out the silt. The whole operation was most effective. The scraper is now preserved in the Exeter Maritime Museum.

The aircraft industry emerged from the 1914–18 War with vastly increased technical competence. Experience gained in bomber design enabled large airliners to be constructed, so that serious commercial operations could begin. New airfields were built around the great cities of Europe and America and as aircraft weights rose during the 1920s concrete or tarmac runways began to replace the grass. Distinctive towers were erected to control aircraft movements. The modern airport had been born.

But even the most important airfields of the 'twenties and 'thirties were comparatively small, since the largest machines could operate comfortably from runways 3000 ft long. The new breed of aircraft thrown up by the Second World War was more demanding. Existing airports had to be enlarged or replaced. Croydon, the centre of Britain's commercial aviation between the wars, was one of the casualties. Its suburban setting prevented expansion and its position as London's chief airport passed to the former Royal Air Force station of Heathrow. For a little over a decade Croydon struggled on, before it was finally closed to air traffic in 1957. Its runways have now disappeared beneath an industrial estate, and its famous old control tower, once the most advanced in the world, has been converted to offices [Plate 22(a)].

Military aviation provides a rich field of study for the industrial archaeologist. Many of the aerodromes which throbbed with life during the crucial war years of 1939 to 1945 now lie open and deserted [Plate 22(c)]. Aviation, though reaching for the sky, has left its imprint on the ground.

FURTHER READING

BIRD, ANTHONY, *Roads and Vehicles* (London: Longmans, 1969)

BIRD, JAMES, *The Major Seaports of the United Kingdom* (London: Hutchinson, 1963) (Although primarily a geography text, this contains much useful historical information.)

COPELAND, JOHN, *Roads and Their Traffic 1750–1850* (Newton Abbot: David and Charles, 1968)

JACKMAN, W. T. *The Development of Transportation in Modern England* (London: Frank Cass, 1962)

PANNELL, J. P. M. *An Illustrated History of Civil Engineering* (London: Thames and Hudson, 1964)

Plate 23

DRINKSTONE MILL (*136/TL 964622 – 5 Miles north-west of Stowmarket*). The mill is still worked and has two cloth-spread common sails and two shuttered spring sails which replaced two common sails during the last century. The twelve pictures show the methods of setting them in readiness for work. (a) Shows the side of the mill body with the rope controlling the brake to enable each sail to be brought round to the lowest position in turn for setting. (b) The brake is released and a common sail is being pulled down with a window hook. (c) Shows the sail with its leading board and frame on which the sail cloth is spread. (d & e) The brake is applied and the cloth is unfurled. (f) The cloth is set on the sail frame by pointing lines, to (g) full sail, (h & i) and secured in position. The sail can also be set to first reef, sword point and dagger point, according to the strength of the wind. (j) Next a spring sail is brought round. (k) The tension in the spring is adjusted. (l) As long as the velocity of the wind does not increase it does not overcome the effect of the spring. If it does, the shutters will open and spill the wind, acting as an automatic speed control.

a	b	c
d	e	f
g	h	i
j	k	l

Plate 24(a)

FOUR-HORSE GIN (*86/NZ 570075 – Drummer Hill Farm, Great Ayton, 8 miles south-east of Middlesborough*). In the north-east of England and in Scotland, circular buildings designed to house horse gins are common; but the machinery has disappeared from virtually all of them. This gin retains the timberwork almost complete, although the gearing and shaft, which used to drive a threshing machine and other implements, were disposed of some years ago. The building is unusual in that it is square in plan and thus hardly recognizable from outside for what it is. The gin was last used during the 1939–45 war and the present owner vividly recalls being made to stand in the building to prevent the horses slowing from their usual 2 miles per hour.

Plate 24(b)

DONKEY WHEEL (*169/SU 688386 – opposite Old Farm, Beech, 2 miles south-west of Alton*). Standing under a small tiled roof, this wheel is typical of most and in better repair than many. The donkey walked inside the drum making it turn like a squirrel-cage; the rope from the bucket was wound directly onto the wheelshaft. To let the bucket descend the animal had to be removed temporarily from the wheel, so the spokes were arranged to allow rapid exit and entry.

Plate 24(c)

GIN HOUSE (*77/NY 931695 – at Planetrees Farm, Wall, 3 miles north of Hexham*). This gin house is unusual in being built as a hexagon instead of the more usual circle. In the northeast a large number of circular buildings or walls still exist. Some were used for agricultural purposes, but the majority were associated with mine workings of various kinds. In the Scottish central highlands many circular gin houses still remain as part of farm buildings.

5. Natural Sources of Power

REX WAILES

BEFORE THE AGE OF STEAM, industry was entirely dependent on natural sources of energy. Power to drive machinery had to be drawn from rushing streams, plucked from the restless air, or extorted from the labour of animals and even men. Steam, by harnessing the pent up energy of mineral fuels, gave humanity a new command over its environment, but for many years beast, wind, and water remained as useful auxiliary servants.

Horse-gears continued in isolated use as late as the First World War and buildings that once housed them have survived in many localities, most notably in Scotland and Northern England. Single storeyed, frequently hexagonal and on the fringe of a group of farm buildings, such structures possess a design of satisfying symmetry.

Today few contain the actual gear. This was, as a rule, mounted at the top of a substantial upright shaft, which was footed in the floor and supported above in a bearing on a cross beam. The wooden spur-wheel of large diameter, normally from sixteen to twenty-four feet, drove through a small pinion such machines as threshers, chaff-cutters, turnip-choppers, apple-crushers or churns. It was mounted high up on the shaft to allow from one to four horses to be hitched below it, and the low gear-ratio transformed the slow plod round the track to a speed high enough to drive the machines [5.1 and Plate 24(a)].

Another type of wheel, like an enormous wooden squirrel-cage, was worked by a donkey confined within it. As the animal attempted to walk forwards the wheel turned and a rope was wound up on the extended wheel-shaft, so raising a bucket of water from a deep well [Plate 24(b)].

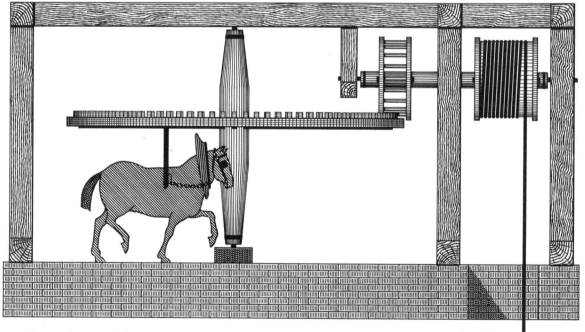

5.1   HORSE GIN

5.2

HORSE-GEAR, STOWMARKET (*136/TM
047585 – Abbot's Hall Museum of Rural Life,
Stowmarket*). This is a typical gear manufactured for driving threshing machines, chaff-
cutters and other farm machinery. One or
two horses could be hitched to horizontal wooden beams which, through a crown wheel
and pinion, drive a long iron shaft with
universal joints to the machinery either
outside or inside the farm buildings. Additional gearing increased the speed by giving
a final ratio of about 100:1.

In the nineteenth century, the cast-iron horse-gear was introduced [5.2]. An inverted
bevel-wheel contained in an iron housing was bedded into the surface of the ground
and turned by a horizontal wooden shaft to which a horse was hitched. The wheel
drove a pinion mounted on an almost horizontal shaft just above ground level and this
transmitted the power for the farm machinery, frequently an elevator feeding a threshing machine. The horse was trained to step over the shaft as it went round. These gears
were made right up to the First World War. Many were installed in the open and have
thus attracted the attention of the scrap merchant but a few are still to be found.

Water power has been put to many uses over the twelve centuries and more that
water-mills have worked in Britain, though it is with corn grinding that most people
associate them. One of the most famous corn-mills still remaining is that known as
Brindley's Mill at Leek in Staffordshire [5.4], now in the hands of a Trust formed to
undertake its preservation. The stone building faces on to Mill Street and on its front
bears the inscription

JAMES BRINDLEY CANAL ENGINEER WORKED HERE 1742–1765

87

At the back of the building in an open-sided wheel-house [5.3] is an undershot-wheel (A), 15 ft 8 in. diameter by 5 ft 6 in. wide, with a turbine alongside. Inside the mill is a large iron-bevel pit-wheel (B) on the wheel-shaft, driving a smaller bevel-wheel known as the wallower (C) on the upright shaft (D). On the floor above, this shaft carries the great spur-wheel (E) and drives three pairs of stones through pinions known as stone nuts.

Where there is a good fall of water, an overshot-wheel with its supply meeting the wheel at the top is frequently used. Instead of flat or curved floats which are moved by the current, there are closed buckets and the wheel is moved by the weight of the water. Very often there was more than sufficient water for one wheel and two were driven either side-by-side or in tandem from the same mill-leat. At the mill at Pont-y-Felin [5.5], six miles west of Portmadoc, the sluices are horizontal in the pentrough above and either one or both wheels can be used; each one drives a single pair of stones through an independent set of gearing. The rear wheel is of wood and of clasp-arm construction with two pairs of four wooden-arms forming a hollow square at the centre and clasping the wheel-shaft. The other wheel is of iron with two sets of six

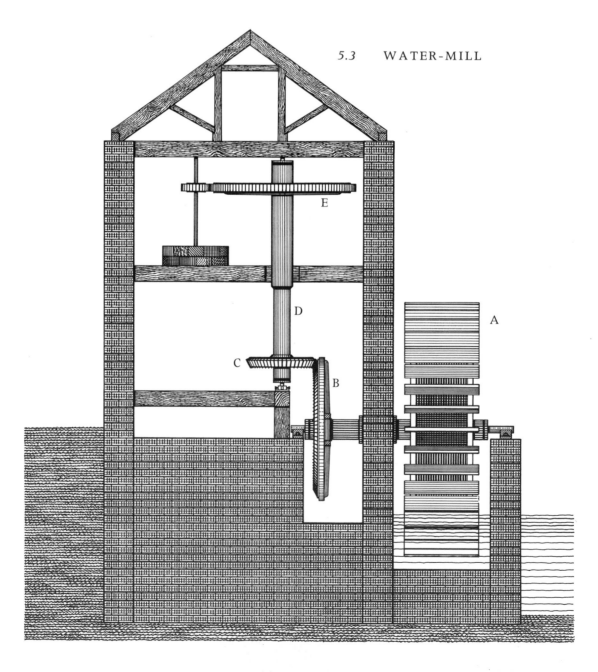

5.3   WATER-MILL

5.4
BRINDLEY'S WATER-MILL (*110/SJ 979569 – in Leek*). Designed and built in 1752 by James Brindley, the celebrated engineer. As seen from Mill Street, the building is barely recognisable as a mill. Inside the machinery illustrates millwrighting practice over the period of approximately one hundred years from the original upright shaft seen in the picture and the great spur-wheel on the floor above, to the iron wallower and pit-wheel and the 16 ft diameter undershot water-wheel outside. A Trust has been set up to restore the mill to workable order.

5.5
PONT-Y-FELIN WATER-MILL (*115/SH 480435 – 6 miles west of Portmadoc*). There are two overshot water-wheels in tandem fed by simple individual sluices in the floor of the trough of the wooden launder. Each wheel drives a single pair of stones direct through a pit-wheel and wallower; the stones were never out of gear and sluice controls were used to start, stop and regulate the speeds. The front wheel has cast iron hubs and shrouds but is otherwise of timber, while the rear wheel is entirely of timber construction.

wooden-spokes radiating from hubs. The wheel is mounted on a massive wooden shaft and probably replaces an earlier one; it last worked about 1958.

Frequently the water-wheel is housed inside the mill as, for example at Deben Mill, Wickham Market, Suffolk [5.6–5.9]. The present undershot-wheel replaced an earlier wooden one and was built and installed by the local firm of Whitmore and Binyon, now defunct. It is of excellent design with cast-iron shaft, hubs, arms, and starts which hold the wrought-iron curved buckets. The wheel is cast in halves and hung on the square end of the wheel-shaft with packing and wedges. The control for the sluice is operated from a covered way inside the mill and, when the river is in flood, is let down to start the wheel and then drawn up later.

Here also three pairs of stones are driven from above or overdrift, while sacks of grain are lifted up into the top of the mill through a sack-hoist operating in the lucam, which can be seen projecting from the gable end. To the right of this is the roller-mill, now empty of machinery, which once contained a small roller-milling plant made by Whitmore and Binyon; one set of rollers is now preserved at the Bridewell Museum, Norwich.

Further down the River Deben is the tide-mill at Woodbridge [5.10–5.12], first mentioned in 1170 when the canons of Woodbridge Priory granted to Baldwin de Ufford a

5.6, 5.7, 5.8 and 5.9

DEBEN MILLS (*150/TM 306566 – in Wickham Market*). They are still at work. *5.7* shows the breast-wheel from inside, the wrought-iron buckets are supported by cast-iron starts; note the small clearance between the ends of the buckets and the wall. *5.8* shows how the wheel is cast in halves and bolted together as well as the end of the wheelshaft. *5.9*, taken from the tailrace, shows the pit-wheel on the left.

The water is controlled by the sluice on the upstream of the wheel. Above the pit-wheel is the wallower, a bevel gear which transmits the power from the horizontal wheelshaft to the upright shaft passing to the stone floor above [5.6]. Here the compass-armed great spur-wheel drives four pairs of stones over-drift; the nut shown in the centre of the picture is out of gear. Behind it can be seen the hopper covered with a sack which delivers the grain to the shoe below it, and the square on the quant carrying the nut which vibrates the shoe to keep grain flowing into the eye of the runner stone. The tun or stone casing is in place round the stones and covered with sacks to keep down the dust. Above the spur-wheel are several layshafts and gears to drive the sack-hoist and auxiliary machinery.

plot of land which gave access to his mill. In the present mill structure eighteenth century ships' timbers are used, as well as some naturally grown oak knees under the ends of the floor beams. A valuation of the machinery, fixtures, and fittings, taken in 1841 gave a total of £299 12s 4d. The mill ceased work in August 1951, when the wheel-shaft broke after about one hundred years of use and the mill is now derelict and owned by a Trust which hopes to restore it. It will not, however, ever work again by tidal power for the mill-pond was not sold with the mill and the sluice-gates have been filled.

The operation of the mill was as follows. A pond was formed by enclosing an area of tidal creek with a wall in which automatic lock-type gates were set. As the tide rose, the pressure of water opened the gates and the pond was filled through them; when the tide turned, the pressure of the water in the pond was greater than that outside and the gates closed automatically. The impounded water was used to drive the mill-wheel and, because of the fall in water level as the mill-pond emptied, the wheel was varied from breastshot to undershot by the use of a sluice in two sections. The $7\frac{1}{2}$ acre mill-pond gave a 6 ft head. The wheel was 20 ft in diameter by 5 ft 10 in. wide. Within the mill, four pairs of underdrift stones are grouped together at one end of the first floor. The drive is through a mortise pit-wheel, i.e. one of iron with wooden cogs, driving an iron wallower at the lower end of the large, wooden, upright shaft; just above this is an iron great spur-wheel which drives the four pairs of stones on the first floor through mortise stone nuts. A crown-wheel, i.e. an upturned bevel-wheel, at the upper end of the upright shaft, provides the drive for the sack-hoist through an iron bevel-pinion mounted on the same horizontal layshaft as a wooden pulley. The belt passes up from the second to the third floor of the mill and is normally slack; the pull of a cord, however, raises a bearer, tightens the belt and the drive is taken up, winding the sack-chain and anything attached to it up to the grain bins on the top floor.

The fabric of the mill is clad in red-painted corrugated iron which, at the present time, acts as a stressed skin and helps to hold it together, and there is a tiled mansard roof. It is much to be hoped that sufficient money can be raised to put the mill into good order both inside and out.

Plate 25(a)

FRAMSDEN MILL, FANTAIL (*137/TM 192597 – 3 miles south-east of Debenham*). Larger than Drinkstone, this post-mill had its roundhouse added in 1841 during modifications. Until about a hundred years earlier substructures of post-mills were unprotected; the roundhouse, not only protects these timbers but at the same time forms a convenient store. The iron wheels at the base of the ladder run on a stone track round which they are driven by the fantail through gearing. The mill is being restored by a few enthusiasts and, when completed, will be more or less in working condition.

Plate 25(b)

BILLINGFORD MILL (*137/TM 167786 – 3 miles east of Diss*). This tower-mill was built in 1860 on the site of a post-mill blown down in a storm. Clearly visible is the prominent fantail which keeps the sails automatically into the eye of the wind and thus prevents the mill being tail-winded like its predecessor. The fantail, invented in 1746, relieves the miller of the constant trouble of watching for change in direction of the wind.

Plate 25(c)

DRINKSTONE MILL (*136/TL 964622 – 5 miles north-west of Stowmarket*). This post-mill dates from 1685 and is one of the oldest in the country. Although some timbers have been replaced and slight extensions incorporated, the mill has changed very little in almost three centuries, although at one time the body was turned head to tail. It is still regularly worked, and runs very well driven by two common and two spring sails [Plate 23(a) to (l)]. These show how the sails are adjusted according to the wind velocity; unusually they turn clockwise. Close by stands the tower of a small smock-mill, the lower portion of which once housed a horse-gear.

Plate 25(d)

UNION MILL, CRANBROOK (*172/TW 779359 – in Cranbrook Town*). Built in 1814 by James Humphrey of Cranbrook, it is the finest smock-mill in England and is 75 ft high to the ridge of the cap, the shape of which is in the Kentish tradition and resembles the roof of a post-mill. The mill stands on the edge of the town and, when seen from the main road as in this picture, looks much smaller than its actual size on account of its excellent proportions. The sails (called sweeps in the south-east) span 68 ft and are double shuttered patent sweeps, originally put up in 1840 as replacements for common sweeps by Medhurst of Lewes and renewed a number of times since. The mill is now in the care of the Kent County Council.

Plate 26(a)

ALBERT MILL, KEYNSHAM (*156/ST 657678 – 5 miles east of Bristol*). This mill was equipped to chip and grind log wood used in dyeing and part of the machinery is still in place. The external breastshot-wheel is 18 ft 6 in. diameter and the metal spoke construction is unusual. A second wheel of the same diameter but different in construction is inside the mill. A sluice can be seen immediately to the left of the wheel. The mill ceased work in 1964.

Plate 26(b)

LEAD ORE CRUSHING PLANT (*84/NY 927429 – Killhope, Weardale, 7 miles south-east of Alston*). Water power was widely used for heavy duties such as crushing ores, and this impressive 30 ft overshot-wheel is an excellent example. It has been tidied up by the Civic Trust, and the site is to be developed as a picnic area.

5.10

WOODBRIDGE TIDE-MILL (*150/TM 275488 – in Woodbridge*). This eighteenth-century mill on a twelfth-century site was the last tide-mill to work in the whole of the North Sea area. These water-mills worked by impounding water in a large pond as the tide rose and letting it out through the wheel race as it fell. The bank of the mill-pond is seen on the right of the picture with the culvert taking the water to the wheel in the centre. The wheel, which was originally covered, varied from breastshot to undershot when at work as the level of the water in the pond fell. Twin iron racks and pinions controlled the flow through the sluice to the wheel and are visible in the middle of the picture. A shed at the front of the mill housed a small oil engine used as a standby. The timber-built mill is at present covered in red painted corrugated iron sheeting.

5.11

STONE FLOOR, WOODBRIDGE TIDE-MILL. The timber construction of the mill is clearly seen and the casings of all four pairs of stones have been removed. The crane on the left is installed for raising the runner stones for dressing. On the extreme left is the chain of the sack hoist operated by a bevel-pinion driven by a crown-wheel at the top of the upright shaft on the floor above. The stones are underdrift from below.

5.12
WHEEL-PIT, WOODBRIDGE (*150/TM 275488 – in Woodbridge*). The wheel is seen in the background; the wheelshaft runs below the level of the photograph to the wheel-pit in the centre of the picture. It drove the bevelled wallower on the upright shaft on the extreme right. The great spur-wheel is just visible at the top and drove four stone nuts. The governor, seen at the centre, controlled the gap between the stones and hence the fineness of grinding.

Abbeydale Works, Sheffield [*9.16* and Plates 27(a), (b) and (c)], made scythes from c. 1714, as well as other products; it was leased by W. Tyzack & Sons from 1849 until 1933, and in 1935 was privately purchased by Alderman Graves and presented to the city. Nothing was done to it until 1964, when a private organization, the Council for the Conservation of Sheffield Antiquities, negotiated a seven year lease and undertook to raise money to restore the whole complex and the machinery.

There were four water-wheels, one each for the bellows, the tilt-forge [Plate 27(c)], the grinding shop, and the drilling machine. The tilt has two hammers for steeling and plating blades, and these worked at 66 and 126 strokes per minute. The undershot water-wheel driving them is 18 ft diameter by 5 ft 6 in. wide and has a wooden shaft, spokes, and buckets and iron hubs and shrounds. The pivoted helves of the tilt-hammers are of wood and are operated by iron cams on the shaft which tilt the tail ends of the helves down and let them go, enabling the heads to fall on to the work-pieces on the anvils. The smith sits in front of the hammer in a swing seat suspended from a roof beam, so that he can forge the complete length of a scythe blade in one movement, while the blows are varied by a suspended pole which operates the sluice control. The tilts were used to rough-forge steel blades to shape prior to hand finishing, drilling, hardening, grinding, and polishing.

The cam-shaft carries a cast-iron flywheel at one end and beyond it is mounted a cast-iron spur-pinion driven by a large clasp-armed wooden spur-wheel mounted on the inner end of the water-wheel shaft. Heavy cast-iron cross-tail gudgeons are let in to the ends of each shaft and both machines and drives are of massive construction.

The tilt is again in working order, the water-wheels and shafts have been repaired and rebuilt, and the whole industrial complex is open to the public and well on the way to being restored to its original appearance.

Albert Mills, Keynsham, near Bristol [Plates 26(a) and 45(c)], consist of extensive buildings in local stone with slate and tiled roofs, and behind the mill an outside water-wheel, sluices and, beyond them again, a weir. At the end of the eighteenth century the mill was probably used for cotton. Later it became a corn-mill, and today it contains the incomplete machinery of a dyewood-mill.

Wood, sometimes known as Brazil wood, was used for dyeing and the logs were reduced to a usable sawdust first by chipping and then grinding with edge runner-stones. The rasping barrels for the final operation have been removed, as have two steam engines, but the outside wheel which drove the grinding pans, the inside wheel, and two sets of rasping barrels remain. Both are breast shot-wheels 18 ft diameter by 10 ft wide but are of different construction.

At just over 1500 ft elevation, near the head of Weardale, stands the Killhope Wheel [Plate 26(b)], derelict for perhaps fifty years until freed and painted by the Civic Trust Youth Volunteers in 1966. The overshot-wheel is 33 ft diameter and was used to drive four sets of crushing rollers for lead ore from a nearby mine. Trucks of ore were hauled up a ramp by a power take-off from the wheel and tipped into a hopper feeding the rollers. After crushing, the ore was washed in buddles and transported to Allenheads for smelting.

About five-hundred years after the first reference to a water-mill in England, the wind-mill appeared here. The earliest type was the post-mill [5.13], built of timber, which had a box-like body carrying the sails (B) and containing the machinery. It was mounted on an upright post (A) (socketed into a horizontal crown tree (I)) on which it could be turned in order to face the sails (B) square into the wind. The post was supported by a trestle of four diagonal timbers called quarterbars (C), which transmitted its weight to four brick or stone piers (D) via two horizontal timbers called crosstrees (E). From the eighteenth century this sub-structure was frequently enclosed by a roundhouse (F), which protected it from the weather and served also as a store for grain. At the back of the mill, a ladder projecting downwards gave access to the mill body and normally rested on the ground. A tailpole (G), also fixed to the bottom of the mill body, projected downwards through the ladder to which it was connected by a lever and chain. This enabled the ladder to be raised when it was necessary to turn the mill into the eye of the wind. The sails were mounted on an inclined windshaft which carried the brake wheel (J), so called because a contracting brake acted on its rim.

This drove the wallower which, in a small mill, drove a single pair of stones (L) direct.

The tower-mill [*5.14*] of brick, stone or timber was a later development and the earliest reference in England is some three-hundred years after that for the post-mill. In it the machinery is contained in a fixed tower, of which only the roof or cap carrying the sails is turned into the wind. Timber-built tower-mills, called smock-mills [*5.15*] from their fancied resemblance to a smock, were introduced as far as is known, by the Dutch when Fen drainage was undertaken in the seventeenth century.

5.13   POST-MILL

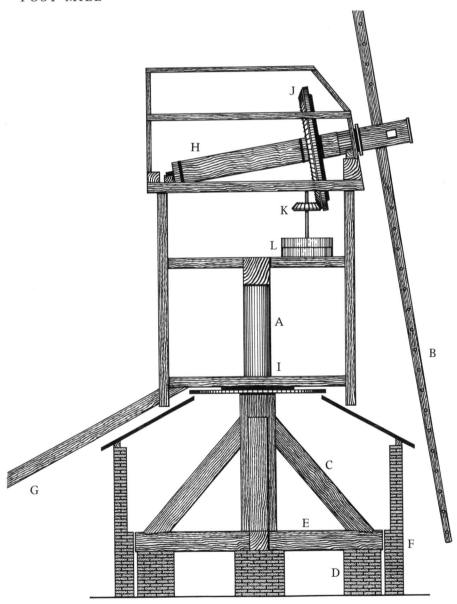

5.14

TOWER-MILL – Of large size, with thick brick or stone walls. The cap alone revolves. (Note the vertical line of windows, one above the other – a bad design feature leading to structural weaknesses causing the cap to jam.)

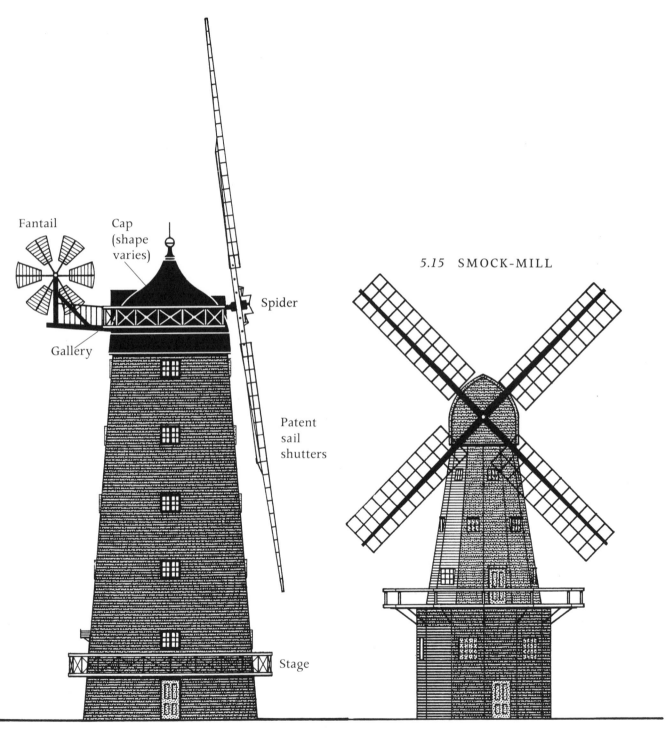

Fantail

Cap (shape varies)

Spider

Gallery

5.15 SMOCK-MILL

Patent sail shutters

Stage

5.16

HEAGE MILL (*111/SK 366508 – 2 miles north of Belper*). A six-sailed tower-mill with a tower in local stone and an ogee cap, which is being repaired as a landmark by the Derbyshire County Council. In Lincolnshire the six-sailed Trader Mill at Sibsey, north of Boston, is now under the guardianship of the Department of the Environment; the five-sailed mill at Burgh-le-Marsh, near Skegness, has been preserved by the Lindsey County Council and the eight-sailed mill at Heckington, near Sleaford, by the Kesteven County Council.

Plates 27(a), (b) and (c)
ABBEYDALE, SHEFFIELD (*111/SK 326820 – 3 miles south-west of the centre of Sheffield*). The breastshot-wheel [27(a)] has been restored so that it can be run to demonstrate the working of its associated machinery. Behind the site is a large pond which feeds the pentrough seen above the wheel. The whole has been restored, the original construction has been followed rigorously, and much of the metal-work has been rescued.

From the wheel, the massive shaft takes the motion to the pit-wheel, seen on the left of Plate 27(b), and, more completely, on the right of Plate 27(c). This pit-wheel is of clasp arm construction, with crossed timbers strengthened with iron ties, and transmits the power to the smaller wallower; both are spur gears. In a cornmill, where the final drive is vertical to a horizontal stone, the pit-wheel and wallower are usually at right angles. In Plate 27(c), the wood shaft which carries the cams and the wallower is behind the tilt hammers themselves; a pair of shears, seen on the extreme left could be put into action as needed. Note the cross-tail gudgeon at the end of the shaft. The right-hand hammer, worked by a larger number of cams gives more blows per minute. Each cam in turn strikes the end of the hammer, which is lifted and falls under its own weight onto the work. Here, a piece of carbon steel was welded into a sandwich between two pieces of wrought iron to make edge tools.

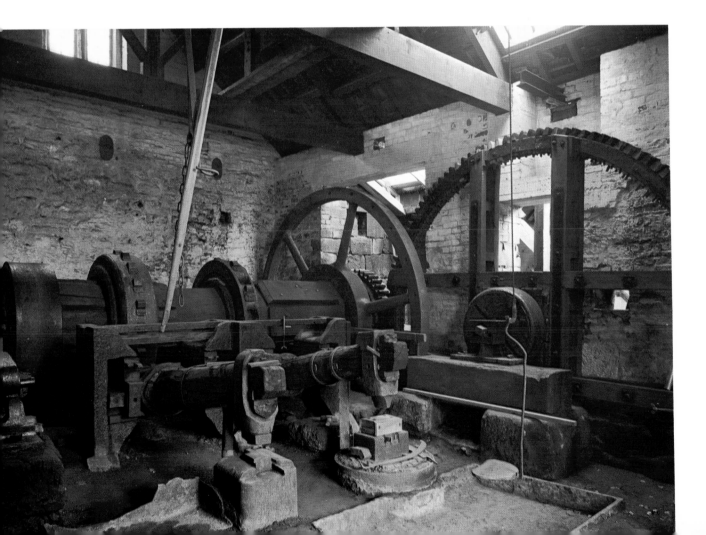

Plate 28(a)
HAYSTACK BOILER (*Seen at Blists Hill Museum site – 119/SJ 696036*) is an unusual object to be found in one piece today, especially out of its housing so that its shape can be seen clearly. Capable of evaporating only a relatively small amount of water per hour, to provide steam at low pressure, this kind of boiler was used with the earliest steam engines of the atmospheric type. The drawing [6.4] shows how such a boiler was used.

Plate 28(b)
EAST POOL ENGINE (*189/SW 674416 – 2 miles west of Redruth*). One Cornish engine to have survived is at East Pool, and there is another nearby. The East Pool (1887) engine was used for winding copper and tin ores from depths of 200 fathoms. This winding engine was last used in 1949, and is now preserved by the National Trust in conjunction with the Trevithick Society. This 30 in. engine and the 90 in. pumping engine at Taylor's shaft are open to the public, and well worth a visit.

Plate 28(c)
CROFTON BOILERS (*167/SU 262623 – at the canal pumping station, 2 miles south-west of Great Bedwyn*). The original boilers at Crofton were of the wagon type, two being used with a third in reserve. These were later replaced by the two boilers seen here, which were made at the Swindon works of the Great Western Railway.

Plate 28(d)
CORNISH ENGINE HOUSE, MARY TAVEY (*175/SX 510812 – 5 miles north of Tavistock*). There are many engine houses of this type in Devon and Cornwall, almost all of them empty and derelict, like this one on the fringe of Dartmoor. The walls were always substantially built and the bob-wall which supported the beam or 'bob' was of particularly massive masonry construction. The bases of the chimneys, also of masonry, usually survive, but the boiler houses were of much less strong construction, and have almost always disappeared. [see also Plate 28(b)].

Like post-mill bodies, tower-mill caps were first turned into the wind by means of a long tailpole at the rear, but in 1746 the automatic fantail was invented by Edmund Lee. This consists of a number of small vanes set at right-angles to the mill sails and connected by gearing to wheels on the bottom of the ladder in the case of a post-mill, or to a geared rack on the top or cap of the tower of a tower- or smock-mill. When the wind veers, it strikes these vanes at an angle; they turn and, in doing so, rotate the mill or the cap back into the eye of the wind.

It is necessary to provide for hand operation to turn a mill fitted with a fantail if there is no wind or the mill is likely to be tail-winded in a thunderstorm. To enable this to be done, a clutch is provided to throw the fan drive out of gear, and various methods are employed to enable the final drive to be operated with a handle, either from the ground in the case of a post-mill or from the cap in the case of a tower-mill. In Kent, for example at Cranbrook, a chain-wheel was sometimes provided instead and an endless hand chain hung down to the stage.

Framsden post-mill, Suffolk [5.17–5.19 and Plate 25(a)], has been rebuilt at least twice and the fantail probably dates from the last rebuilding around 1841, when the round-house was constructed. The driven wheels of the fan carriage at the bottom of the ladder of a post-mill are set on a curve to follow the levelled track around the mill and, as can be seen, this entails an ingenious split drive to each wheel, involving the use of bevels.

At Drinkstone post-mill, Suffolk [Plates 23 and 25(c)], the fantail was added during the Second World War and came from Thurston Mill not far away. For almost three-hundred years before that it had been winded by means of a tailpole. Strangely, the body of this mill has at some time been turned end for end; the breast is now the tail and vice versa.

Not only is Drinkstone one of a handful of wind-mills in private hands and still worked by wind but it is also one of the very few on which the cloth-spread common sails have survived. When not in use, the cloths are drawn back like a curtain, twisted up rope-fashion and tied to the outer end of the sail. When being set, they are untied and spread across the sail frame at the top. Loops of cord on the selvedge of the leading edge of the cloth are hitched over cleats on the sail frame and, by means of cords called pointing lines, the cloth is spread over an area of the sail according to the power required. The four self-explanatory settings are 'sword-point', 'dagger-point', 'first-reef'; and 'full-sail'.

Each sail has to be set and furled individually by hand from the ground whenever the wind freshens or slackens to any considerable degree, as well as at the start and finish of the day's work. The invention of the spring sail by Andrew Meikle in 1772

5.17, 5.18 and 5.19

FRAMSDEN POST-MILL (*137/TM 92597 – 3 miles south-east of Debenham*). Built in 1769, the mill, after considerable rebuildings over the years, is now being restored by some volunteer enthusiasts. At the time the photograph was taken only two sails were in place, and it can be seen [*5.17*] how the stock is passed through the poll end, wedged in position, strengthened at the sides with clamps and carries two sails which are bolted to it.

Inside [5.18] the brake-wheel is seen mounted on the iron windshaft. It is a clasp arm wheel, the four arms forming a square round the shaft. The iron skew gear and horizontal wood shaft across the centre of the picture drove the bolter at the tail of the mill by belt. The sack-hoist was driven from the wood pulley in front of the brake-wheel up to the chain drum in the room.

5.19 shows the stone floor with the iron wallower taking the drive from the wooden brake-wheel to the floor below, where the great spur-wheel drives the stone nuts for two pairs of stones. The governors regulating the stones can be seen behind the upright shaft and were driven from the pulley below the wallower.

was, therefore, a very great advantage. Hinged shutters, like those of a Venetian blind, are fitted into the sail frame and connected by a wooden shutter bar which is controlled by a single spring on the whip or backbone of each sail. With the mill at rest each spring can be tensioned, according to the power required, by an adjusting device at the tip of the sail. This done, the speed of the sails is automatically regulated since the shutters open under increased wind pressure and 'spill-the-wind'.

Both types of sail are made with a weather or twist analogous to that of a propeller but the construction of the common sail lends itself more easily to an efficient shape than that of the shuttered type. It was therefore common practice to have two cloth-spread common sails to get a good driving power and two shuttered spring sails to obtain a certain amount of self-regulation, since in any case the mill had to be at rest for initial adjustment.

In 1807 Sir William Cubitt invented and patented what has ever since been known as the patent sail. He used hinged shutters but, by means of cranks and levers, connected all shutter bars to a spider coupling in front of the wind-shaft which carries the

104

5.20

BUTTRUM'S MILL (*150/TM 264494 – ½ mile north of Woodbridge*). This plate shows the inside of the cap of a fine tower-mill typical of the work of Whitmore and Binyon of Wickham Market, now defunct. It has been preserved by the East Suffolk County Council. The framing of the ogee cap is well shown, together with the fine brake-wheel of cast iron with wood cogs, the rim separate from the arms and bolted on. In the foreground of the picture can be seen the striking gear for the patent sails. The endless chain hanging over the chain-wheel was used to operate the striking rod controlling the shutters through twin racks-and-pinions, and by this means the operation could be carried out from inside the mill, an unusual refinement.

sails. The shaft was either drilled down its whole length or a longitudinal hole was cast down the centre when made and a striking rod was passed through it and connected at the tail end to a geared rack engaged by a pinion. On the pinion spindle was a chain wheel with an endless chain which hung down to the ground or to a stage round the mill. By pulling the chain one side or the other, the rack-and-pinion moved the striking rod backwards and forwards to open or close the shutters simultaneously, and it was thus possible to regulate them according to the power required, without stopping the mill. A weight on one side of the chain held the shutters open and varying weights on the other side kept them closed.

Early wind-shafts were of wood and the portion projecting from the front of the mill to carry the sails was known as the poll. The sail [5.17] frames were built up of bars mortised into a whip or backbone and the frame was completed with longitudinal laths or uplongs, the outer one on the trailing edge being known as the hemlath. Much longer and stouter timbers called stocks were mortised at right-angles through the poll of the wind-shaft and wedged in place. Each stock carried two sails whose whips were bolted and strapped to it. John Smeaton, of lighthouse fame, experimented with wind-mill sails and came to the conclusion that five sails were more efficient than four. To enable five sails to be fitted, he used a cast-iron shaft with a five-armed cross [5.16]. Instead of stocks, he used a back the same length as, but stouter than, a whip, and bolted and strapped it to the arms of the cross. Sail bars were mortised through the back, which thus took over the function of the whip. Eventually, this was employed for four, six and eight sails but the method was comparatively little used. Instead cast-iron poll-ends were let in to the nose of existing wooden wind-shafts and iron shafts were cast with the poll-end incorporated; the stocks and whips continued to be used as before.

105

Inside the mill the power of the wind on the sails turned a wheel, which was located on the forward end of the wind-shaft and known as the brake-wheel [*5.18* and *5.20*] from the fact that a contracting brake acts on its rim. In the case of some post-mills, a second wheel, called a tail-wheel, is located in front of the tail end of the shaft, as at Drinkstone. Each wheel drives a single pair of stones through a pinion known as a stone nut. However, indirect drive is used in tower-mills and in many post-mills, with the brake-wheel driving the wallower on an upright shaft passing down to the stone floor below, where a great spur-wheel mounted on it drives the stone nuts, as at Framsden post-mill [*5.19*].

The stones are, as a rule, mounted at floor level and the bedstone is supported on a heavy timber frame. The stones are enclosed by round or octagonal wooden casings, also known as vats or tuns. On the top of the casing is mounted a framework known as the horse, usually with four legs. This supports the hopper which holds the grain for the stones and an inclined trough or shoe feeds it from the hopper to the eye of the runner stone.

To raise sacks of grain to the top of the mill, a sack-hoist is provided. In tower-mills the drive can be by gear from the upright shaft and then by slack-belt or chain, while in the case of post-mills a pulley is usually fixed to the wind-shaft either in front of the brake-wheel as at Drinkstone, or behind it as at Framsden [*5.18*], the drive being by slack-chain and slack-belt respectively.

Mills may be appreciated for their undoubted aesthetic appeal or the mechanical ingenuity of their machinery but for the industrial archaeologist they hold an additional lure. They are fossilized, industrial history − beautiful relics of man's skill in harnessing the forces of nature.

FURTHER READING

BENNETT, RICHARD, AND ELTON, JOHN. *History of Corn Milling.*
    Vol. I – *Hand Stones, Slave and Cattle Mills* (1898)
    Vol. II – *Watermills and Windmills* (1899)
    Vol. III – *Feudal Laws and Customs* (1900)
    Vol. IV – *Some Feudal Mills* (1904)
    (London: Simpkin Marshall)
DARBY, H. C. *The Draining of the Fens* (Cambridge: Cambridge University Press, 1940)

FARRIES, K. G. AND MASON, M. T. *The Windmills of Surrey and Inner London* (London: Charles Skilton, 1966)
Newcomen Society Transactions, Vol. XXII (1941–42) to date.
Society for the Protection of Ancient Buildings, Annual Reports from 1930 to date.
WAILES, REX. *The English Windmill* (London: Routledge and Kegan Paul, 1967). Still in print.

6. Power from Steam

N EIL C OSSONS

S TEAM POWER WAS WITHOUT DOUBT the most important technological factor in bringing about the huge social and economic changes which have been called the Industrial Revolution. From the early 1700s until near the close of the nineteenth century, the steam engine was unchallenged. It powered machinery, drained mines, propelled ships and locomotives, and helped transform Britain and many other countries into highly industrialized societies. Even today, though the older reciprocating steam engine has been largely replaced, a high proportion of the nation's energy demands are still satisfied by steam-driven turbo-generators. The importance of the history of the steam engine transcends its purely technical aspects; its evolution was the first major step in the liberation of mankind from toil.

In the late seventeenth century mines had become sufficiently deep to create serious problems of drainage, a difficulty overcome in some instances by the use of water-powered pumps but more often by men or horses. Severe limitations were imposed on further deep mining by the small capacity and great expense of mine-pumping equipment. It was against this background of outstanding need that the discovery of atmospheric pressure led on to the development of the steam engine. The pressure of the atmosphere had been demonstrated in the middle of the seventeenth century by Evangelista Torricelli, a pupil of Galileo, who in 1643 claimed that the atmosphere exerted pressure because of its weight. Numerous demonstrations, by Otto von Guericke of Magdeburg and the Dutch scientist Christiaan Huygens and his assistant Denis Papin, showed that a useful and powerful engine could be made to utilise this atmospheric pressure if a vacuum were generated under a piston in a cylinder. In 1690 Papin condensed steam beneath the piston in a $2\frac{1}{2}$ in. diameter enclosed cylinder, producing a partial vacuum and raising a weight of 60 lbs [6.1]. Papin did not pursue his experiments but Thomas Newcomen (1663–1729), an ironmonger of Dartmouth working on similar principles but almost certainly without knowledge of the Dutch scientist's work, was actively pushing towards a practical application [6.2].

A steam-generated vacuum was in fact used as early as 1698 in a mine drainage pump patented by the Cornish engineer, Thomas Savery (c. 1650–1715). In this device a steam-filled vessel was cooled by cold water poured on its outside and the resultant partial vacuum was used to raise water in a suction pipe through a non-return valve. Steam pressure was then used to eject the water up a delivery pipe. Savery's pump was only suitable for moderate lifts and consumed an enormous quantity of coal. It also required a boiler capable of withstanding a pressure of several atmospheres and this could not be made satisfactorily at that date.

Thomas Newcomen was also aware of the drainage problems of the Cornish mines and, after experiments lasting some fifteen years, he built an atmospheric steam engine incorporating a piston, connected to a rocking beam, working in an open-topped cylinder [6.2]. The cylinder was mounted above a boiler which was little more than a tank of water with a fire beneath it. The end of the beam distant from the steam cylinder was connected to the pump rods of the mine shaft. The first recorded New-

107

Plates 29(a) to 29(f)

STRETHAM OLD ENGINE (*135/TL 516730 – 4½ miles south of Ely*). This engine, built in 1831, has been preserved by a trust, and is chosen as an example of the many beam engines which were once so important as providers of power for different purposes. It can be visited every day on payment of a small charge, and is recommended as an excellent site, from which an understanding can be gained of the workings of a typical Boulton & Watt type engine. 29(a) shows the outside of the engine, and makes clear that its use was to drive a very large (33 ft) scoopwheel, to drain the surrounding countryside, which lies below the level of the river. The boiler house is on the right, the engine in the centre and the scoop wheel on the left. Each revolution of the scoop raised 30 tons of water, and the engine ran at about four revolutions per minute. It was last run in 1941. 29(b) shows the Watt parallel motion from its uppermost floor. This connects the end of the piston rod with its simple reciprocating motion to the end of the beam which describes an arc. When the engine was running, each oiling point had to be filled up once an hour; the longest non-stop run was during floods in 1919, for a total of forty-seven day and nights.

The other end of the beam is seen in Plate 29(c), after the engine had been turned. The beam is 24 ft 8½ in. between centres, and the connecting rod is 21 ft long. Note the brass oil-drip catcher under the bearing. The cylinder top is shown in Plate 29(d), with the 4¼ in. diameter piston rod emerging from its gland. The cylinder is of 3 ft 3 in. diameter, with an 8 ft stroke. A steam pressure of about three pounds per square inch was originally provided by the wagon boilers first fitted and this was increased to the present 8 psi in 1888, after new Lancashire boilers had been installed. 29(e) shows the eccentric and the 24 ft diameter flywheel. The crankshaft was replaced in 1892, but the eccentric, which drove the valves, is the original. 29(f) shows the valve chest, standing in front of the cylinder and with the pipe to the condenser (out of sight below the floor) alongside. The valves were altered in 1909, to give greater efficiency. On the inlet side within the main valves are two more, driven by a rod from the beam; the others are driven from the eccentric. The new arrangement of the valves allowed for variation in the cut-off, resulting in a saving of fuel and an increased horse power.

Plate 30(a)

HESLOP'S ENGINE, 1795 (*Science Museum, London – 170/TQ 268793*). This is a rotative beam engine, with two open-topped cylinders. The hot cylinder is near the connecting-rod end of the beam, and steam at about 2 psi raised the piston to make the upstroke. The steam was allowed into the other, cold, cylinder by an eduction pipe. This cold cylinder, immersed in water, condensed the steam allowing atmospheric pressure to force the piston down for the power stroke. An air pump replaces the original snifting valve to remove air from the cold cylinder. In effect – the cold cylinder was exactly the same as the separate condenser of the Watt design, and was indeed held to infringe his patent. The hot cylinder is of 34·4 in. diameter by 34 in. stroke, the cold 25·4 in. diameter by 39 in. stroke.

Plate 30(b)

ATMOSPHERIC ENGINE, 1791 (*Science Museum, London – 170/TQ 268793*). The beam was originally of wood, the present cast-iron one being fitted in 1841. The piston is of $57\frac{1}{4}$ in. diameter and 11 ft. stroke, and the piston rod is fixed to the beam by the typical forged iron-link chains. The other end of the beam is attached in a similar manner to the pump rods, as the engine was used for colliery drainage. Three separate lifts raised 220 gallons through 360 ft per minute. The open top of the cylinder can be clearly seen. Steam was provided by a haystack boiler at about 3 psi.

Plate 30(c)

PARSONS STEAM TURBINE (*Science Museum, London – 170/TQ 268793*). The development of the steam turbine was particularly significant in the fields of electricity generation and marine propulsion. In the former case the reciprocating steam engine could not match the high speeds possible with the turbine. This small turbine of 1901 is direct-coupled to a 60 KW generator. It is of the axial-flow single-ended compound condenser type with a stepped rotor and seven sets of individually inserted blades. Operating speed was 4000 r.p.m. at a steam pressure of 110 psi.

Plate 30(d)

DINORWIC AIR-COMPRESSOR (*107/ SH 593598 – 1 mile east of Llanberis*). In slate quarries such as this, material was always moved by gravity if possible, and although this machine has the appearance of a steam-engine, it is actually an air-compressor. A 170 hp electric motor drove the machine through a 20 in belt, to feed the vertical receiver at the back of the picture at a pressure of about 100 psi. So far as can be determined, this compressor, and about five others like it, was installed about 1920. The name-plate bears the details 'Ingersoll Rand Co. – New York – Imperial Type 10'.

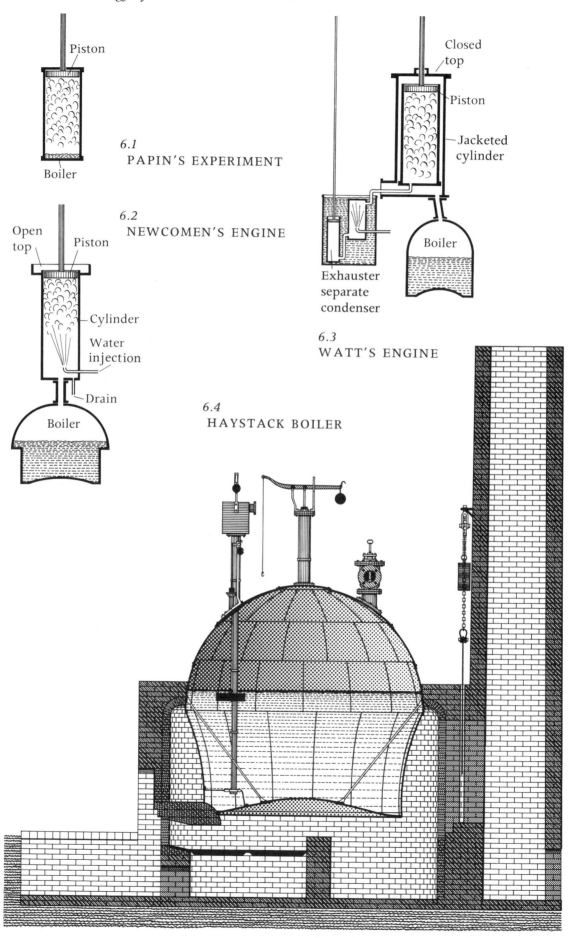

Piston

Boiler

6.1
PAPIN'S EXPERIMENT

6.2
NEWCOMEN'S ENGINE

Open
top

Piston

Cylinder

Water
injection

Drain

Boiler

Closed
top

Piston

Jacketed
cylinder

Boiler

Exhauster
separate
condenser

6.3
WATT'S ENGINE

6.4
HAYSTACK BOILER

6.5

NEWCOMEN TYPE ENGINE, ELSECAR (*102/SE 388000 – 5 miles south-east of Barnsley*). The open cylinder top is shown here, indicating that the engine is of the atmospheric kind, relying on air pressure to force down the piston to do the work, as the steam below the piston condensed and created a partial vacuum. The engine dates from 1787, and was last worked in 1930. Steam pressure was about 2 psi, and the engine made between 6 and 8 strokes per minute. The piston is packed with spun yarn and the pipe for running in water to act as a seal is seen above the 48 in. diameter cylinder [see also 6.6].

comen engine was erected in 1712 at Dudley Castle in the Black Country where it was used for draining a coal mine. This engine had a cylinder 19 in. diameter, a stroke of 6 ft, and developed some $5\frac{1}{2}$ horsepower. The principle of operation was both simple and extremely reliable; important factors influencing the widespread adoption of Newcomen engines. When steam, at slightly above atmospheric pressure, was admitted into the cylinder the piston was drawn up by the weight of the pump rods. At the same time any air in the cylinder was ejected through non-return valves. Closure of the steam inlet-valve was followed by condensation of the steam in the cylinder by a jet of cold water which created a partial vacuum and allowed the unbalanced atmospheric pressure on the top of the piston to push it down, raise the pump rods, and thus make a working stroke.

Undoubtedly the most important surviving memorial to Thomas Newcomen is the Hawkesbury engine, re-erected in the Royal Avenue Gardens, Dartmouth (188/SX 879515) and opened to the public in July 1964 to commemorate the 300th anniversary of its inventor's birth. This engine probably dates from the mid-1720s. It was originally installed at Griff colliery, Warwickshire, later moved to Measham, and in 1821 installed on the bank of the Coventry Canal at Hawkesbury Junction (132/SP 363846) where it was used to raise water from a sump into the canal itself. The engine was occasionally worked until 1913 and in 1963 was given to the Newcomen Society by its owners, the British Transport Commission. A number of modifications have been made to the

6.6

CYLINDER, ELSECAR ENGINE (*102/SE 388000 – 5 miles south-east of Barnsley*). The body of the cylinder showing the cold water injection valve box on the right and the pipe to the injection inlet. Beneath the cylinder is the box of the hot well and condensate drain pipe.

engine, the most significant of which is the 'pickle-pot' condenser below the cylinder, an improvement designed to increase thermal efficiency and at the same time avoid an infringement of Watt's separate condenser patent. Another surviving engine of New-comen type stands at Elsecar [6.5 and 6.6] in the West Riding of Yorkshire where it was used for colliery drainage from 1787 until 1923.

The most important single contribution to the evolution of the steam engine was the invention of the separate condenser by James Watt (1736–1819), the Scottish instrument maker who was to become responsible, in association with the entrepreneur and industrialist Matthew Boulton (1728–1809), for the widespread adoption of steam power in all types of industrial application. In 1765, when employed at Glasgow University, Watt had appreciated the fundamental inefficiency built into the Newcomen atmospheric engine – the thermal losses resulting from raising and lowering the temperature of the working cylinder during the cycle from steam-inlet to condensation. His, in principle, simple solution was to remove the area of condensation from the cylinder to an evacuated chamber – the separate condenser – so that the temperature of the working cylinder was not significantly lowered [6.3]. By keeping the condenser clear of the water with a pump, and the cylinder as hot as possible with a steam jacket, Watt brought about a major increase in thermal efficiency and absolute power. This was further enhanced by the use of steam instead of air to push the piston down. Watt patented his condenser in 1769. Relics of this period of his career include the model Newcomen engine on which he carried out experiments, the cylinder and condenser which were probably used by Watt in his original experiments, and the contents of his garret workshop from Heathfield, Birmingham. The model is housed in Glasgow University; the latter remains are in the Science Museum, South Kensington.

In 1782 Watt patented the double-acting engine in which steam is applied alternately to both sides of the piston thereby obtaining double the power from the same size of cylinder. In the same year he took out a patent for a rotative beam engine incorporating a curious sun-and-planet motion between the connecting-rod and flywheel shaft, devised to avoid infringing a patent of 1780 obtained by James Pickard for the common crank. These features, together with his parallel motion which provided a positive linkage between the reciprocating end of the piston rod and the beam, meant that Watt had an engine capable of a much wider range of applications than mere mine pumping. With the advent of rotary power generated by steam, industry was on the verge of a major technological breakthrough. By 1800 when Watt's partnership with Boulton ended and the patent on the separate condenser expired, 496 engines had been built of which 308 were rotative. A few of these were rated at 40 horsepower. but most had an output of between 15 and 20 horsepower, well within the existing capa-

6.7
NAMEPLATE, PAPPLEWICK ENGINES (*112/SK 583522 – 3 miles north-east of Hucknall*). It is always useful to note nameplates on engines and other machines, since they are often very helpful, if used with some caution, in establishing the dates of machinery. This particular name plate bears an especially honoured name in steam engineering.

cities of the water-wheel. The major advantage of the steam engine, however, was its freedom from both the tight locational factors and the unreliability of stream flow which restricted the widespread application of water power.

The rotative beam engine enjoyed greatest popularity for driving machinery between 1800 and 1850 but both the rotative and non-rotative forms remained in vogue for water and sewage pumping until the early 1900s. Few non-pumping beam engines are still in active use although a number are preserved. An early example of a Watt engine, dating from 1788 and complete with sun-and-planet gear, wooden beam and the centrifugal governor which Watt patented in that year, may be seen in the Science Museum, South Kensington. A pair of engines, still in regular use, drive mashing and milling machinery in the Ram Brewery, Wandsworth (170/TQ 256747). Built by Wentworth and Sons in 1835 and 1867 these compound engines exhibit all the classic

6.8

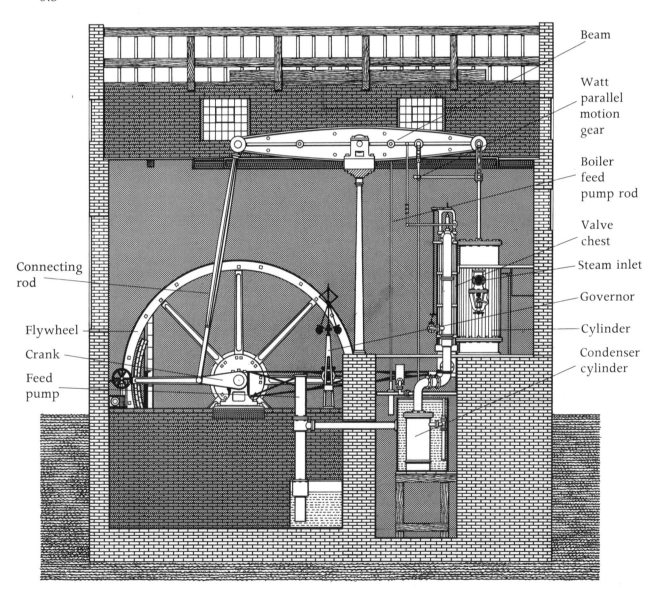

Beam

Watt parallel motion gear

Boiler feed pump rod

Valve chest

Steam inlet

Governor

Cylinder

Condenser cylinder

Connecting rod

Flywheel

Crank

Feed pump

features, including slide valves and lattice eccentric rods (introduced by Murdoch in 1799), cast-iron beams, timber-lagged cylinders, and the immaculate cleanliness so typical of steam engine maintenance.

The mechanical fascination and tremendous visual impact of the large beam engine have led to numerous examples being preserved *in situ*. At Stretham in Cambridgeshire [*6.11* and Plates 29(a) to (f)] is the last surviving beam engine used for fen drainage. The robust reliability of the beam engine made it popular with water supply companies and for sewage pumping, and in these roles it reached a high degree of development by the latter years of the nineteenth century. Two late engines of this type are preserved at Papplewick, Nottinghamshire [*6.7* and Plate 31(b)]. Built by James Watt and Co. in 1884 these rotative engines with their 46-in. diameter cylinders and 7 ft 6 in. stroke, each raised 1 500 000 gallons of water per day from the Bunter sandstone to supply the city of Nottingham. The iron pillars supporting the engine are covered in intricate decoration which recurs throughout the interior of the engine house in tilework and stained glass windows. The whole effect is heightened by the landscaped setting and ornamental pool beloved of waterworks companies at this period. Also preserved in the East Midlands are four ornate sewage pumping engines at Abbey Lane, Leicester (121/SK 589066) built in 1891 by Messrs. Gimson, a local firm. They form the centrepiece for a museum of technology of the East Midlands, currently under development. In County Durham Ryhope pumping station (78/NZ 403523), with its two 1868 rotative compound engines by Hawthorns of Newcastle, is under the care of the Ryhope Pumping Engines Preservation Fund, whilst in Hampshire Portsmouth City Museums are restoring two James Watt sewage pumping engines of 1887 at Eastney (181/SZ 675989).

A specialized, and in many cases very large, type of beam engine was the Cornish pump developed by Richard Trevithick (1771–1833) from an engine he erected in 1812 at Wheal Prosper tin mine in Cornwall. The Cornish engine was a single-acting, usually non-rotative beam engine in which steam applied above the piston lifted, through the beam, pump rods in the mine shaft. At the end of the piston's down stroke the equilib-

6.9

INDICATORS, ROSTOWRACK ENGINE (*In Holman's Museum, Camborne – 198/SW 647401*). Such indicators, acting on the movement of a pendulum relative to the motion of the beam, were a vital part of the arrangements of early engines, at least so far as Boulton and Watt were concerned. They took payment for their engines as a percentage of the estimated savings in coal consumption as compared with a Newcomen engine doing the same amount of work, and so they needed to know how many strokes the engine had made per year. The indicators were locked to prevent tampering. Similar counters can be seen on much later engines providing a simple record of operation.

6.10

CORNISH ENGINE AND STAMPS (*In Holman's museum, Camborne – 189/SW 647401*). This model shows a complete Cornish boiler house, engine, and ore-crushing stamps, arranged as they were normally worked. The model is particularly interesting as no site still survives with all components intact to illustrate their arrangement. The model can be rotated to show the action of the stamps. Numerous exhibits relating to the history and technology of mining in Cornwall make a visit to the museum well worthwhile.

rium valve was opened allowing steam to be transferred from the upper to the lower side of the piston as the unbalanced weight of the pump rods caused it to ascend. At the end of this stroke the equilibrium valve was closed and, with the piston at the top, the next cycle proceeded. At the same time the exhaust valve was opened to the condenser, the steam below the piston condensed, and the resultant vacuum below was added to the effect of the steam above the piston. Cornish engines were extremely efficient for draining mines but also found widespread favour for water supply pumping and other drainage applications as in the Severn railway tunnel. As their name suggests they were most numerous in Cornwall where five engines were preserved by the Cornish Engines Preservation Society and are now in the care of the National Trust. These include one of the largest, with a 90 in. diameter cylinder, built at Taylor's Shaft, East Pool (189/SW 674416) in 1892 and an early rotative winding engine of 1840 at the Levant mine (189/SW 375346), six miles from Land's End. In Scotland the Cornish engine at Prestongrange Colliery, East Lothian (62/NT 374737), built by Harvey and Co. of Hayle, Cornwall in 1874, is being restored to form the centre of an historical

6.11

WATER LEVEL INDICATOR, STRETHAM OLD ENGINE (*135/TL 516730 – 4½ miles south of Ely*). As the boilers worked at a low pressure the old water level indicators from the original 1831 wagon boilers were reinstalled. The indicator works from a float inside the boiler, the counterbalance weight being seen in the picture. The water level is both indicated and controlled by this mechanism as the float connects with rods which open or close a valve in the bottom of the cistern, which was filled with the hot condensate from the cylinder. When the steam pressure was raised in 1888, this system was unworkable, but fortunately the indicators were allowed to remain.

Plate 31(a)

DEE MILL ENGINES (*101/SD 944090 – in Shaw*). Typical of the larger engines installed to drive spinning mills in the cotton areas of Lancashire, this magnificent pair of twin tandem-compound mill engines by Scott & Hodgson were built in 1907, and represent the near ultimate development of the steam engine for factory use. The Corliss-valve high pressure cylinders are of 21 in. bore and the low-pressure 44 in. bore. The stroke is 5 ft. The boilers supplied steam at 200 psi and the engines were designed to develop 1500 h.p. at 65 r.p.m. The larger low-pressure and the smaller high-pressure cylinders of both engines are plainly visible in this picture. The valve chests in front are shown in more detail in *6.19*. The 84-ton flywheel is grooved to take the drive ropes which run direct to the shafts on each floor of the factory. Messrs Courtaulds have co-operated with the Northern Mill Engine Society to preserve this notable engine (see page 2).

Plate 31(b)

PAPPLEWICK PUMPING ENGINES (*112/SK 583522 – 3 miles north-east of Hucknall*). This pair of engines was installed in 1884, with 46 in. diameter cylinder of 7 ft 6 in. stroke, using steam of 50 psi from six Lancashire boilers. Each engine, developing 160 h.p. at $11\frac{1}{2}$ strokes per minute, can raise $1\frac{1}{2}$ million gallons per day. The photograph shows the cylinder tops and the parallel motion, while in the background can be seen the ornate detailing of the engine house. The engines were last used regularly in 1969 but are still kept in steam on standby duty. The flywheel and governor are seen below; in the background is the stained glass of the upper parts of the windows. Outside, the ornamental pool and landscaped setting are characteristic of the flamboyant style still to be seen in many Victorian water supply installations.

116

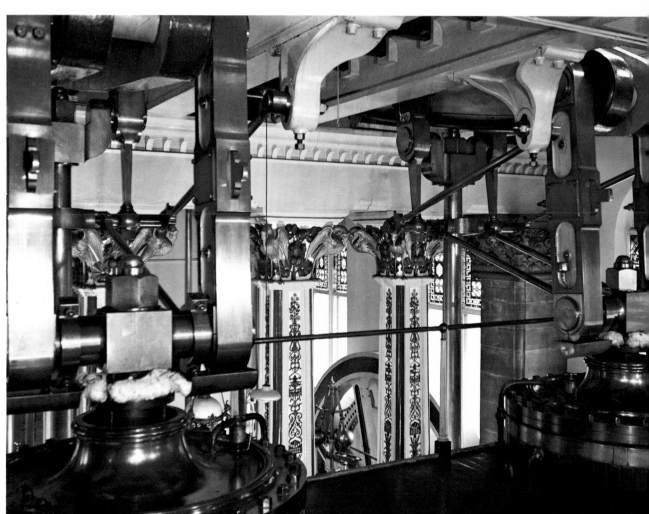

Plate 32(a)

PARSONS BRUSHGEAR (*preserved in the Science Museum*). This brushgear is on an early three-phase turbo-alternator. The machine was built by C. A. Parsons & Co. in 1900, and remained in use in a colliery until 1934. Running at 2520 r.p.m. it generated 150 kilowatts at 350 volts and 42c/s. A small DC generator directly coupled to the main machine provides the excitation current for the bipolar field magnet. The output current is taken from the three 300 mm diameter slip-rings by the copper gauze brushes shown here. Four 45 mm wide brushes bear on each slip-ring, two near the camera and two behind the machine. In this machine the armature rotates and the field is static, so that the brushgear has to carry the entire output current. Carbon brushes, now universally adopted, were suggested as early as 1885, but metal gauze was used on some machines until well into the twentieth century. The current-carrying capacity of the brushgear determined the maximum size of generators of this pattern. For higher powers the machine was inverted, with the armature windings static; the brushes then had to carry only the much smaller exciter current. In modern machines even this is too great, and brushgear is avoided altogether by generating the excitation current in an auxiliary machine on the same shaft and rectifying it with semiconductor rectifiers mounted on the rotating system.

Plate 32(b)

KENSINGTON COURT GENERATING STATION (*160/TQ 258797 – Kensington Court, London W.8*). The first generating plant erected to serve the new development of Kensington Court was in a temporary building, but the generating station shown in this picture was erected in 1887, and designed to blend with the estate. The terraced houses were arranged round an open green, and linked with a subway, through which Crompton ran his mains of bare copper strip supported by insulators on the wall. Nothing remains of the original plant, which consisted of Willans engines directly coupled to Crompton DC generators and used accumulators to supply the load in off-peak periods. Coal was supplied to the station through a pavement hole similar to those provided for the coal cellars of the houses. The building is now used as offices and a transformer substation.

Plate 32(c)

GREENWICH POWER STATION (*171/ TQ 388781 – next to the Royal Naval College*). This photograph was made from the coaling pier of Deptford West power station, and shows the last important British power station to be built with reciprocating engines rather than turbines. It was built to supply the trams and railways operated by the London County Council, and was opened in 1906 with four generators rated at 3500 kilowatts each. The 'Manhattan' engines had a speed of only 94 r.p.m.; the crankshaft carried a flywheel at its centre and was driven by two cylinders, one vertical and one horizontal. The original intention was to complete the station with a further four engines of the same kind, but this was not done. Within a few years four 5000 kilowatt turbo-generators had been installed, and by 1922 all the original engines had been removed. The station is fired by coal brought by river (note the coaling jetty on the left of the picture) and uses river water to cool its condensers.

site devoted to the Scottish coal industry. Last worked in 1954 this pumping engine has a steam cylinder 70 in. in diameter with a stroke of 12 ft.

The opening years of the nineteenth century saw several alternatives to the beam engine introduced to achieve greater efficiency, simplicity of erection and higher speeds. Direct-acting engines, dispensing with the heavy rocking beam between connecting rod and crankshaft began to appear [*6.13*]. An early form was the table engine introduced in 1807 by Henry Maudslay (1771–1831), and this was followed, after about 1825, by numerous designs of the soon to be popular horizontal engine, with its single

6.12

TREVITHICK HIGH-PRESSURE ENGINE (*In the Science Museum*). This engine was built by Hazeldine & Co. of Bridgnorth between 1803 and 1808, and marks a very notable advance in steam engine construction. James Watt's engines operated on low-pressure steam but Trevithick's use of higher pressures together with expansive working led to a great increase in efficiency. This engine worked at about 52 psi with a cylinder 6·37 in. diameter by 30·5 in. stroke. At 50 r.p.m. it developed 7½ h.p., not far short of the output of the much larger beam engines using low-pressure steam. The complete unit, of which the boiler was an integral part, was now small enough to be moved from place to place as requirements dictated. The cylinder is sunk inside the boiler, steam being admitted by a four-way valve worked by a tappet from the crosshead. The 9 ft diameter flywheel has a cast-in balance weight.

6.13

MAUDSLAY TABLE ENGINE (*In the Science Museum – 170/TQ 268793*). This engine was used to pump water to supply a hospital, and was made about 1815. The table engine was one of the earliest direct-acting types which avoided the use of a cumbersome rocking beam. The cylinder is mounted vertically on a table and the piston rod is connected to the crankshaft beneath by two return connecting rods. The crosshead at the end of the piston rod is guided by small rollers running between vertical slide bars. The cylinder has a 12 in. bore and 24 in. stroke and at 60 to 80 r.p.m. developed about 7 h.p. For over half a century this compact and easily portable type of engine was favoured for driving workshops and similar duties.

6.14
PORTABLE STEAM ENGINE (*In the Bressingham Steam Museum collection – 136/ TM 080808, 2 miles west of Diss*). The portable engine has a locomotive-type firetube boiler, on top of which is mounted the power unit consisting of one or two cylinders driving a crankshaft on which is a belt wheel. Portable engines were not powered but had to be towed to their place of work.

6.15
BEAMISH WINDING ENGINE (*78/NZ 220537 – 1 mile east of Stanley*). Dials of indicators which provided the engineman with information on the position of the cage in the shaft.

cylinder, slide-bars and crankshaft bearings on a cast-iron bedplate of box-girder section. Examples of both these types may be seen in the Science Museum, South Kensington. High-pressure steam engines [*6.12*], pioneered in Britain by Trevithick, achieved higher efficiencies and led the way to railway locomotives and steamships, both of which used direct-acting engines in a variety of configurations. This was a most important advance.

Compounding, applied successfully on beam engines, was also used in a variety of other types and developed throughout the nineteenth century to form the basis for the most efficient and sophisticated reciprocating engines ever constructed. These were used in textile mills and for electricity generation. Watt had exploited the expansive properties of steam by cutting off inlet at an early stage in the stroke of the piston. Arthur Woolf (1776–1837), a versatile Cornish mine engineer, developed the idea further by putting two cylinders of different diameters on a beam engine. Steam was admitted from the boiler to the smaller cylinder, allowed to expand partially, and exhausted into the larger diameter cylinder where further expansion occurred, with the result that great increases in efficiency could be obtained. The Ryhope engines mentioned above are of this type.

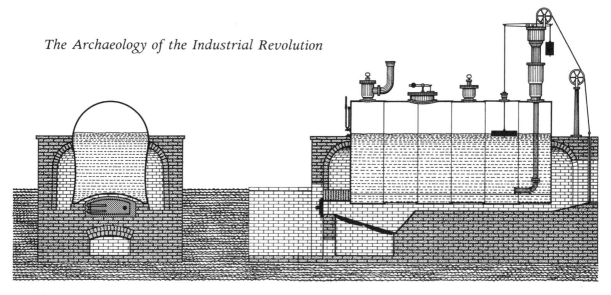

6.16
WAGON BOILER

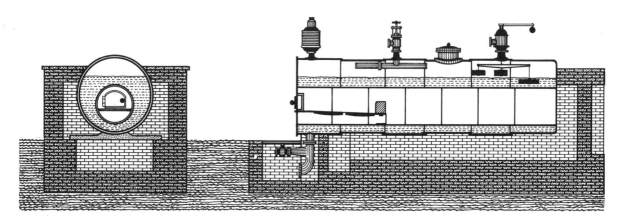

6.17
CORNISH BOILER

6.18
RAILWAY LOCOMOTIVE BOILER

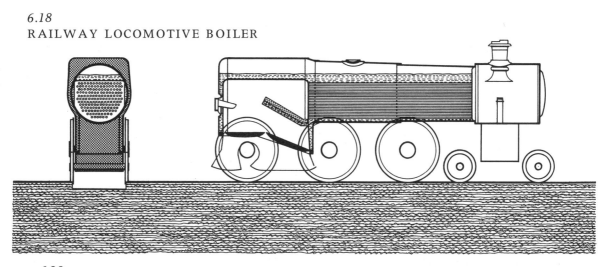

With high-pressure direct-acting engines compounding was still more successful, eventually being achieved in three or even four stages through cylinders of successively increasing size. The triple expansion type with three cylinders mounted vertically above the crankshaft found favour not only for marine use but also as a replacement for beam engines in water pumping stations. Two of the largest land-based triples ever built are still in use at Kempton Park Waterworks, Hounslow, (170/TQ 110709), while another pair of triples remains operative at Otterbourne pumping station in Hampshire (168/SU 468233); both pairs are by Worthington and Simpson of Newark and date from the 1920s.

By the end of the nineteenth century the big textile mills of Lancashire and Yorkshire were demanding higher and higher horsepowers to drive their vast numbers of machines and a specialized type of engine, the mill engine, was developed to satisfy this need. Almost invariably horizontal compounds, these were built to give as much as 4000 h.p. The two most popular layouts were the tandem-compound in which high- and low-pressure cylinders lay one behind the other with a common piston rod, and the cross-compound in which the high-pressure cylinder drove one end of the crankshaft and the low-pressure the other, while between the two was the fly-wheel with its broad face cast in grooves for the cotton drive ropes which powered the mill. The engine of Dee Mill, Shaw, near Rochdale [6.19 and Plate 31(a)] is an example of the ultimate in mill engine design. A small tandem-compound mill engine by Pollitt and Wigzell of Sowerby Bridge is displayed in the Birmingham Museum of Science and Industry.

In the 1880s demand arose for engines to power electrical dynamos. A number of high-speed types were developed which could be direct-coupled to the generator shaft, the Willans single-acting compound central-valve engine and later the double-acting vertical compound by Bellis and Morcom achieving considerable success. Indeed

6.19
VALVE ARRANGEMENT, DEE MILL ENGINES (*101/SD 944090 – in Shaw*). The semi-rotary Corliss inlet valves of one of the high-pressure cylinders and their drive rods.

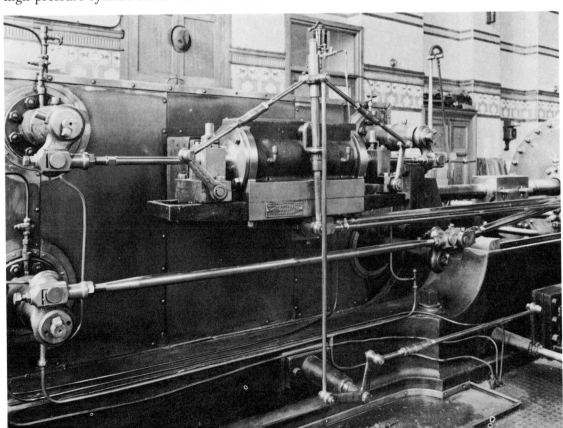

engines of the latter variety are still employed in large numbers to generate electricity in factories and hospitals where steam is needed anyway for heating and process work. The patenting of the steam turbine in 1884 by C. A. Parsons (1854–1931) marked the beginning of the end for the reciprocating steam engine although the internal combustion engine and electric motor have been much more significant factors in its demise. Parsons' original 1884 turbine and bipolar dynamo are in the Science Museum, South Kensington; others of his turbines may be seen at the Abbeydale industrial museum, Sheffield and, appropriately, in the Newcastle upon Tyne Museum of Science and Engineering. Plate 30(c) shows a Parsons turbine of 1901.

FURTHER READING

BARTON, D. B. *The Cornish Beam Engine* (D. B. Barton, 1965)

DICKINSON, H. W. *A Short History of the Steam Engine* (Cambridge University Press, 1938; reprinted, Frank Cass, 1963)

LAW, R. J. *The Steam Engine* (HMSO, 1965)

ROLT, L. T. C. *James Watt* (London: Batsford, 1962)

ROLT, L. T. C. *Thomas Newcomen: The Prehistory of the Steam Engine* (Newton Abbot: David and Charles, 1964)

WATKINS, G. *The Stationary Steam Engine* (Newton Abbot: David and Charles, 1968)

7. Electric Power

BRIAN BOWERS

THE ELECTRICITY SUPPLY INDUSTRY has not left many relics comparable with those of wind, water, and steam power. This is not just because it is a young industry, for several 'generations' of equipment have come and gone since electricity supply began about 1880. Redundant wind-mills and water-wheels have usually been in sites of little value, where they were just abandoned. The early electricity supply stations were in more expensive urban areas and so were often stripped and re-equipped, or demolished altogether. Another contrast is that while wind and water power require buildings of a special character, the electricity generator and a steam engine to drive it could be installed almost anywhere. Crompton's station at Kensington Court [Plate 32(b)] was purpose-built, but designed to harmonize with the surrounding houses. Only the inscription over the door reveals the original purpose of the building.

Although remains are scanty, there are detailed records of many of the early public supply systems in the electrical journals of the time and the sites may be found from local records. With private generation the position is different. From an early date some country-house owners and some businessmen installed their own generating equipment. At first such installations were equipped with steam-driven plant similar to that used by the public supply companies; later petrol or diesel prime-movers were used. Sometimes the private plant was just left, abandoned, when the public supply arrived, and such remains are largely unrecorded.

The supply industry really began when there was both a practical source of electricity, the generator, and a useful application for electricity, initially the arc lamp and then the incandescent filament lamp.

7.1
EARLY COMMERCIAL SWAN LAMP

7.2
TYPICAL SWITCH FROM A MAIN SWITCHBOARD. As the switch opens (b) a small spring-loaded auxiliary contact makes the final break of the circuit. Any damage by sparking is confined to the replaceable auxiliary contact.

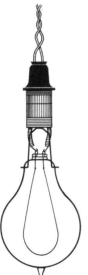

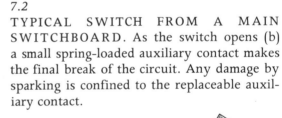

123

Plate 33(a)

BANK BELL-PITS (*camera position 102/SE 275139; bell pits 1 mile away at SE 267129 – 6 miles south-west of Wakefield*). Where bell-pits survive nowadays, they do so as a series of pimple-like protrusions on the surface, each perhaps 10 yd across, perhaps 10 ft high, and with a central depression [see *8.1*]. At Bank there are the remains of about 60 such pits, associated with Bank Furnace. Although these pits were for ironstone, the same type was used for coal. In the background is a spoil heap of typical form. Both such surface remains are subject to erosion, while in addition bell-pits are vulnerable to ploughing, as can be seen in the case of some of those shown in the plate. About ten miles south of this site, upwards of forty such pits were exposed during the construction of the M1 motorway at Tankersley, north of Sheffield. Many are plainly visible from the motorway.

Plate 33(b)

WORSLEY COLLIERY ENTRANCE (*101/ SD 748005 – 6 miles west of the centre of Manchester*). The outstanding example both of underground water transport for coal and of sough drainage of a colliery is that system which starts from the delf in Worsley, at a terminus of the Bridgewater canal. The system was begun in 1759, the main canal running four miles northward to Farnworth, intersecting various seams. At the north end a second canal was made 35 yd above the first, connection being by a self-acting underground incline. Today all that can be seen to remind us of this fantastic early subterranean system are the two tunnel entrances, plainly visible from the road, the reed-grown canal basin, and the remains of two of the sluices which when opened provided a current to help move the boats underground. On the other hand, the whole Midlands canal complex may be taken as a memorial to the success of the Bridgewater Canal. James Brindley first came on the scene in July 1759, construction having begun in April, under John Gilbert. By the end of the year 150 yd had been driven underground, and 2 miles of surface canal had been cut towards Patricroft and the site of the famous aqueduct over the Irwell [see *2.3*].

Plate 34(a)

ELSECAR PUMPING ENGINE (*102/SE 387000 – about 7 miles north of Sheffield*). A Newcomen-type atmospheric engine dated to 1795 (the date 1787 on the engine house is erroneous and a warning to all industrial archaeologists), this pump worked regularly until 1923, was brought back into use in an emergency during 1928 and last worked in 1931. Originally the beam was of wood with chains connecting it to the pump rods (parts of which are still hung beneath the cast-iron beam and parallel motion of 1836–37). The engine made between six and eight strokes per minute, lifting 50 gallons through 43 yd per stroke. This machine is a fine example of the engines which made deeper mining possible. (Further details are shown in *6.5* and *6.6*).

Plate 34(b)

PIT GEAR, DAWLEY (*119/SJ 678078 – just outside Dawley, although now dismantled for re-erection at the Blists Hill site*). This small pit was one of many hundreds in the area, although very few have any headgear remaining, and most are now filled in. Besides coal, which was sold locally until the last war, the shaft also produced good quality brick clay. The wooden gear is typical of small scale workings of earlier date, and represents a stage in evolution just past the bell pit. The shaft was only about fifty feet deep.

Plate 34(c)

BEAMISH WINDING ENGINE (*78/NZ 220537 – 1½ miles east of Stanley*). In 1800 Phineas Crowther, of Newcastle upon Tyne, patented a vertical single-cylinder engine, which dispensed with the usual beam, and which remained in use in the Newcastle area for many years. The winding drum was placed above the vertical cylinder, so necessitating the typical tall engine-house shape, shown in the plate. J. & G. Joicey of Newcastle built their No. 20 in 1855 for Beamish No. 2 pit, where it continued in use until 1952. The wooden pithead gear remains in good order, while the machinery is still in place inside [see *6.15*]. Although several other such engine houses can be found, none of these retain their machinery. This engine is reserved for the open-air museum, and so will be on display at Beamish in the future.

The generator stems from Faraday's discovery in 1831 that an electric force is induced in a piece of wire moved so as to cut the 'lines of force' of a magnet. A variety of magneto-electric machines ('magnetos' for short) were devised in the 1830s and 1840s, but their output was small. Their main application was for electro-chemical work, such as electro-plating.

In 1857 the Englishman F. H. Holmes demonstrated to Trinity House a magneto and arc lamp for use in lighthouses. On Faraday's advice two Holmes machines and an arc lamp were installed in the South Foreland lighthouse in 1858. Each machine weighed over five tons, but its output was very small.

The enormous weight-to-power ratio of magneto-electric machines was inevitable because they depended on permanent magnets. The substitution of electro-magnets for the permanent magnets had been suggested at least as early as 1845 but the idea was not developed until the 1860s. The final step, which made the modern generator possible, was the realization that a generator could use electro-magnets whose energizing current was taken from the output of the generator itself. The current which could be generated was no longer restricted by the strength of the permanent magnets available. This discovery, which became known in 1867, was made independently by Siemens, Wheatstone, and Varley, and possibly by others also.

The intense light produced by an electric arc between two carbon rods was demonstrated by Davy in 1808. The carbons burn away in the heat of the arc and in the first arc lamps they were moved together manually to compensate. Automatic regulators were then devised in which the mechanism was controlled by an electromagnet connected either in series with the arc, so as to respond to variations in the current as the carbon burnt away, or in parallel with the arc, so as to respond to variations in the voltage across it. Usually the carbons were arranged one above the other, the upper one falling under gravity but restrained by a brake.

The brilliant light of the arc lamp made it ideal for illuminating large spaces, though it was quite unsuitable for domestic use. In the second half of 1878 a number of electric lighting installations appeared in London. The Victoria Embankment between Westminster and Waterloo Bridges was illuminated, as was Holborn Viaduct. Both were abandoned after a short trial period and gas lighting restored on grounds of economy. Within a year, however, the incandescent filament lamp was devised, independently, by Swan in England [7.1] and Edison in the U.S.A. The filament lamp was ideal for domestic use.

The first power station supplying consumers – though its principal purpose was street lighting – was probably the hydro-electric station at Godalming, Surrey, installed and run by the Siemens Company in 1881. In 1882 Edison, through his London agent, obtained permission to light the Holburn Viaduct with incandescent lamps; he also gave a supply to private consumers nearby and subsequently to the General Post Office in Newgate Street and the City Temple at the west end of the viaduct, the first church to have electric lighting.

The Godalming company used cables laid in the gutters along the streets. Edison had a main consisting of two segment-shaped copper conductors fixed in iron pipes and each consumer was connected to this main by an insulated cable [7.3].

During the next twenty years a large number of supply companies were formed. One of the earliest whose generating station building (though not the machinery) still survives was the company formed by R. E. B. Crompton to supply Kensington Court, then a new residential development just off Kensington High Street. The houses in

126

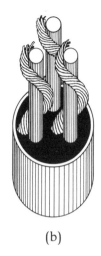

(a)   (b)   (c)

7.3

TYPES OF CABLE (a) Edison main of 1882 with two segment-shaped copper conductors in an iron tube. (b) Edison three-core main of 1884. The conductors are copper rods wound with rope and placed in an iron tube filled with pitch. (c) Ferranti 10 000 volt tubular main of 1890. The conductors are concentric copper tubes with impregnated paper between them and whole cable is encased in an iron tube.

Kensington Court were all linked by a subway, thus avoiding the need to obtain Parliamentary powers to dig up the road.

The electric lighting legislation adopted had the effect of encouraging the proliferation of a large number of companies each supplying only a small area, usually with direct current. The man who made the most significant contribution to the development of the supply industry as we know it was Sebastian Ziani de Ferranti (1864–1930). His arguments – which were strongly disputed by many engineers – were that electricity should be generated by large machines, which were more economical than small ones, and transmitted at high voltage over much greater distances than had been the case until then. The use of high voltage meant that a smaller current was needed for a given power and lighter and cheaper cables could be used. It also meant in practice that the system had to use alternating current, rather than the direct current used in most of the earlier systems, because the alternating current transformer provided the most reliable and efficient method of converting the supply to high voltage on leaving the generating station and back to low voltage in substations near the consumers. In 1886 Ferranti entered the employment of Sir Coutts Lindsey who, three years earlier, had established a station for lighting the Grosvenor Gallery in London. This station soon began supplying other people in the area and in 1887 it became the London Electric Supply Corporation Ltd. Ferranti planned a power station which was built at Deptford and transmitted electricity to central London at the unprecedented pressure of 10 000 volts. He designed transformers and cables [7.3] for the purpose, his cables being the first to use oil-impregnated paper insulation. Not all engineers accepted Ferranti's ideas, and the 'battle of the systems' – a battle of words conducted in the engineering journals and societies on the relative merits of AC and DC systems – continued for some years until Ferranti's ideas prevailed.

In the first steam powered generating stations the generators were usually belt-driven from the steam engine, which rotated at a much lower speed than the generator. From 1885 onwards the higher speed Willans engine enabled generators to be coupled

7.4

DEPTFORD WEST POWER STATION
(*171/TQ 374779 – Stowage, London S.E.8*).
This generating station is not old in comparison with many of the other sites described in
this book, but it is one of the oldest generating stations still in service. Although it was built
as recently as 1928, the station has been at least partly superseded, allowing opportunity
to see a 1920s power station in virtual operational order.

7.4 shows the control room, where two men were normally on duty. When compared
with the control room of a modern power station, the main differences are that the
controls are several times the size of their modern counterparts, and that the indicator
lights are 'on' to show satisfactory operation, whereas in modern practice indicator lights
come on only to indicate a fault. A variety of obsolescent equipment is shown, the most
obvious being the semaphore-type indicators (above the switching panels) showing which
switches are closed. The free-standing equipment resembling a ship's telegraph has much
the same function; each of the six generating sets has its own Chadburn indicator unit in
front of its control panel. This unit incorporates a Dicks intercom. The instrument towards
the right of the picture, and encased in a glass-fronted panel, is a Tirrill regulator, which
controls the output voltage of the generator. As with the indicator lamps, this is constantly
operating to give a series of clicks; modern regulators operate only when a voltage change
has to be made. At the far end of the room, on a swivel mount directly under the clock, is
the synchroscope by means of which the engineer could bring the outputs of two sets
into synchronism before any switching was carried out – failure to do this could cause
considerable instantaneous damage to the generating equipment.

directly to the prime mover. The speed R (revolutions per minute), output frequency f (cycles per second), and number of pairs of poles P of a generator are linked by the formula

$$R = \frac{60 f}{P}$$

so that a 50 c/s (cycles per second) generator directly coupled to a 300 r.p.m. (revolutions per minute) Willans engine would have ten pairs of poles and be a large and complex machine.

The steam turbine, developed by Sir Charles Parsons, rapidly replaced reciprocating engines. The turbine is essentially a high-speed machine and if it is directly coupled to a generator running at 3000 r.p.m. the generator needs only a single pair of poles (in a single phase system) and can be of much simpler and more robust construction.

7.5

A general view of the turbine house, showing the six sets of turbo-generators. Number 1 and 2, nearer the camera, were installed in 1928; the others were put in successively as demand required, the furthest set being used from 1939. In the well between the sets the condensers are visible (cooling water is taken from the Thames); auxiliary equipment is arranged along the far wall. Behind this wall is the boiler house, containing an interesting range of equipment, starting with 1928 Stirling chain-gate boilers. The control equipment is still in situ, and it is notable that very few instruments are provided compared with modern installations.

The last important British power station to be built with reciprocating engines was the one at Greenwich, opened in 1906 by the London County Council to supply London Transport [Plate 32(c)]. Within a few years this was re-equipped with turbines and turbines have been used in all later British power stations. The main changes since then have been in the size of plant. Parsons' first three phase turbo-generator installed in a colliery in 1900 was rated at 150 kilowatts. In 1935 the largest was 105 megawatts at Battersea. In 1970 the Central Electricity Generating Board was commissioning units rated at 500 megawatts.

FURTHER READING

DUNSHEATH, PERCY *A History of Electrical Engineering* (London: Faber, 1962)

PARSONS, R. H. *Early Days of the Power Station Industry* (Cambridge University Press, 1939)

There are numerous biographies of electrical engineers like Ferranti, Crompton, Edison, Swan and others.

8. Coal and other Fuels

WILL SLATCHER AND BRIAN BRACEGIRDLE

COAL

Any account of the archaeology of the coal trade in Britain in a short compass must needs be superficial. One can only hope to indicate trends and the reader must not be surprised if the generalizations do not seem to apply to his part of the world. Indeed it is extremely difficult to generalize about an industry with traditions and practices as diverse as this; local practices, accidents of history, and sheer perversity combine to upset the would-be commentator.

Of the coal measures, the numerous coal seams form only a minute proportion and of those only a small number ever had economic significance. Workable seams have varied from the 10-ft Staffordshire Thick and Barnsley coals to the 2-ft coals of West Yorkshire and Wales. The coals themselves vary very widely in quality and have found widely differing applications. Among steam-coals those of South Wales have been highly regarded, whilst the Tyneside High Main was once a favourite house-coal. South Durham coals have produced the strongest metallurgical cokes, whilst other bituminous coals have yielded town gas and fed a once vigorous by-product coal-tar industry. The high ash content of poorer coals has led them to be used for lime burning, salt boiling, and modern electricity generation. Coal-measure sandstones, typically forming the roof of a coal seam, have been of economic importance, whilst the seat-earths below the seam have yielded refractory ganisters or brick-making fireclays. Seams of clay ironstone, now abandoned but once forming the backbone of an industrial revolution, are found in the coal measures. On a smaller scale alum has been extracted in Yorkshire and oil distilled from Lanarkshire shales [8.13]. Many, indeed most, of the traditional uses of coal are fast declining and urgent activity on the part of the industrial historian is necessary if what was once commonplace is to be recorded or preserved.

The chief technical aspects of working a colliery may be put into five categories: sinking the shafts; getting the coal; moving it; keeping the workings dry; and ventilating them. Usually the coal seams dip gently from the horizontal and they, and the rest of the coal measures, are extensively cut up by faults which, together with the varied make-up of the measures, provide vigorous relief and often affect the local techniques and history of exploitation [8.2]. Small-scale outcrop working of coal in quarries, short day-holes or adits, have been of local significance from the earliest times. The land today has generally recovered from the passage of this activity but not all such workings belong to the remote past. Until this century many a northern textile mill had its day-hole for engine coal and the thin coals above the limestones in the Yorkshire dales have been convenient for the local burning of agricultural lime. Next in sophistication comes the bell-pit [8.1 and Plate 33(a)], where the coal was reached by numerous shallow shafts, often no more than fifty yards apart. If the seam outcropped on a hillside, sough drainage through what might once have been a day-hole could be employed. Otherwise some form of simple pump might have been used if the workings penetrated the water table. New workings were to the rise of the old and water was let down into or through the abandoned dip-side pits.

Extension of exploitation beyond these limits raises most of the technical problems

Plate 35(a)

STEEL HEADGEAR, USHAW MOOR (*85/NZ 220428 – 3 miles west of Durham*). National Coal Board rationalization policy has led to the abandonment of many mines and the subsequent filling in of their shafts and destruction of their surface installations. Such sites tend to offer only uninterpretable concrete and twisted steel, although the headgear is sometimes retained, as in this case at Ushaw Moor. The headgear is of steel construction, and shows a fairly typical design of the present.

Plate 35(b)

ABANDONED SHAFT, HALESFIELD COLLIERY (*119/SJ 704052 – 5 miles south-east of Wellington*). When the headgear and other buildings have been removed, all that may remain is a square hole such as that shown in the plate; the shaft will have been filled in but settling may have allowed the level to fall a couple of feet or so. The shaft here was about 600 ft deep, and was worked from about 1850 until the General Strike in 1926, after which it was used only for pumping from an adjacent mine. Besides coal, ironstone was mined for many years. This was taken along the Shropshire Canal to Blists Hill blast furnaces, about one and a half miles away. The headgear was removed in 1969.

Plates 35(c) and 35(d)

DRIFT MINE, SWANSEA VALLEY (*153/SN 767078 – on the mountainside above Ystalyfera*). This mine used to employ about thirty men, but was closed by the National Coal Board some years ago. It has recently been re-opened to salvage some of the gear for use further up the mountain side in a privately operated drift. The track for the coal tubs is in situ at the lower end, and can be seen in Plate 35(c), looking back up towards the surface about half a mile away. The winding cable is visible between the rails, while to the far side of them is the pipe used for drainage, there being no sough lower down. The telegraph wires are still present, and at this point a vein of iron ore is exposed. 35(d) was made nearer the surface, where the track had been lifted. Relatively few props were needed here, the rock being firm enough to be safely self-supporting. A natural cavern had been passed through, the height of the drift itself being seen to be quite low – about five feet for most of its length. Water in such a mine is a considerable nuisance, for it pours from the roof and runs down the floor constantly, demonstrating vividly the great need for pumps if mining is to proceed.

Plate 36(a)

COKE OVENS, ROWLANDS GILL (*78/ NZ 152582 – about 4 miles north-west of Stanley*). By the middle of the eighteenth century coke ovens were in use in Northumberland, venting from the charging hole at the top. From the mid-nineteenth century the off-gases were collected in a common flue and used to waste-heat a boiler. Attempts were made to use the gases as a source of by-products such as tar and ammonia, and the first battery of by-product ovens was erected at Crook in Durham in 1882. The last coke ovens of the non-recovery beehive type to operate in this country were situated at Rowlands Gill and remained in use until 1958. They owed this late survival to the fact that although vertical machine-charged ovens were much more efficient, the coke from beehive ovens was in certain ways superior. Some of the original set of more than 100 ovens that stood at Rowlands Gill have, as shown in the photograph, been preserved in good order, enabling an excellent idea to be formed of their mode of working. Ovens of a similar type, but in a derelict condition, may be found at the other side of England, immediately north of the station in Whitehaven, between the site of the colliery and the sea.

Plate 36(b)

HORIZONTAL RETORTS (*76/NY 364844 – Langholm gas works*). In about six largely independent gas works in southern Scotland horizontal retorts were still in use to make town gas in 1971 – although they were not expected to be used for much longer. The pattern has not changed in a century except for a degree of standardization, and the operating methods are still the same [see *8.3* and *8.5*]. Here in Langholm are two benches of five retorts, as originally built. The rest of the works is on a similar small scale so that all the technology of town gas manufacture can be seen in a five-minute stroll round an area of about an acre.

Plate 36(c)

DIESEL ENGINE, STRETHAM (*135/TL 516730 – 4½ miles south of Ely*). This engine is still in working order for standby duties, and, unlike the fine beam engine at the front of the building, may not be visited without special permission. Engines on Diesel's original air blast system are now quite rare, most of those called diesel not having the high pressure air bottles required for fuel intake employed by the early system. This example is by Mirrlees and Co., and was first run on 20 February 1925. The original air pump remains in place for charging the bottles, which are still insured for their full working pressure. Although only about one tenth of the size of the beam engine it replaced, it could work at about three times the pumping rate.

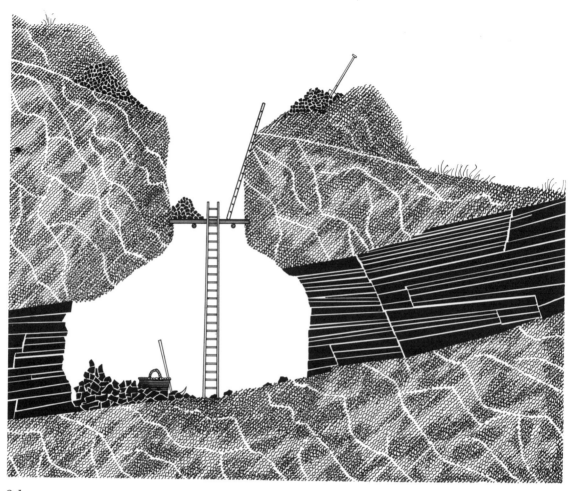

8.1

BELL-PIT. The seam was excavated from the central shaft until the danger of collapse made it necessary to follow the seam by digging another shaft nearby.

mentioned above. The method of getting the coal fell into two broad categories. In long-wall working, all the coal was removed, save pillars left to support the roadways. Props supported the roof at the long working face but were knocked out in the rear and the roof allowed to fall. This method was widespread in Shropshire and the coal-fields dependent on its technology but was not suitable for gas-rich coals or where roof and floor were weak. Creep tended to crush the coal and reduce its value. In the other method, pillar and stall, between half and a quarter of the coal would be left to hold the roof as the colliery was worked away from the shafts. At the end of a pit's life these pillars might be robbed out and subsidence suffered. This method was widely adopted on Tyneside and its technically dependent coalfields. From the working stalls the coal would usually be moved down the dip to a level working road and so carried to the shaft. In earlier workings of this kind shafts were frequent, for the cost of a long underground haul was greater than that of a shallow shaft. This sort of shallow colliery,

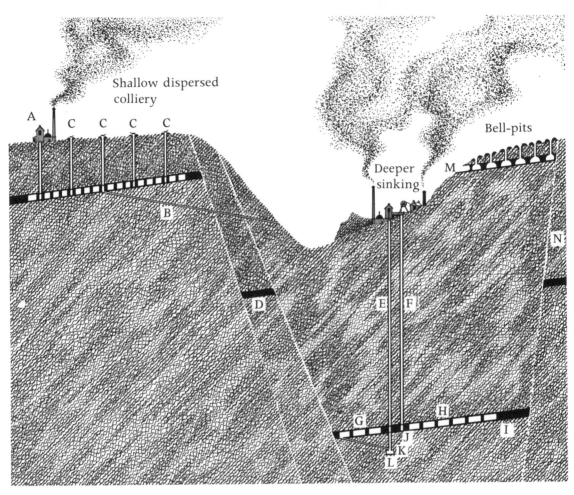

8.2

TYPES OF PIT. The various features of the pits are labelled as follows: A pumping shaft; B sough; C winding shafts; D coal between faults which is not worth working; E pumping shaft; F winding shaft; G dip side; H rise side; I working face; J working level; K water level; L water lodge; M day hole; and N fault.

usually drained by a sough, or tunnel, leading to a suitable surface watercourse, is not infrequently exposed by modern opencast mining, and the archaeologist is offered a rare glimpse of it at a point of final destruction. Record work at this stage is clearly important but rarely undertaken.

Drainage by sough has been mentioned and occasionally their tails can be found; sometimes they have been navigable, as at the famous Worsley Delf [Plate 33(b)]. When workings went deeper, pumping was necessary. Sometimes water power was used but more commonly the atmospheric steam engine or one of its successors was employed [Plate 34(a)]. A second level in the mine, just to the dip of the working level would take the water from the workings to the pumping shaft, which would remain essentially static during the life of a colliery. Its site, occasionally with buildings and workshops, can often be found. The many drawing shafts of these collieries are often represented by spoil-heaps similar to those of bell pits, but bigger and standing alone. Each hill consists of the spoil from a shaft and sometimes a little waste coal. Occasionally the horse-gin circle, used to wind coal from the pit, may be found; on the other hand the stacks were often filled into the shafts when the colliery was abandoned and all that may remain is a soil-mark or, after a wet winter, a depression where the shaft has dropped in a little. When the sites have not been cleared, nature has often reclaimed them and many remains may be found in coppice covered bell-pit or pit-stead ground. Sometimes entry to shallow workings is possible but this can be most dangerous and should never be attempted.

In early days the ventilation of collieries was often inadequate but with increasing numbers of explosions from deeper workings in the nineteenth century, practices were improved. We shall not detail the methods here as the industrial archaeologist will see little of the critical underground paths. A favourite method was to draw air by a furnace at the bottom of an 'upcast' shaft and a short chimney may remain over this shaft at the surface. Often this upcast shaft was also the pumping shaft, and the arrangements were modified. Less frequently the furnace was on the surface. At a later date large fan-houses – looking like water-wheel pits in impossible places – replaced the furnaces. The winding-shafts were used as the 'downcast' shafts.

As collieries became deeper and the cost of sinking shafts rose, fewer were sunk and transport underground had to be improved. In places basket-corves on sleds were dragged over the floor of the mine if it were solid and on boards if it were not. Small wooden railways with wheeled rollies were used on Tyneside and its technical colonies but it was left to John Curr to introduce his system of cast-iron plate rails with wheeled tram-corves into the Sheffield collieries in 1787. Light L-section plates of this type can sometimes be seen on older pit waste-tips. The plate-rail soon came to the surface and in the Midlands, Shropshire, and Wales was in vogue for feeder systems to the canals from the 1790s. As these and other improvements cheapened transport underground – and incidentally led children into extended employment – innovations came in the methods of drawing coals up the shafts. The industrial archaeologist will no longer meet the Scottish bearer-women who carried the coals out of the pit on her back but he may see signs of the gin-circles already mentioned or the water winding-engines sometimes employed. Curr drew his new tram-corves by the small steam engines or 'whimseys' which came into use about 1800 in the Midlands. He also introduced guides to steady the corves in the shaft and the principle was later adopted for pit-cages. The rate of winding could be increased by their use and deep collieries more efficiently worked.

These, and other developments in sinking techniques, paved the way for a new phase in coal mining, that of the deep sinkings. At first the cost of the shaft was such that pumping, drawing, and ventilating were often done from one shaft, divided by brattices, though later two shafts or more became essential. Colliery conveniences and pitmen's cottages clustered round the now fixed pitheads. As the shifting nature of the exploitation of a coalfield came to an end, a change occurred in the pattern of pitmen's settlement. Many deep sinkings in the Tyne basin date from the early nineteenth century. Elsewhere, with reserves of shallow coal remaining, the transition did not come for several decades, though Tyneside had no monopoly of deep early sinkings. With these developments and the enlarged scale of the collieries there is often less of interest for the industrial archaeologist. Few original buildings or machinery from this period survive and, with the screening and cleaning of the coal transferred from the pit-bottom to the surface, spoil heaps began to grow. With the coming of coal-cutting machines from the 1870s much waste was brought to the surface and left there.

It has been in this last century that parts of the British coalfields have become moon-scapes of dereliction, with acres of burning, burnt red, or grey shales lying in untidy heaps. Occasionally, it is true, they do make positive contributions to the landscape but few will mourn their passing. Subsidence has affected drainage and extensive water flashes add to the depression and dereliction. The Wigan Alps seen across the Ince flashes will surely attract no preservationist. The run down in the coal industry in recent years has led to the abandonment of many collieries, sweeping away older buildings and machinery, and even whole colliery sites. With these closures whole communities are swept away too, their memories and spirit with them. The classic movement of the industry to the deeper seams of the concealed coalfield east of the Pennines has been greatly accelerated and large new winnings sunk. The modern work-ing collieries may retain some old installations but today they tend to have up-to-date equipment. Often little of the old order is to be seen. Vast areas of land are taken for coal stacking, spoil dumping, and for settling the slurry emanating from coal washing and preparation plants.

Today's industrial archaeologist will probably be at his happiest working out the complicated transport arrangements of older collieries. Cheap access to the markets has always been paramount in determining the viability of a coalfield. Coal, of low bulk value, has always suffered the burden which overland transport puts on its price. With specialized markets to hand, such as Sheffield cutlers or Nottingham house-holders, substantial inland sales were possible in the seventeenth century. But the coalfields which prospered from that time were those having water-carriage com-munication with the markets. The Tyne and Wear pits were closest in transport economic terms to London, whilst Coalbrookdale on the Severn dominated that river valley market. New river navigations in the late 1600s and the eighteenth century opened many coalfields where the river courses cut the bassets of the seams. Canals continued the process throughout the industrial revolution, save on the Tyne and Wear. There wooden railways flourished and, as pits were wrought out, so the rails penetrated further inland, opening new collieries to the water. Wooden ways fed the trunk routes of river navigations and canals elsewhere too. Oversimplifying the situa-tion, iron railways followed the wooden ones and steam-locomotives ventured onto the metals. In 1825 the Stockton and Darlington Railway linked South Durham coal with the navigable Tees. Though it was of iron, had locomotives, and was open to the public, its chief raison d'être was just that of the wooden Tanfield Way, opened in 1725 to feed new coal to the Tyne. A number of early steam railways were of this kind, feeding canals or harbours; then they became feeders to the new trunk railways. Not until the age of aggressive railway expansion in Victoria's reign were competetive railway systems designed, trunk and branch, to connect the pit and the distant customer.

GAS

The experiments which led to the development of the gas industry were spread over more than a century. Coal was distilled as early as 1690 by John Clayton, an enter-prising English clergyman, who described in a letter to Robert Boyle how 'first there came over only fleghm, afterwards a black oyle, & then likewise a Spirit arose. . . .' Clayton collected his 'spirit' in bladders, which when pricked and squeezed gave out a jet of inflammable gas that could be lit in a candle flame to amuse the assembled company. No commercial possibilities seem, however, to have crossed Clayton's mind.

During the eighteenth century several researchers interested themselves in the gas which issued from coal mines. In 1764 Gabriel Jars, a member of the French Academy of Sciences, made the far-sighted suggestion that mine-gas be used to provide lighting for nearby communities. Practical difficulties prevented the implementation of this scheme but in the following year James Spedding, the manager of Lord Lonsdale's Whitehaven colliery in England, seems to have achieved a small-scale success by lighting his works office with gas piped from the mine.

It is difficult to decide who was the first person to distil coal for the express purpose of producing an illuminating gas. There are a number of claimants and documentary evidence is slender. Englishman George Dixon appears, however, to have a good case. He certainly founded a works for extracting tar from coal in 1779 and this lends considerable credence to the report that in the same year he used a gas distilled from coal to light one of the rooms in his house. Another contender is the Dutchman Jean Pierre Minkelers, who experimented with coal distillation while a professor at the University of Louvain. It is said that from 1783 onwards Minkelers gave a once-yearly demonstration of the illuminating powers of coal gas by employing it to light his lecture room. But leaving aside the question of priority there can be no doubt that the key figure in the early history of gas was the Scots engineer William Murdoch, for it was he who first produced the new fuel in commercial quantities.

Murdoch became interested in gas while working for Boulton and Watt as their chief engine erector and supervisor in the West Country. Despite an incredibly heavy work load he found time to experiment by heating a variety of mineral and vegetable substances, and in 1792 succeeded in lighting his office at Redruth in Cornwall with a gas distilled from coal. He was recalled to Birmingham in 1798 to manage the Soho Foundry and it was there that he built the first large-scale apparatus for producing, purifying, and storing coal gas. Celebrations for the Peace of Amiens in 1802 provided an opportunity to show gas lighting to the public at large. The Soho manufactory was illuminated overall by 2600 coloured oil lamps but pride of place was given to two spectacular gas-fed flares positioned one at each end of the building. By 1804 Boulton and Watt were offering complete gas-lighting installations for sale. These had special appeal for the owners of textile mills, because gas light proved safer than oil lamps or candles and was bright enough to allow work to go forward at night as well as during the day.

The first major contract for gas-making equipment came from the cotton-spinning concern of Phillips and Lee whose fire-proof factory at Salford, the first in Lancashire to be built with cast-iron beams and columns, had been engined by Boulton and Watt in 1801. This history of successful co-operation must have helped the mill owners in their decision to adopt gas lighting not only for the factory proper but also for its counting-houses, store-rooms, and even the adjacent dwelling-house of Mr. Lee himself. Between 1805 and 1807 Murdoch installed 900 gas lights which were supplied by a battery of six small vertical retorts (later replaced by horizontal). Lighting bills were reduced to about one third of those previously incurred with candles and the whole project won wide praise and publicity. Boulton and Watt were established as undoubted leaders in the manufacture of gas-making plant but, although Murdoch continued to improve the apparatus, his firm failed to exploit its advantage to the full.

Murdoch had shown gas lighting to be a viable proposition; now came the turn of those prepared to exploit the new illuminant. Foremost amongst such entrepreneurs was the flamboyant German-born Frederick Albert Winsor, who erupted onto the English scene in 1803 as the self-appointed champion and inventor of gas. Winsor's enthusiasm actually stemmed from a visit to Paris in the previous year when he had witnessed Philippe Lebon's experiments with a gas distilled from sawdust. Convinced of the commercial possibilities Winsor built a wood-distillation plant of his own but he quickly recognized cheap British coal as a more promising raw material and it was possibly this which lured him to London. On arrival in England he began a programme of lectures and demonstrations at the Lyceum Theatre with the intention of arousing interest in the formation of a national gas-lighting company. In June 1807 he gas lit the garden walls of Carlton House in honour of the birthday of its owner, the Prince Regent, and towards the end of the same year he erected thirteen gas lamps in Pall Mall. It was largely due to his efforts that the London-based Gas Light and Coke Company was started in 1812 but by this time he was becoming an embarrassment to his financial backers who managed to exclude him from the original board, although later he was elected to a directorship. Winsor's share in promoting what was the first company in the world to provide a public gas supply from a central works deserves full recognition and it is regrettable that he tarnished his image in the eyes of both his contemporaries and posterity by claiming a priority in invention which was rightfully Murdoch's.

Although the gas industry had been launched, it had yet to become established. Public suspicion and prejudice were strong and for several years the very existence of the Gas Light and Coke Company hung in the balance. No dividend was paid until 1817. Fortunately, however, the company had acquired in Samuel Clegg a chief engineer of considerable talent, who was able to steer it through all its initial technical difficulties.

Clegg first made acquaintance with gas while apprenticed to Boulton and Watt at Soho where he learnt his trade from no less a person than William Murdoch. In 1805, his training complete, he set up in business for himself and over the next few years installed several private gas-making plants, amassing invaluable experience. Appointed chief engineer to the London company in December 1812, he at once threw himself with great vigour into his work. He encouraged the manufacture of improved gas pipes and other fittings and was responsible for the gradual replacement of earlier mains with new ones of greater capacity. Not content with administrative activity Clegg contributed several inventions, the most important of which was the horizontal rotary retort, first used in the gas-making plant installed at the Royal Mint in 1817. He also drew up preliminary plans for a gas-meter. By the time Clegg resigned his position in 1817, he had lifted the company from the verge of ruin to a position of reasonable financial security. It is with some justice that he is regarded as the first professional gas engineer.

The progress of gas was rapid from now onwards. Coal-distilling plants sprang up in all the major provincial cities to satisfy an ever-growing demand for gas street lighting. London will serve to give a picture of the tempo of advance. In the eleven years from 1823 to 1834 the length of gas main in the capital leapt dramatically from 122 to 600 miles. Public buildings and factories were also increasingly lit by gas but it was not until the late 1840s that the new illuminant was at all widely used for domestic lighting. It was only when gas had won through to this final acceptance that the industry achieved real prosperity.

8.3

DISCHARGING A HORIZONTAL RE-
TORT (*75/NX 184974, Girvan gas works*).
This works has five benches of seven and one
of eight retorts, fired by hand. The charge is
changed every four hours, and each time the
central retort is emptied into a special barrow
which funnels it into the furnace below, which
heats the retorts. The others are discharged,
by 11 ft rakes, into the barrow shown, and
quenched under a water jet after some initial
water has been thrown onto the barrow. The
hydraulic main passes across the tops of the
retort benches, on the way to the exhauster.

One of the most serious difficulties which faced the early gas engineer was the puri-
fication of his product. The carbonization of coal gave rise to a mixture which, besides
the desired gas, contained tar, ammonia, hydrogen sulphide, and other smelly impurities. Tar could be easily removed by condensation; the rest required greater
expertise. Washing seems to have been one of the first expedients tried. Murdoch
wrote of his installation at the Phillips and Lee factory that the gas was conveyed into
reservoirs 'where it (was) washed and purified.' This crude method would have dis-
solved out much of the ammonia but as the industry grew up standards became more
demanding. Eventually, in 1846, George Lowe introduced the forerunner of the modern

140

8.4
RETORT HOUSE, NORWICH GAS WORKS (*126/TG 236091 – near Palace Street, Norwich*). Photographed during demolition, for its typical retort house appearance. The walls of pierced brick are the usual method of ventilating a vertical retort house, and the height is also that normally found in moderate-sized installations.

8.5
INTERIOR OF HORIZONTAL RETORTS (*76/NY 364844 – Langholm gas works*). While the bench was closed for servicing it was possible to photograph the interior of a retort, to show its shape and 10 ft length. The exterior fittings are now standard in those horizontal retorts remaining, but this is a recent development which simplifies servicing. In use, the retorts, are heated with coke, fed into the low central floor. To remove the ashes from the furnace, steel plates normally present to form a floor are removed to uncover the ashpit door below. In use the retort doors are covered with tar, but these have been cleaned for inspection.

tower scrubber and the ammonia problem was solved. Sulphur compounds were far more intractable. The slurry of slaked lime used to remove them proved relatively inefficient, while the heaps of spent lime left by the process gave off a foul odour. As early as 1817 Reuben Phillips suggested the use of almost dry slaked lime but this improved method was not widely adopted until the 1870s. Meanwhile, in 1849, Frank Clark Hills had discovered that hydrogen sulphide could be removed by iron oxide. This outstandingly successful process was pirated by many companies and is still in use today [*8.10*].

For the first sixty years of its manufacture, the heating properties of gas were seldom

141

8.6 and 8.7
IPSWICH GAS WORKS (150/TM 170436
– on the east side of Ipswich dock). The two
gasholders shown in 8.6 are typical of those
built in the last quarter of the nineteenth
century. The earlier one is in front, and the
later and larger one, operating to the same
design is behind.

The tops of the vertical retorts are shown in
8.7. Arranged vertically in the retort house
is a series of tubes, into the tops of which
the coal is loaded. As the coal moves down the
length of the tube it is progressively heated
(in this case by producer gas) and so is distilled, the volatile products passing out
through the necks shown here and into a
main, before being purified. The long rods
are used to break up any blockages at this
upper side. The coal is kept in bunkers above
the retorts, and this continuous production
arrangement is much more efficient than the
old hand fired horizontal retorts seen in Plate
36(b).

142

At the bottom of the retort are the doors seen in *8.9*. One is open and the ashes have been poked away to show the intense flames of the producer gas. Care in operation of the dampers is needed to ensure that adequate air is provided for the combustion of the producer gas but too little for the coal itself to burn instead of being distilled. Although on a larger scale the process is exactly the same as that used by William Murdoch to produce gas to illuminate his office at Redruth in 1792.

One of the most valuable products of the dry distillation of coal, apart from coal gas, is tar. Being a viscous substance when cool, special pumps have to be used to draw it from the condensing system and pass it out to the storage tanks. The pumps shown in *8.8* are near the feet of the vertical retorts at Ipswich, and were in action while the photograph was made – as they had been for over half a century.

8.10 and 8.11
IPSWICH GAS WORKS (*150/TM 170436 – on the east side of Ipswich dock*). *8.10* shows the purifier boxes, containing iron oxide through which the town gas is led to remove the hydrogen sulphide. Such boxes form no part of plant connected with natural gas, and are thus comparative rarities. Although operating at the time this photograph was taken, the works is scheduled for closure, so that in this sequence of pictures we are seeing industrial archaeology in the making.

8.11 is of another now unusual sight, the loading of gas tar into rail tankers which were once a commonplace on the railways. Of the original range of storage tanks for the tar only two remain, but demand for the tar is still high, since it is a source of valuable by-products. In the background is the retort house, showing clearly how the original small building on the left was extended to take larger retorts.

exploited and the various attempts made to interest the public in gas cooking met with scant response. Alfred King's surprisingly modern-looking cooker received disappointing support when offered for sale in 1850, nor could James Sharp provoke more than passing attention by preparing a meal for 120 persons with the aid of gas. As King sadly recorded: 'The manufacturers who had embarked in the business found it either impossible or unwise to continue.' The gas industry was content with its role as chief purveyor of light and felt little need to expand its market.

It was shaken out of this mood of complacency by the advent of electric light in the early 1880s. Gas companies soon found themselves forced to adopt new commercial practices and to tighten up their efficiency if they wished to stay in business. Coin-in-the-slot meters were introduced in 1889 to appeal to householders in the lower income brackets and companies began to hire out cookers to their customers. This long overdue

144

8.12

TOWN-GAS LAMP (*150/TM 171436 — at the side of Ipswich Gas Works*). Gas lamps such as this were once commonplace throughout the country, but are now rarities in their original form complete with incandescent mantle. Examples occur locally, but they are more likely to be found modified for electric light and installed outside some front door.

expansion into the field of heating was facilitated by the use of the extremely hot flame which had in fact been available ever since the German chemist Robert Wilhelm Bunsen had devised his burner in 1855. Gas even fought back on the lighting front. The Welsbach incandescent mantle came onto the market in large numbers in 1893 and was sufficiently successful to stave off the challenge of electric light for another twenty years. Gas engines, which came increasingly into vogue from the 1870s, proved a valuable additional outlet. 50 000 of them were in use in Europe by the end of the nineteenth century.

Since the Second World War the gas industry has been gradually revolutionized by the introduction of gases other than those produced from coal. The development of cracking methods to reform heavy oil fractions and the use of North Sea gas have caused the removal of all those small works which once served only their own immediate neighbourhoods. If a coal-gas plant can still be seen at work it is an example of industrial archaeology in the making [see *8.6–8.11*]. Houses for horizontal retorts, recognizable from their relatively low profiles, are now extremely rare [*8.3*, *8.5* and Plate 36(b)], and even the later vertical retort houses are being quickly felled. Gas-holders, however, remain prominent, for they are just as useful as they ever were, although many are well over seventy-five years old. The No. 2 holder at Fulham Gasworks was built in 1830 and is probably the oldest in the world.

OIL

Mineral oil has been known since ancient times but its large-scale exploitation dates only from 1859 when Edwin Drake's experimental drillings in Pennsylvania began to show a yield. The crude oil or petroleum derived from oil wells is a complex mixture

145

8.13

SHALEOIL DISTILLERY, LANARK, (*61/ NS 899435 – near Lanark golf course*). Early remains of oil workings are rare in this country. Some abandoned oil wells can be seen in Nottinghamshire but, apart from these, little of archaeological interest can be found. Occasionally, however, it is possible to seek out relics of the early oil industry in quite unlikely spots, and this is one such site. The Caledonian Mineral Oil Works, still known locally as 'The Paraffin', has left scant remains, but a retort house (shown in the plate), slag heaps and railway sidings, some workers' cottages, and the manager's house can be identified with some certainty. Built about 1865, the works operated until the early 1900s, being just remembered by some of those living nearby. Shale, brought from Tarbrax and the Lothians, was distilled for its oil content.

of hydrocarbons, which is normally refined by distillation to give a series of fractions of different boiling points. In the early days petroleum was valued mainly as a source of kerosene or paraffin for use in oil lamps, the light mineral oil (petrol) fraction being discarded as dangerous. Paraffin could also be obtained by distilling certain shales and this industry assumed local importance in parts of Britain before eventually succumbing to competition from cheap American oil [see *8.13*].

The oil industry went from strength to strength as other of its products were found to possess commercial value. Liquid paraffin took on medicinal properties; petroleum jelly, sold under the name of Vaseline, made its proprietors a fortune; paraffin wax proved useful for candles. By 1900 world production of crude oil had reached 20 million tons and, just when it seemed that electric lighting might reduce demand, petrol-engined cars appeared in growing numbers to make use of the previously despised light mineral oil. The subsequent relentless advance of mechanical transport has

146

necessitated an almost fantastic increase in production. New fields have been explored and new techniques devised. In 1965 alone 1500 million tons of petroleum poured from the world's oil wells. Man is consuming one of his most valuable natural resources at an alarming rate.

The oil industry did not originate in Britain, nor does this country possess any significant inland deposits. The industrial archaeologist will, therefore, find little concerned with primary production other than a few abandoned oil wells in Nottinghamshire and the heaps of shale left behind by the Lanarkshire paraffin manufacturers. Most existing installations are concerned with oil refining and are extremely up-to-date. An industry as vital as oil cannot allow its equipment to become obsolete. It may be more rewarding to concentrate on consumption rather than production. The diesel engine at Stretham, for example, still works on the now-superseded air blast system and is a real piece of industrial history [Plate 36(c)]. Even humble petrol pumps deserve a second glance. They are sometimes much older than they seem [4.16].

FURTHER READING

CHANDLER, D. AND LACY, A. D. *The Rise of the Gas Industry in Britain* (London: British Gas Council, 1949)

STEWART, E. G. *Town Gas: Its Manufacture and Distribution* (London: Science Museum, HMSO, 1958)

9. Iron and Steel

W. K. V. GALE

IRON IS THE MOST USEFUL and universal of all the metals produced by man. It is very widely distributed, being the fourth most abundant element in the earth's crust, but with the exception of meteoric debris, it is found only in the form of ores, which have to undergo considerable processing before they are of commercial use. The exception – meteoric iron – is so rare as to be only a curiosity so that iron throughout its long history has been obtained from one or other of the naturally-occurring ores.

Any consideration of the development of the iron industry must be based on a clear understanding of the various forms which the manufactured metal may take. These are, in order of antiquity, wrought iron, cast iron, and steel. Wrought iron is a commercially-pure form of iron. It can be forged, rolled, and shaped, when both hot and cold, but cannot be cast in a mould. Cast iron is really an alloy of iron with, principally, carbon. It can be melted and cast in a mould but cannot be forged or worked when either hot or cold. Steel in its commonest form, is again a commercially-pure iron, though it is physically different from wrought iron. It can, however, also exist in the form of alloys of varying degrees of complexity. Many steels can be cast, forged or rolled but the greatest tonnage is rolled into a large variety of shapes.

The origins of iron making are unknown but its history can be divided into periods which are fairly clearly definable, though overlapping. From prehistoric times until about the fifteenth century is the direct-reduction period, when wrought iron was made direct from the ore in small charcoal-fired furnaces known as bloomeries. The product was wrought iron only and the output from several hours of work was a piece of iron – a bloom – weighing only a few pounds.

The indirect-reduction period began in Continental Europe about the year 1400, a century before it started in Britain. Wrought iron was still the final product, but the ore was first smelted in a blast furnace ([9.3 and Plate 38(b)] show eighteenth century examples and [9.17] a nineteenth century site and [9.14] shows a typical nineteenth century masonry furnace) and cast into pig iron by running the molten metal into a sand bed in the form of a comb – fancifully likened to a sow and its litter. Hence the name pig iron, which is still with us, though pig is now the product of a machine and the sand bed has gone.

Pig iron was decarburized in a charcoal-fired hearth called a finery, to produce a bloom of wrought iron which, after reheating in another furnace, the chafery, could be hammered out as required.

The important point about the indirect process – which is still the basis of iron and steel production – is that it marked the beginnings of mechanization. Bloomeries were operated manually. Blast furnaces, tiny though the first ones were by today's standards, were too big for the muscular power of man. Mechanical power, at first that of water, had to take over to blow the blast furnaces. As larger pieces of iron were being made, power hammers were also necessary. Power hammers varied widely in details ([Plate 40(b)] shows two power hammers at Wortley, near Sheffield). Heavy pieces of iron were handled by manually powered cranes such as that at Wortley [9.13].

148

So iron making took the first steps towards becoming an industry. No use was found at first for cast iron but after a time it was discovered that useful shapes could be made by letting molten cast iron solidify in shaped sand moulds. Firebacks were among the earliest castings but the first cannon was cast at Buxted, Sussex, in 1543.

The growth of the iron industry was inhibited largely by the fact that water power was neither abundant nor particularly reliable; it suffered from droughts and frosts. Where nature did provide all the requisites for iron production – iron ore, timber for charcoal, streams for power – iron making became an industry. The Weald, in Surrey and Sussex developed into Britain's biggest iron-making area in the sixteenth century.

But there was another trouble ahead. As the trade grew, timber shortage made itself felt. The nation's forests were not unlimited and there were other demands on the best timber resources. Shipbuilders and others competed with the charcoal burners for supplies of oak. Charcoal shortage was serious by the early 1600s, and more than one attempt was made to find a solution.

It was not, however, until 1709 that the answer was found. In that year Abraham Darby converted his little charcoal blast furnace at Coalbrookdale, Shropshire, to use mineral fuel. There were technical reasons why coal – although quite well known at the time – could not then be used 'raw' (as mined) in the blast furnace. Darby instead carbonized coal by subjecting it to controlled burning, like charcoal burning, and used the resulting coke as his fuel. Darby did not invent the coking process but he was the

9.1
THE WAREHOUSE, COALBROOKDALE
(*119/SJ 668047 – 4 miles south of Wellington*).
As one would expect, this warehouse (built in 1792, with the rather fine clock tower added in 1843), has cast-iron door heads, window frames and sills, and internal columns. It is an interesting part of the museum site [see Plate 38(b)].

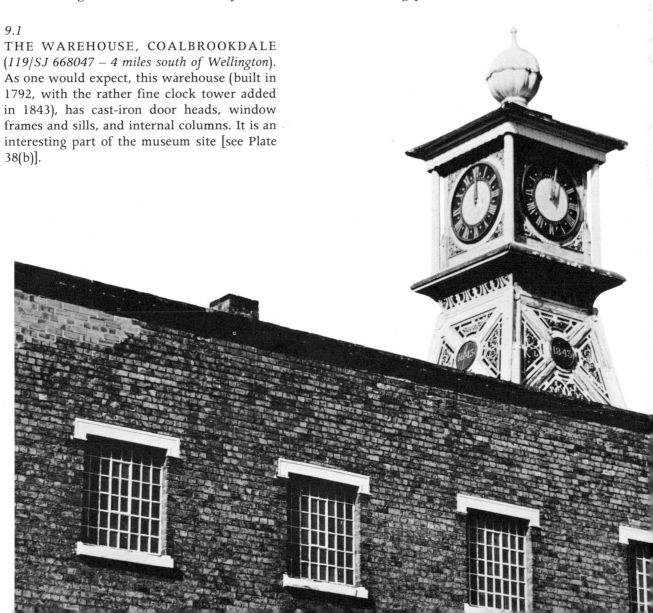

first to use coke in the blast furnace. The 1709 furnace no longer exists but a coke fired furnace of 1777 is preserved on the Coalbrookdale site [Plate 38(b)]. It was used to make iron for the Iron Bridge [*9.4, 9.5* and Plate 38(a)].

The introduction of mineral fuel smelting was the greatest single step forward in the history of iron making. It freed the iron trade from its dependence on the dwindling supplies of charcoal and gave it the basis for expansion at a time when expansion seemed impossible and contraction appeared likely.

The industry continued, however, to suffer from a chronic power shortage until reliable steam engines became available in the latter half of the eighteenth century. This is not the place to deal with the development of steam power, which, in any case, had far-reaching effects in many fields besides iron making. It will suffice to say that by 1784 the work of Newcomen, Watt, and others had produced engines capable not only of blowing blast furnaces but also of working power hammers and rolling mills. Dependence on the fickle power of streams was over and iron works could be built where nature had deposited the ores and coal. Some of the nineteenth century blowing engines were very large, as the Lilleshall engines show [Plate 39(c)].

As steam began to take a grip on technology the iron trade experienced another important development – the last in the chain of events leading to the great advances of the nineteenth century. The success of coke smelting had dramatically reduced the

9.2 and 9.3

MORLEY PARK BLAST FURNACES (*111/SK380492 – 2½ miles north-east of Belper*). This site has been worked for coal and ironstone since 1372, but the furnaces (cold-blast coke-smelted iron) were erected by Francis Hurt in 1780 and 1818, the older one being probably the first of its type in Derbyshire. *9.2* shows the top of the furnace from the bank behind, and indicates how the site was chosen to minimize the difficulty of charging. *9.3* shows the front of the older furnace, built as a square pyramid in gritstone, about 36 ft high. The works was once large, having about 400 employees in 1846. The furnaces were last in blast in 1874.

150

9.4 and 9.5
THE IRON BRIDGE (*119/SJ 672034 – 5 miles south of Wellington*). These two pictures show the date cast into a rib and details of the construction of this remarkable bridge which weighs 378 tons. The few ties and bolts which are present are not original, but have been added during repairs. The original dovetail construction is clearly visible. [See also plate 38(a)]

demand for charcoal without completely eradicating its use. For many years this increasingly scarce material was required in the finery. A new process was urgently needed for the production of wrought iron. The breakthrough which released the industry from the last vestiges of its reliance on charcoal was the invention of the puddling process by Henry Cort in 1784 [9.8 and 9.9]. Cort used a furnace of known form, the reverberatory, and, with raw coal as his fuel, succeeded in converting pig iron to wrought iron. The process was known as puddling, from the fact that the iron was stirred or 'puddled' manually during part of the operation. Cort also improved the mills for rolling wrought iron. A small mill of about Cort's period has survived at Wortley [9.7].

So far steel has not played much of a part in our story. In fact it was to remain of relatively small significance for some time but it is now appropriate to examine steel's position in the increasingly mechanized and developing iron trade.

It was known as long ago as about 900 B.C. that wrought iron, heated in contact with a carbonaceous material such as charcoal, acquired on the surface the properties of what we now call carbon steel. The metal, case hardened by this process, was useful for making cutting tools. Slow to operate, case hardening never did amount to much as long as iron itself was only available in small quantities.

151

9.6

CEMENTATION FURNACE (78/NZ 131567 – 4 miles north-east of Consett). An early process for making steel (with a controlled amount of carbon) was to pack iron bars into fireclay chests, with a filling of charcoal [see 9.11]. The chests were heated inside a furnace by coal, and since the chests were sealed, the impurities from the coal did not affect the steel. The fire at the base of the furnace heated a relatively small chamber, the cone above containing flues in its lower part. This cementation furnace at Derwentcote near Rowlands Gill is one of only two remaining in the country (the other in Sheffield), and is reserved for eventual transfer to the open air museum, Beamish.

However, if the heating were kept up long enough, a piece of wrought iron could be carburized more or less right through and this was known as cementation [9.6 and 9.11]. It was practised certainly as early as 1722 and probably earlier. Cementation produced a kind of carbon steel called shear steel. This could be cut into pieces, reheated, and hammer-welded together to form double shear-steel, which had improved qualities.

A valuable advance was made in 1740 when Benjamin Huntsman melted shear steel in a crucible and so produced a much more homogeneous carbon steel, which could be hardened more reliably than shear or double shear. Plate 40(a) shows the surviving crucible furnaces at Abbeydale, Sheffield; 9.16 is a general view of the same works. But steel was still expensive and used only when essential.

However, if steel remained for the time being of specialized value only, the opposite was the case with iron. From the beginning of the nineteenth century the iron trade made tremendous strides. With the ability to use the vast deposits of coal and iron ore in various parts of Britain, and with mechanical power at their bidding, the iron makers offered a cheap, strong, and convenient raw material for the developing engineering, railway, and shipbuilding industries throughout the country and, increasingly, overseas.

9.7

IRON ROLLING MILL, WORTLEY TOP FORGE (102/SK 294999 – 9 miles north-west of the centre of Sheffield). This rolling mill, which enabled iron to be formed directly into rods without the need to tilt it under the hammer, is the oldest known survivor in this country. Although now rather heavily restored, it is in essence the same as that originally introduced by Henry Cort under his grooved rolls patent of 1783. This mill was originally at the nearby Lower Forge, but is of later date than the original mill there, which was installed about 1790.

152

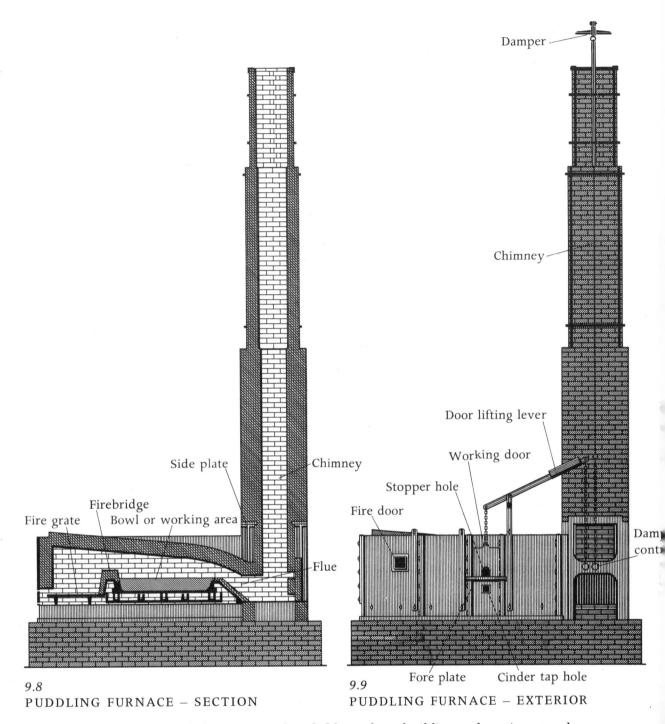

9.8
PUDDLING FURNACE – SECTION

9.9
PUDDLING FURNACE – EXTERIOR

The use of iron expanded too into other fields such as building, where it not only provided the utilitarian (and often hidden) girders and stanchions which supported a building but also appeared in the form of the decorative and other visible castings [9.1, 9.10, 9.18 and Plate 39(a)] which became so popular as the century wore on.

In the first quarter of the nineteenth century there was little technical development in iron making. Some increases in the scale of operation came from bigger furnaces and machinery but most of the expansion was from the multiplication of producing units. There were more integrated plants too in which coal and iron-ore mines, blast furnaces, forges, rolling mills, and sometimes foundries, were brought together under a single owner.

153

The year 1828 saw the next important technical development. In that year the Scot J. B. Neilson introduced the use of the hot blast for blast furnaces. Prior to that date the air for combustion had always been blown in at ambient temperature. Blast temperatures were very low at the start – around 150 °C – but economies in furnace fuel resulted. Improvements in the blast heating-equipment raised the temperature and improved the fuel economy. Today all blast furnaces are hot blast and the air temperature is sometimes as high as 1300 °C.

While Neilson was improving the blast furnace others were at work on the puddling process. Cort's puddling process was effective but because it was wasteful several experimenters were led to attempt modifications. The most successful was Joseph Hall who, in about 1816, modified Cort's process producing great economies in both fuel and iron. Hall's process was altogether quicker and more vigorous than Cort's and it became known as pig boiling or wet puddling. The older method continued in use for many years but was finally abandoned in favour of Hall's wet puddling. To avoid confusion the older process is now known as dry puddling.

Iron making and processing were great users of fuel but while coal remained cheap few bothered very much about exercising fuel economy. Nevertheless, in the first half of the nineteenth century there were two developments which were the first manifestations of the concern over fuel economy which, perforce, is so important today. These were the waste-heat boiler and the use of blast furnace gas.

9.10
CAST-IRON LAMP (*160/TQ 306807 – by the side of the Savoy Hotel, London*). Many iron gas lamps remain, even though town gas is being rapidly supplanted by other fuels for illumination. This particular example is not only elegant, but burns a gas which is not generally supplied to the public. In 1895 J. E. Webb patented a street-lighting column which extracted sewer gas and burnt it – this lamp being one of the few remaining, although over 2500 were sold. Originally fitted with fish-tail burners, it now has the usual incandescent mantle. Town gas is burnt from a mains supply, and a tube through the lamp column carries sewer gas up to the flame, where it is consumed.

J. U. Rastrick interposed a boiler of his own design between a puddling furnace and its chimney stack in 1827 and so used for steam generation much of the heat which would otherwise have passed straight out into the atmosphere.

Using the waste gas produced by a blast furnace was a different proposition. There was a lot of gas and it burnt in a great flame at the top of the furnace. That the gas was inflammable was obvious and more than one attempt was made to collect and burn it under boilers or in hot-blast stoves.

The trouble was that to collect the gas effectively it was necessary to close the top of the furnace and yet leave means for charging the raw materials. When this was done by the bell-and-cone apparatus of George Parry in 1850 the working of the furnace was affected adversely [9.14]. But the problems were solved and the recovery and use of blast furnace gas finally became standard practice.

Such were the major technical developments in iron making up to the middle of the nineteenth century. There were others, of course, not always of much apparent significance at the time but all adding to the great total of change in the period. A use was found for blast furnace slag, for example, sometimes in blocks for building [Plate 39(b)], later for road making and concrete aggregate.

It is important to note, too, that the very long period of empiricism in iron making was beginning to show signs of change. For many centuries iron makers had made discoveries by trial and error. They knew what they had to do but not why. But now

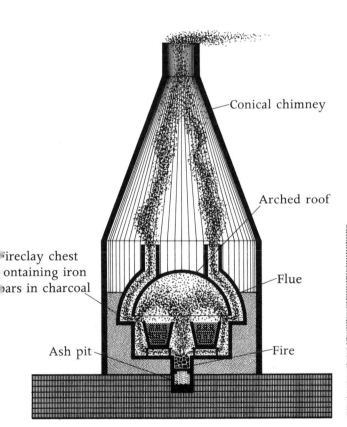

9.11
SECTION OF CEMENTATION
FURNACE

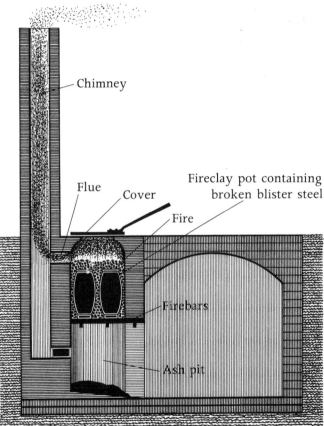

9.12
CRUCIBLE OR POT FURNACE

Plate 37(a)

HODBARROW HAEMATITE MINES (*Camera position 88/SD 179787 – 1 mile south of Millom*). This impressive site, at which operations ceased only in 1968, has as its most staggering features two enormous sea walls – visible in the picture, the inner one (broken) at the extreme left, the outer one visible in the distance just above it. The inner wall, built in 1888–90 with Sir John Coode as consultant, protected the then workings, many millions of tons of ore being extracted from underground using a pillar-and-stall technique. The mine had been exploited since 1856, and an annual output of almost 350 000 tons was achieved by 1880. Subsidence followed the extraction of the ore, and the sea threatened the workings, hence the sea wall was made. By any standards, the sea wall is a most remarkable feat of engineering. In 1898, when it was penetrated, the decision was made to build a mile-long outer barrier from 25-ton blocks of limestone with clay infilling and steel or timber piling. This was constructed between 1900 and 1905, and is most spectacular. Within these barriers remain the most complete iron-mine survivals in the country, and it is to be hoped that some plan will be formulated to preserve at least part of the site. Visible in the photograph, in addition to the two walls and the inundated centre, are the surface remains of No. 2 shaft ('Annie Lowther') in the immediate foreground, and just to the right of the chimney, in the distance, the square buildings of the Company's offices. Next to the offices are the houses of Steel Green (1880), built as homes for some of the many immigrant workers. The chimney in the far distance is that of No. 1 shaft. This site is tremendously evocative, and is highly recommended for a visit while there is yet time.

Plates 37(b)

CHARCOAL FURNACE, CHARLCOTTE (*130/SO 638861 – 6 miles south-west of Bridgnorth*). This furnace is a rare survival in good condition of a once-common type of furnace, dating from the seventeenth century. As the furnace stands it is possible to see the charging bank at the back, but the pig bed and the site of the water-driven blowing apparatus have disappeared. It is likely that this furnace may be transferred to the Ironbridge Gorge Museum site (see page 5).

Plate 38(a)

THE IRON BRIDGE (*119/SJ 672034 – in Ironbridge, 5 miles south of Wellington*). This bridge, the first in the world to be made from cast iron, was designed by Abraham Darby III, the grandson of the Abraham Darby who smelted iron with coke [see 38(b)]. It was erected in 1779, and has a span of 100 ft. Bolts were not used for fixing the parts, instead the bridge was assembled using interlocking joints and wedges [see *9.4* and *9.5*]. As first built, the side arches were not of metal, but of masonry. This proved too heavy for the banks, and the present metal arches were added later. Although now open only to pedestrians, the bridge is still threatened by moving banks, and urgent efforts are required to secure its preservation. This bridge is a most interesting structure, spanning the Severn with an airy grace and allowing plenty of headroom for the numerous boats which then plied the river. Nowadays, one can still see the occasional coracle pass beneath, but the trading craft are only a memory.

Plate 38(b)

THE OLD FURNACE, COALBROOK-DALE (*119/SJ 667048 – 4 miles south of Wellington*). This furnace was originally built as a charcoal burner in 1638 and was well sited since supplies of timber and ironstone were close at hand. In 1709 Abraham Darby successfully smelted iron with coke in this furnace – and it is true to say that the industrial revolution started here. The furnace was rebuilt in 1777, to give it greater capacity for the casting of the members of the Iron Bridge, but the site is little changed since then. The entire site is now preserved by the Ironbridge Gorge Museum Trust and is a 'must' for those interested in industrial history, for a number of very important 'firsts' happened here, all of them being well documented and illustrated in the museum displays. In 1723 the first cast-iron cylinders for Newcomen engines were made here, while in 1797 the foundry produced the cast-iron beams and posts used in the construction of the first fireproof textile factory [see Plate 46(a)]. In 1802 Trevithick worked at Coalbrookdale to build the world's first steam locomotive (his second ran on the Penydarren track, see Plate 10(a)). In 1851 the Company contributed the great iron gates to the Crystal Palace exhibition (they still stand between Hyde Park and Kensington Gardens in London). This collection is of great importance, and is incorporated into the complex of sites of the industrial museum to be set up in the area (see page 5).

157

9.13

WORTLEY TOP FORGE CRANE (*102/SK 294999 – 9 miles north of the centre of Sheffield*). Early forges had only a small output by present-day standards, and the equipment with which they worked was primitive. This crane is typical of such locally-made machines, and the details of its swivel mechanism and cast-iron winch are worth study.

enquiring minds were turning to the scientific study of iron and its processing. Such men as David Mushet, John Percy, and H. C. Sorby brought science to bear on various aspects of the subject. It was on their work and that of others who followed them that the modern science of metallurgy was founded.

By the 1850s a pattern had emerged which seemed likely to continue for a long time. Iron was made by mineral fuel smelting in the blast furnace and the major part of the pig iron so produced was converted into wrought iron, principally by wet puddling. Some of the pig iron went into castings. Crucible steel was still made but iron, both cast and wrought, remained king.

Into this comfortable and apparently settled scene there came, in 1856, an interloper, Henry Bessemer. He proposed to make what he called 'malleable iron' (it was a misnomer in fact) cheaply and without fuel. It all looked rather unlikely and since Bessemer's process involved blowing *cold* air through molten iron many people refused to believe in it. And when things went wrong for Bessemer at first, the unbelievers were jubilant.

But Bessemer was right and when his early technical troubles were eliminated, the Bessemer process became not only a British but an international success [*9.15*]. What Bessemer did was to decarburize molten cast iron by means of the oxygen in the air blown through it. No heating fuel was needed because the reaction was exothermic and the iron actually became hotter.

The process was fast. While the puddling furnace took about 2 hours to make 5 cwt of wrought iron, a Bessemer converter could make the same quantity of the new metal in about 20 minutes. It was not long, either, before Bessemer converters were scaled up, to make several tons, not hundredweights, in less than half an hour.

Bessemer's metal was not like crucible steel or (physically) like wrought iron though chemically it had much in common with the latter. It was in fact what we now call mild steel and since it was as good for most purposes as wrought iron it became a formidable competitor for the older material.

158

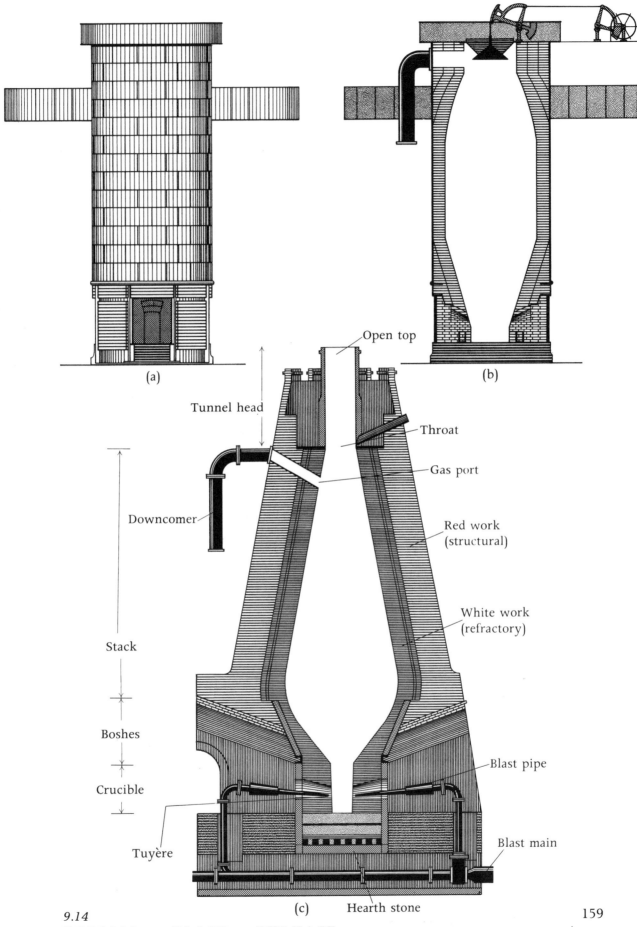

(a)

(b)

Open top

Tunnel head

Throat

Gas port

Downcomer

Red work
(structural)

White work
(refractory)

Stack

Boshes

Crucible

Blast pipe

Tuyère

Blast main

(c)

Hearth stone

9.14
TYPICAL BLAST FURNACE
MASONRY (a) Iron cased, typical of the
second half of the nineteenth century, (b) a
section through (a) showing the bell and cone
apparatus, and (c) a section through a typical
masonry furnace.

159

The Bessemer process was not suitable for all types of pig iron or for all circumstances and another method of steel making, the open-hearth process, commercially available from about 1866, also found favour. The open-hearth furnace, developed by C. W. Siemens, could be considered as complementary to the Bessemer converter. Between them the two processes eventually superseded the puddling furnace, and wrought iron was effectively no more, though it took a long time to die.

Both the open-hearth furnace and the Bessemer converter not only made steel in large quantities; they made it possible to produce it in larger individual pieces than the older wrought-iron blooms which each weighed about 1 cwt. This was important in the context of engineering development, since uses were soon found for the larger girders and plates made available by the new processes.

So began the last of our historical periods, the steel period, in which we are still living. The last quarter of the nineteenth century also saw the beginnings of several branches of the steel industry which are important today. In 1868, for example, R. F. Mushet introduced tungsten into steel, so making a self-hardening metal ideal for engineers' cutting tools and, albeit unknowingly, starting the alloy steel industry. In 1887 R. A. Hadfield developed manganese wear-resisting steel and so took alloy steels a stage further. These two steels – and stainless steel introduced by Harry Brearley in

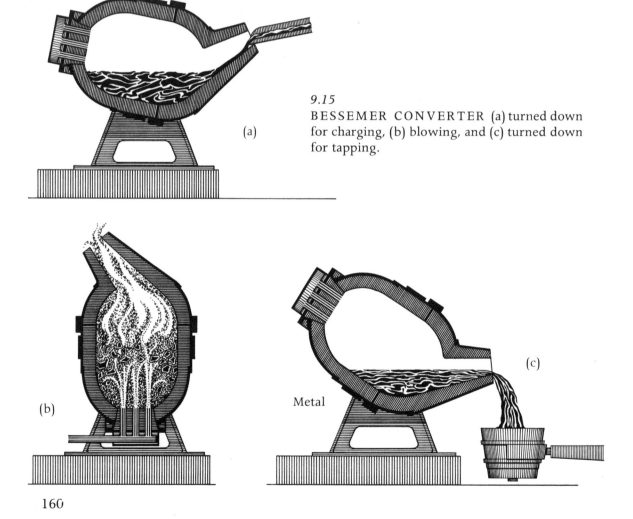

9.15
BESSEMER CONVERTER (a) turned down for charging, (b) blowing, and (c) turned down for tapping.

(a)

(b)

(c)

Metal

9.16

ABBEYDALE INDUSTRIAL HAMLET
(*111/SK 326820 – 3½ miles south-west of the
centre of Sheffield*). This general view of the
restored buildings of this remarkable museum
shows, from left to right, the crucible steel
melting shop with the steps up to the door to
leave room for the fire places beneath, the
hardening shop with its ample window and
water trough, and the large gable-end of the
tilt shop [see Plates 27(a), (b) and (c)]. The large
water-wheel is seen in the opening next to the
tilt shop, and there are also two other wheels
in this recess. The boring shop is at the right-
hand side, with another small water-wheel.

1913 – were the direct ancestors of the tremendous range of alloy and special steels
which, mostly unseen in countless places from car and aero-engines to nuclear applications, are so essential today.

From around 1900 to the present day, development in plant, processes, and products
has been fast; indeed in the last twenty years or so it could only be described as fast and
furious. This is not the place to detail the many changes that have taken place but it
is worthwhile summarizing the present position.

The main route for all tonnage steels (that is general-purpose steels made in large
quantities) is via the blast furnace and the oxygen converter. The Bessemer converter
is virtually extinct and the open-hearth furnace is steadily being phased out. Much of
the steel is cast by a continuous process (which is spreading rapidly) into billets,
blooms, and slabs for rolling into bars, sections, and plates and sheets. Rolling is highly
mechanized and computer control is developing quickly.

Alloy and special steels are mostly made in electric furnaces and very sophisticated
means are employed to ensure an extremely high standard of quality.

It is reasonable to expect that the iron and steel industry, with such a long history of
technical change behind it, should have left many traces of past activities. This is the
case but the distribution of remains is very uneven in both location and period. In
addition to plant there are also many examples of the products of the industry but these
are dealt with elsewhere in this book.

Of iron-making equipment quite a lot exists, although it is widely scattered geographically. From the early direct-reduction, bloomery period the relics range from mere traces (a small amount of slag or the remnants of a hearth) to more complete iron-making sites where the process can be studied in some detail. A word of warning is necessary here; without specialized knowledge old iron-working sites are easily confused with those used for other metals. Iron-ore mining relics, too [Plate 37(a)] are not usually easy to identify.

The eighteenth and nineteenth centuries provide the largest and most complete examples of iron-making relics. There are several more or less complete brick or stone

9.17

BLISTS HILL IRONWORKS (*119/SJ 695034 – 6 miles south-east of Wellington*). These works were started by the Madeley Wood Company in 1832, and continued in production for nearly a century. There are no remains of nineteenth-century blast furnaces left in the entire country, but on this site several types of cold-blast furnace were once worked, terminating with iron cased ones. The plate shows the two engine houses, between which the furnaces stood, as shown by their foundations about twelve feet below present soil level. The furnaces were filled from the bank behind, where there is also evidence of coking and storage of ore and coal. This site is the centre of the new open air museum. It will be restored with beam engines from Lilleshall [see Plate 39(c)], furnaces etc, and is even now well worth a visit. (See page 5 for details of the proposals for this site.)

9.18
CAST-IRON TOMB, MADELEY
CHURCHYARD (*119/SJ 696041 – 7½ miles
south-east of Wellington*). Although cast-iron
tombstones are not uncommon, few are as
ornate as this example, which belonged to a
prominent local family. The church against
which it stands was designed by Telford.

9.19
CAST IRON SIGNPOST, BRISTOL
(*155/ST 599718 – at the junction of A4 and
A37*). Cast-iron signposts, being especially
hard-wearing, are fairly commonplace
throughout the country. This particular one
is more ornate than most, with Doric column
and openwork lettering.

9.20
ELY CATHEDRAL, CAST-IRON STOVE
(*135/TL 541803 – in the Cathedral*). Church
heating stoves are long-lasting objects, and a
variety of sizes may be found. The one shown
in this plate is certainly of cathedral size, and
made according to Gurney's patent. Other
iron objects in churches include occasional
coats of arms (as at Stoneleigh in Warwickshire, pew doors at Coalbrookdale, and a
Coalbrookdale-made safe at Swinbrook, Oxford.

Plate 39(a)

CAST-IRON WINDOW, FLATFORD MILL (*149/TM 077333 – 7 miles north-east of Colchester*). The use of cast iron for industrial building was widespread, even in places where local ironworks were uncommon. This picture shows a cast-iron window frame, with opening light, of a kind widely found in older industrial buildings.

Plate 39(b)

SLAG WALL, BEDLAM FURNACE (*119/SJ 683033 – 6 miles south-east of Wellington*). Slag was once extensively used for roadmaking and walling in localities round ironworks, so that its presence is a useful indication that a blast furnace was at work nearby. Gibbons introduced a method of forming blocks by running successive tappings of slag into a mould; typical walling slabs were about 4 ft long and made up from layers an inch or so thick to a total of 6 to 8 in. A central hole was left by the removal of the rod or 'dog' embedded during manufacture to help in lifting the slab. If the slag was not wanted for walling, it was simply run into shallow depressions in a sand bed, to cool into random shapes. These were broken up and used as road metal. Near to the site of this slag wall are the remains of the old Bedlam furnaces, erected 1757–58. This site was the first in Shropshire at which coke was made in ovens instead of open heaps. The furnaces last worked in 1832.

Plate 39(c)

BLOWING ENGINE HOUSES, LILLE-SHALL (*119/SJ 703098 – in the Lilleshall Company's works, 3 miles east of Wellington*). On this site, formerly a hot-blast ironworks and Bessemer steelworks but now not used for these purposes, it was once possible to trace a history of the blowing of blast furnaces by steam power. The house on the left still contained two beam engines, built in 1851 by Murdoch Aitken and Co., and named 'David' and 'Sampson' (sic). These first worked on Christmas Eve 1851, when there were four blast furnaces on site, and last worked in 1952, as standby engines. Their total i.h.p. was between 200 and 260, and they are excellent examples of blowing engines of their period. Fortunately, they have been removed to the Blists Hill Museum site for preservation. The right-hand house was demolished in 1970, but before this it sheltered vertical blowing condensing engines, made by the company itself in 1900. Also on site were two 1925 Frazer and Chalmers turbo blowers, making in all a unique succession of three periods of blowing engine.

Plate 40(a)

ABBEYDALE WORKS (*111/SK 326820 – 3½ miles south-west of the centre of Sheffield*). The works, now very well restored by a local organization and open to the public, shows on one site the story of crucible steel production, forging and grinding in full and clear detail. Water provides the power (the wheels are in working order and run for the benefit of visitors) [see Plates 27(a), (b) and (c)], and the whole site is strongly recommended to any-one interested in industrial history. The picture shows the interior of the crucible steel melting shop. Here, using crucibles made in an adjoining room, weighed charges of car-burized iron (and often steel scrap) were heated in a coke-fired furnace, the mouth of which reached to floor level. Heating continued for about four hours, during which time the carbon diffused throughout the molten metal. The pot was then taken from the furnace, the slag skimmed off, the metal poured into moulds, and allowed to cool. This furnace and procedure is that developed by Benjamin Huntsman about 1740, and was the basis of Sheffield's later supremacy in carbon steel production. After testing, the ingot was reheated and forged under the tilt hammers. [See *9.16* for a general view of the buildings.]

Plate 40(b)

WORTLEY TOP FORGE (*102/SK 294999 – 9 miles north-west of the centre of Sheffield*). Reopened in 1955 as an industrial museum, the forge site dates from the early seventeenth century, although iron making had been carried on the immediate vicinity since the twelfth century. The picture shows a helve hammer on the right, a tilt hammer left, and a timber crane overhanging from the right. The water-wheels are visible outside the building, which dates mainly from the eighteenth century. This Top Forge was concerned with the conversion of pig metal into wrought iron by the 'finery' process, while the nearby Lower Forge worked the products of the fineries into bars. Although blast furnaces had been operated much earlier at Wortley, the pig iron at this time was supplied from Bretton. The output was of the order of three or four hundred tons per year, of high quality. This is a site which should be visited by all interested in industrial history [see also *9.7* and *9.13*].

blast furnaces and fortunately their value is now more generally realized. Some are preserved, others are the subject of preservation schemes. In several cases action has come only just in time. Long years of neglect have taken their toll. Wind and weather act insidiously and a tree growing out of a stone structure can do heavy damage. Plain theft by local people in search of a few stones or bricks has helped the process of destruction and more recently senseless vandalism has accelerated the rate of decay.

The old masonry furnaces survived simply because they were not worth the labour cost of removal. After the first quarter of the nineteenth century iron-making plants were almost exclusively made of iron (later steel) and since they then had scrap value, they did not usually survive long after they had ceased to be used. Appropriately they went as raw materials into the newer furnaces which had superseded them.

No nineteenth century blast furnace survives, there are no preserved puddling furnaces, and precious little in the way of machinery from this later period. Of early twentieth century plant there is also nothing of importance, though here and there a little machinery may be found still in use. The rest has long since served its last useful purpose as scrap. Some equipment has been scrapped after less than twenty years of use – and expensive capital plant at that – because technical progress has been so rapid.

Such few relics of iron-making machinery as do survive are either in museums such as those in London, Birmingham or Cardiff, or preserved on site, as at Abbeydale or Wortley, Sheffield, or at Sticklepath, Devon. Iron making will take its place, too, in such developing schemes as the Ironbridge Gorge Museum in Shropshire or the open-air museum at Beamish in Co. Durham.

History is a continuous record and the most modern iron and steel plants of today are the material of tomorrow's history. Nothing is likely to be preserved of such plants when their useful life is over. They are far too big. But a worthwhile job would be to make scale models, so that posterity may at least get an idea of the continuing story. For there will be more developments – some are in the pipeline now. We have not heard the last of iron.

FURTHER READING

ASHTON, T. S. *Iron and Steel in the Industrial Revolution* (Manchester University Press, 1924, reprinted 1963)

BRACEGIRDLE, B. AND MILES, P. H. *The Darbys and the Ironbridge Gorge* (Newton Abbot: David and Charles, 1974)

CARR, J. C. AND TAPLIN, W. *History of the British Steel Industry* .(London: Blackwell, 1962)

GALE, W. K. V. *Industrial Archaeology, Vol. 2 Iron and Steel* (London: Longmans, 1969)

GALE, W. K. V. *The Iron and Steel Industry: a Dictionary of Terms* (Newton Abbot: David and Charles, 1971).

RAISTRICK, ARTHUR *Dynasty of Ironfounders* (London: Longmans, 1953)

SCHUBERT, H. R. *History of the British Iron and Steel Industry* (London: Routledge and Kegan Paul, 1957)

166

10. Building for Industry

Jennifer Tann

Before the Industrial Revolution the typical industrial worker was the village craftsman with his workshop in or near his own home. The spinner, weaver or basket maker could work in a room which might also serve as the sleeping quarters for children. In the district around Huddersfield and Halifax, for example, there are many cottages containing an upper-floor loomshop lit by long windows; similar windows can be seen in Spitalfields, London [*10.1*], Macclesfield [*10.2*], and Hillfields and Chapelfields, Coventry. Some village crafts required separate premises. The forge, mill, and tannery, like the shops belonging to the currier, wheelwright, and carpenter, were generally to be found near the owner's dwelling house. Examples of surviving workshops can be seen all over Britain, for the village and town craftsman did not die out in the eighteenth or even the nineteenth century but in many cases survived until the early part of the present century [*10.3* and *10.17* to *10.19*]. The hand craftsman, like the small firm, complemented the large manufacturer by making what the latter could not or did not want to make.

Nevertheless by the early eighteenth century some manufacturers, notably in the textile industry, were already beginning to concentrate their means of production by gathering numbers of hand-operated machines into their workshops. In the Midlands the merchant hosiers began to assemble knitting frames in their warehouses; one Nottingham hosier employed more than forty apprentices as early as 1720. Spinners began to assemble spinning jennies in workshops and James Hargreaves, inventor of the jenny, which was patented in 1770, and his partner Thomas James built Hockley Mill, Nottingham, to contain fifty jennies. The beginnings of factory production can also be seen in the accumulation of workshops behind the houses of master potters in north Staffordshire during the 1740s and in the hand chain-shops of the Black Country some of which contained more hearths than a single family could work. One such shop has been removed from Cradley to Avoncroft Museum of Buildings.

Although many of the early workshops were purpose-built, the demand for workshop space became so great as the Industrial Revolution progressed that existing premises were frequently converted. Chapels, houses of the aristocracy, lumber rooms, even old barns, outhouses, and outbuildings of all descriptions were repaired, windows were broken through the old blank walls, and all were fitted out as workshops. The early workshops generally had something in common – the absence of power. One power source that could be easily installed was the animal wheel. A horse could be harnessed to drive pumping machinery at a brewhouse, dash wheels at a bleachworks, clay-mixing machinery at a pottery, boring machinery at a forge, and carding and spinning machinery at a textile workshop. The installation of a horse wheel was a useful bridge between the unmechanized embryo-factory and the full-scale factory driven by water or steam power. There is often little evidence of horse wheels left in the few recognizable remains of these embryo-factories but at James Longsdon's workshop/factory at Longstone, Derbyshire, part of the beam survives in the building in which carding was carried out in the late eighteenth century.

10.1
SPITALFIELDS (*160/TQ 338818 – Fournier Street, London E.1*). These silk weavers' houses have rows of well-lit garret workshops above the cornice. The prosperity of the eighteenth century did not last, and by 1830 many of the 50 000 people in the area who were directly dependent on silk manufacture were in desperate straits. The final blow was the 1860 commercial treaty with France, which allowed imports of cheap foreign silks.

10.2
MACCLESFIELD (*110/SJ 923730 – Windmill Street, Macclesfield*). In some parts of the north, Macclesfield for example, handloom silk weavers suffered in the same way. Many three-storey houses, such as those in the picture, were once to be seen in this town, but clearance has drastically reduced their number. Nevertheless a very few hand looms are still operated in the town, and some factories still process silk. [See also Plate 1(a)].

The water-mill was another focal point for development. In the early stages of industrial expansion an existing water-mill was often converted to a new purpose with little or no adaptation being made to the exterior. This can make deductions based solely on field work misleading, for what may appear to have been a corn-mill might in fact have been, at different times, an iron forge, a saw-mill, and a fulling-mill. In many cases, such as in a number of south Westmorland mills, the old building became a multiple mill, the owner retaining one or two pairs of corn stones and installing, in addition, snuff grinding machinery, bobbin making machines or fulling stocks. Dursley Mill, Gloucestershire, is a very small two-storey, eighteenth-century combined corn- and fulling-mill. At a time of industrial expansion diversification was a way in which the mill owner could attempt to insure against possible future adverse trade conditions.

The date at which the purpose-built factory first appeared varied from industry to industry and although there were early exceptions in almost all industries the chronology of factory building followed, on the whole, the innovation of powered machinery within each industry. In some industries techniques changed little during the Industrial Revolution and there was little difference, for example, between the buildings used for lead smelting or logwood in 1770 and those of a hundred years later [Plate 45(c)]. There was variation even in related trades. On the one hand the iron forge and foundry were organized on a factory basis by the 1780s whereas chain and nail manufacture were only slowly mechanized and there is still a hand chain-works in the Black Country. Silk throwing machinery was introduced in 1719 when Lombe began his large Derby mill yet hand silk-weaving survived until the present century; hosiery frames were only put into factories on a large scale from the 1850s when they were first steam driven and this accounts for the number of late nineteenth century factories in Leicester.

An important part in the movement towards factory production in the cotton industry was played by Richard Arkwright who in 1769 patented the water frame. His first horse-powered workshop in Nottingham has long since disappeared but his first water-powered factory (1771), subsequently extended in length and robbed of its top storey, survives at Cromford. He added a second Cromford mill (burnt down in the nineteenth century) in 1777 and in the early 1780s built factories (which still stand) at Wirksworth, Matlock Bath [*10.25* and Plate *47*(a)], and Rocester. Arkwright sold licences to a very few other spinners permitting them to use his machine, but it seems certain that the water frame was widely pirated in the 1780s. There are many remains of early spinning mills, especially in the north Midlands, and their remarkable conformity to the standard width of approximately thirty feet set by Arkwright's own factories suggests that they were built to house water frames. After 1790, when mule spinning was gradually adopted, new cotton mills were built fifteen or more feet wider to accommodate the new machines. This was the beginning of the urban steam-factory phase in the cotton industry. Because the majority of these early mule-factories were built in the Lancashire towns, where there has been much mill demolition, few of them survive but some early nineteenth century buildings do remain in the Chorlton Mills complex in Manchester.

The factory was a later phenomenon in the woollen industry [*10.12–10.15*] in spite of the fact that large workshops had emerged early in the eighteenth century. From the late eighteenth century technological innovation was rapid in the cotton industry

10.3

STAYS FACTORY (*111/SK 181464 – Compton Street, Ashbourne*). This works, an unpretentious three-storey brick building, was erected in 1864 for Cooper and Smith. Despite its modest appearance, a revolution was effected here, for in 1898 the corset-making process was broken down into separate operations for the first time.

10.4, 10.5 and 10.6
BROOKS No. 9 MALTINGS, MISTLEY (*150/TM 117320 – 1 mile east of Manningtree*). Built in 1901, these maltings incorporated many up-to-date features to increase production without employing extra labour. *10.4* shows the two upper floors, originally used for barley storage; below are the four working floors. For comparison with *10.10*, the width is approximately four times that of the Old Maltings. *10.5* shows the interior of one of the kilns – on a much larger scale of construction than those at the Old Maltings [see Plate 45(a)]. In 1901 two innovations were included – a wiremesh floor instead of perforated tiles, and a mechanical revolving traversing rake to fling the grains about in the kiln and so accelerate their drying. Later still a fan was added at the top, to draw through more air, and nowadays very powerful fans are fitted, making the use of mechanical rakes obsolete. *10.6* shows the barley screening plant installed in 1915. This removed small grains, seeds, and half kernels, which, if left, tended to mildew during germination on the working floor and taint much of the batch. The design is traditional, and the building has a strong 'agricultural' flavour due to its wooden construction. Reciprocal self-cleaning sieves and indent cylinders form the main part of the machine, but there are also elevators and a variety of accessory parts; the whole is an unusual example of an early large-scale machine still in good working order.

171

Plate 41(a)
INDUSTRIAL HOUSING IN GOOLE (*97/SE 748235 – Ouse Street, Goole*). Goole grew from 1825 onwards as a frontier town of the Yorkshire fenland and the only port of the West Riding. The Aire and Calder proprietors exercised some paternal oversight over the town, and the dwellings, though plainly built in brick with slate roofs, were of reasonable standard and laid out according to an overall plan. By 1829 there were already 178 houses, and by 1841 the population had grown to 3200. Unfortunately the houses were built at the extremities of the docks, which meant that later extensions to the docks had to be made further and further away from the river. Currently this early housing is being demolished to allow for expansion in the logical place nearer the Ouse.

Plate 41(b)
INDUSTRIAL HOUSING IN CROMFORD (*111/SK 295567 – North Street, Cromford*). Arkwright erected substantial industrial buildings at Cromford [Plate 47(a) and *10.25*], and by 1777 he had also built North Street to house his workers. Of gritstone construction, the houses have attics once used as stocking-knitting rooms by the families of employees. The spring-fed water faucets are still in the street.

Plate 41(c)
INDUSTRIAL HOUSING IN NEW LANARK (*61/NS 882425 – 1 mile south of Lanark*). A cotton spinning mill commenced operations on this site in 1786, under the partnership of David Dale and Richard Arkwright. It was sold in 1799 to a company formed by Robert Owen, who set out to improve the social conditions of the working people. Owen's ideas on education were far ahead of his time, and his 'New Institution' attracted scores of eminent visitors. The village store was operated on co-operative principles.

Plate 41(d)
INDUSTRIAL HOUSING IN SWINDON (*157/SU 146847 – Exeter Street, Swindon*). Once Swindon had been chosen as the principal centre for building and repairing locomotives and rolling stock for the Great Western Railway, it became necessary to build a new town to accommodate the workers and their families. During the 1840s and 1850s six streets were laid out in the fields, and the elegant little houses still survive. The contractors were J. & C. Rigby, who rented the cottages to the railway company, which then recovered the monies from its employees.

Plate 42(a)

ALLOA GLASS CONE, INTERIOR (55/NS 881924 – in Alloa). This site, still the home of an active glassworks, has two cones in good order; one remains in use although not as originally worked. The cone shown in the photograph dates from about 1750. The skill with which the bricklayers tapered the cone is evident as one looks towards the top of the interior, and the typical floor-level arches are in fine order.

Plate 42(b)

CATCLIFFE GLASS CONE (103/SK 425886 – 4 miles east of Sheffield centre). Glass cones were complete working units in which all processes took place from the founding of the 'metal' to the annealing of the final product. The design of a cone was dictated by the need to restrict the air circulation round the furnace so as to prevent too rapid a loss of heat from the glass during its removal; it was also necessary for the creation of enough draught to sweep away waste gases. During founding the openings at the base of the cone were closed, so as to produce a strong draught through the furnace via the furnace flue below ground level. Cones were first used about 1730, and were the standard glass-making building for a century. The Catcliffe cone dates from 1740, being built by William Fenny who had come from another glass works at Bolsterstone. The cone is approximately 40 ft diameter by 68 ft high. It was closed down between 1884 and 1887, but reopened, unsuccessfully, for about a year in 1901.

Plate 42(c)

POTTERY KILNS, LONGTON (110/SJ 907432 – Edensor Street, Longton). The bottle kiln was a spectacular response to functional requirements. Those illustrated are good examples dating from the nineteenth century, but, like many of their fellows, they are in danger of demolition. The bottle kiln is suitable only for batch working, while more modern kilns are constructed to allow for continuous use, the products passing through them in a tunnel, various zones of which are heated to different temperatures.

whereas few important mechanical inventions were made specifically for woollen manufacture. Instead, machinery that had proved valuable in the manufacture of cotton was adapted, with varying degrees of success, to the woollen industry. Arkwright's water frame, for example, was not successful and power spinning was not adopted until the 1820s–30s when the mule was adapted to woollen spinning. The early woollen mills were finishing mills rather than spinning factories. Fulling and scribbling mills were built on the sites of earlier water-driven mills in the West Riding valleys and about 1790 Crank Mill was built at Morley near Leeds [*10.7*]. This was one of the earliest steam fulling-mills and was powered by an atmospheric engine giving rotary motion through a crank and flywheel. The stone-built, three-storey mill, still survives and is one of the most interesting small Yorkshire factories. The largest English woollen factory of the period was demolished only recently. This was Benjamin Gott's Park Mill at Leeds. Gott, like Matthew Boulton [*10.8*] and Josiah Wedgwood [*10.24*], was exceptional for his day in building a very large factory containing comparatively little powered machinery. There were also some fairly large factories in the west of England which were built before the adoption of power spinning. Stanley Mill, Stonehouse Gloucestershire was erected in 1813 and the new part of Ebley Mill [*10.9*] dates from about 1815. Dunkirk Mill, a massive structure for the area, was built in stages between the 1790s and 1820.

To contemporary eyes the textile factory epitomized the startlingly rapid progress of the Industrial Revolution. It was a readily recognizable feature of the landscape and was undoubtedly the commonest of the new factories to be seen, for both the cotton and woollen industries were far more widely dispersed than they are today. This view is, however, misleading for the metals industries were as important during the Industrial Revolution in terms of capital investment, although their rise was not so meteoric. There was considerable investment in certain sectors of the industry long before the first cotton factory was built; families like the Foleys had about £60 000 invested in

10.7
CRANK MILL, MORLEY

10.8
MATTHEW BOULTON'S SOHO MANUFACTORY, BIRMINGHAM

different ironworks in the mid-seventeenth century. The iron, copper, lead, and other metallurgical industries were highly capitalized by the end of the eighteenth century although the individual industrial buildings remained small [Plate 43(c)]. A large ironworks would consist of several blast furnaces, casting shops, forges, rolling mills, fuel stores, and a warehouse. Taken together the value of the buildings was high but the value of each separate building was small compared with a multi-storey factory. In terms of organization the small-building complex was certainly a factory. Another characteristic of the metals industries was the multiplication of small units under one firm; thus the Coalbrookdale Company owned a series of works along the dale. This was initially a response to the heavy demands for water power for bellows and hammers. The characteristic Pennine lead-smelting mill was small but each large mining company owned several mills located as near as possible to the mines because of the high cost of transporting ore. Where transport facilities were poor or where the value of the raw materials was low in relation to weight it was necessary to process the raw materials on the spot in order to increase the value before transporting them; [Plates 43(a), (b) and (c)].

10.9
EBLEY MILL, STONEHOUSE,
GLOUCESTERSHIRE

MALTINGS, MISTLEY (*150/TM 109319 – just outside Mistley High Street*). The top-floor granary of one of the maltings pictured in Plate 45(a). The details of the timber construction are original, dating from the 1820s.

The multi-storey factory was a characteristic part of the factory complex in two important food processing industries, brewing and corn milling. Expansion in the brewing industry had been taking place before the mid-eighteenth century but the scale of production was determined by the size of the local market because ale could not travel economically for a distance of more than four to six miles. Large breweries such as Whitbreads and Trumans could only develop in London although some large provincial towns had moderate sized breweries. Nevertheless beyond the confines of the large towns the small distiller and brewer and the innkeeper who brewed his own beer continued to flourish well into the railway age [Plates 44(a), (b) and (c)]. The former Rhodes Brewery in Thirsk, Yorkshire, which supplied some of the forty or so local coaching inns, is typical of the small late eighteenth- to early nineteenth-century country-brewery [Plates 45(a) and (b)]. Donnington Brewery, Gloucestershire, is still partly driven by water power.

The country corn-mill survived until this century and a few working water-powered corn-mills still exist. Nevertheless the larger steam-driven mill had appeared following the precedent set by the Albion Flour Mill, London, which was burnt down in 1791. The majority of the early steam-powered flour-mills were built at or near ports such as Hull or in towns well served by inland waterways such as Birmingham. In and near market towns where water power was available large water-powered corn-mills were built to supply a wider market than the immediate locality. Thirsk Town Mill, for example, is a three-storey brick building 120 ft long and 36 ft wide. Steam power was added in 1855 when the mill was run by a co-operative society.

The variations in the size of breweries and corn-mills can be readily understood but are there any general rules which might help to explain the variations in size of other factories? It could perhaps be argued that the magnitude of an industrial building was determined by the amount of power available to it or by the state of the transport facilities in its vicinity.

Power was undoubtedly important. Some early factories like New Lanark Mills, were built in locations where water power was particularly abundant, but others were erected where the power was less adequate. It is necessary to remember, however, that during the early part of the Industrial Revolution the larger factories were only slowly filled with machinery and it was sometimes many years before a building achieved capacity working; some, such as Albion Mills, never did. Often the manufacturer seems to have been content to find sufficient power for his immediate purposes, hoping that supplementary sources would become available as the need arose. The number of enquiries received by Boulton and Watt about steam engines capable of driving machinery suggests that many factories were larger than their natural power resources would have warranted. This is confirmed by field work which, though hampered by the difficulty of estimating changes in flow rates over the centuries, shows that mills and factories of similar dimensions were built beside streams of greatly differing apparent powers. The amount of water power available to an industrial building does not appear to have been crucial in determining its size.

As for transport, although good facilities were vital to the brewing trade in the eighteenth century, and in a sense governed the size of the factory, there are examples in many other industries where access was improved only after the establishment of quite a large factory in a remote area. The Cromford Canal is a good example.

The size of the industrial unit was almost certainly determined chiefly by the amount of capital that could be raised for it and the maximum output that the manufacturer thought he could achieve within the limits imposed by his capital.

10.11

FROST'S MILL, MACCLESFIELD (*110/ SJ 919733 – Park Green, Macclesfield*). This textile mill was built in 1785 and driven at first by water power, later by steam (1811), and finally by electricity (1914). Thrown silk for weaving was its original product (helping to hasten the downfall of Spitalfields by supplying the weavers of Macclesfield where labour was cheaper and better organized than in Spitalfields). Nowadays a variety of synthetic fibres is used, and the building is of great interest being largely in its original form externally.

177

10.12, 10.13, 10.14 and 10.15
OTTERBURN WOOLLEN MILL *(77/NY 888928 – 18 miles north of Hexham)*. This very active small mill manufactures exquisite woollen garments. Output is similar to that of much earlier mills and, since the management encourages visitors, it is possible to follow all stages of production and thus gain a useful insight into the way textile factories were once operated.

10.12 shows the spinning mule with the yarn being twisted under tension, and then wound. The mule in the picture was working, the spindles being momentarily at the end of their travel. Large machines of this kind might have as many as 1000 spindles. *10.13* shows the warping process, where the threads which are to form the warp (the lengthwise component of cloth) are wound side by side on a roller. A dressing is often applied at this stage, to lessen fraying during weaving. The fulling stocks, illustrated in *10.14*, are still in use. Their gears worked by water-wheel below can be seen – the principle of operation being that the large hammer-head is raised by pegs on the side of the wheel and allowed to fall heavily and frequently onto the cloth in the stocks. Fuller's earth may be fed into the stocks and used with a relatively large amount of water for a fairly short time in a process called scouring. This removes excess grease from the cloth, and nowadays is carried out using soap (note the soap barrel next to the stocks). The fulling operation may also be carried on for longer with less water, when it results in felting. The material loses its woven character and becomes thicker at the expense of some contraction in its length and width. Both scouring and felting are called, collectively, fulling.

Teazles, in a gig mill shown in *10.15*, are used to give goods such as blankets a brushing to raise fibres for better insulation. Although teazles were once important enough to be a good cash crop in many parts of the country, they have now been largely superseded by metal machines.

A notable feature of the mill is the use of overhead shafting and belt drives – very reminiscent of early water-powered and later steam-powered mills, and very different from present-day works where each machine has its own self-contained electric motor.

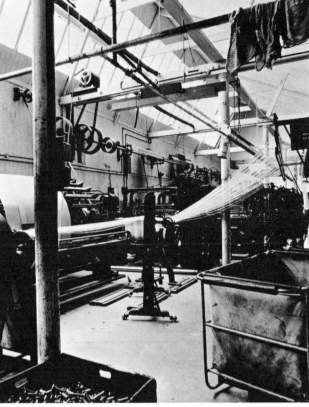

Plate 43(a)

DINORWIC SLATE QUARRY BUILD-INGS (*107/SH 592599 – 1 mile north-east of Llanberis*). In an extended working of the kind associated with slate production, there is need for a large number of small buildings. Here, walls are of slate as well as roofs, and other stone is brought in only for specialized use, such as in the winding gear. The construction of the various inclines is also in slate, giving great solidity but producing a very sombre effect.

Plate 43(b)

SLATE MILL, YNYS PANDY (*116/SH 550434 – 4 miles north-east of Criccieth*). On a larger scale of construction, this mill was used for cutting and smoothing slates brought down from the quarry above. The central water-wheel is no longer in position, but the tailrace opening is plain in this view. The large waste heap by the side of the mill is of typical colour for the slate of this region; so is the slate-built mill-pond dam on the far side of the building.

Plate 43(c)

POLDICE MINE BUILDINGS (*190/SW 741429 – 2½ miles east of Redruth*). The buildings for many of the Cornish mines were individually small, and many have not survived. Occasionally it is possible to reconstruct the entire layout of mine buildings, starting with the substantially-built engine houses [Plates 28(b) and (d)]. On the horizon in this picture, for example, there are no fewer than three engine houses, each of which has lost its subsidiary buildings. At Poldice the smaller buildings are still obvious. The mine was worked for tin as early as the sixteenth century, and for copper from 1750, by which time it was already 100 fathoms deep. For over a century the mine was profitable, but by 1900 only a few miners remained, working the shallow levels. In the left foreground can be seen the condenser chambers, where arsenic fumes were taken around a labyrinth of masonry chambers on their way to the chimney stack. The cooling thus produced allowed the arsenic to condense as an oxide.

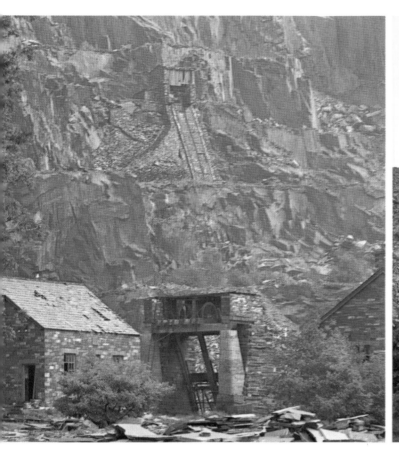

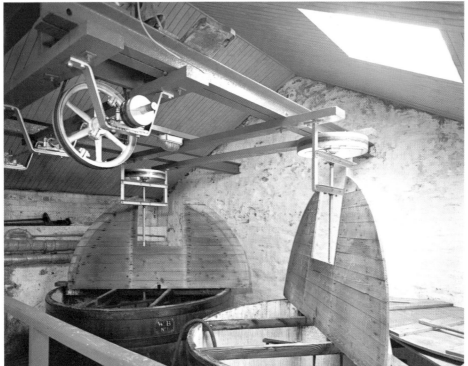

Plates 44(a), 44(b) and 44(c)

EDRADOUR DISTILLERY (*49/NN 959579 – 1½ miles east of Pitlochry*). There are many distilleries in Scotland, producing single malt whiskies for blending into the well-known brands; almost all of them have been enlarged from time to time so as to keep pace with the increasing demand for their products. Edradour is one which is still virtually the same size as it was when built in 1837, and so gives an excellent picture of the earlier form of many of the now-larger distilleries. The works were originally powered by water, and, although the wheel has disappeared, there is still a mill pool. The barley barn and malting house survive, but are no longer used for their original purposes. Plate 44(a) shows the view between the buildings, with the malt kiln at the top of the road; in front of this, out of sight, is the mill pool. A store is to the right of the picture, and the building with the chimneys is the still house. Plate 44(b) shows wooden tuns of the type used for mashing the malted barley with water and for washbacks. Pulley wheels for agitation are also visible. In 1887 these washbacks were recorded as usually holding a capacity of 1000 gallons; their capacity is 1600 gallons. Plate 44(c) shows the interior of the still house, with the copper wash still and low-wines still in position above a coal-fired grate (not now used). In 1887 they usually contained 740 and 420 gallons respectively; they hold 1000 and 500 today. Then the total annual output was 6600 gallons – it is now 28 000 gallons. The cost of the material and labour needed to produce one gallon of pure malt whisky at ten degrees over proof is about 75p.

10.16

LONG SHOP, GARRETT'S OF LEISTON (*137/TM 444626 – in Leiston*). Built in 1853 when Richard Garrett and Sons had established a large trade in portable steam engines (see *6.14* for a similar example). The building measures 80 ft by 36 ft by 25 ft to eaves. The first floor is a gallery, in the well of which a hand-powered travelling crane once ran. Artificial lighting was originally by coal gas batswing burners, and not the electric fittings now in place. The layout was designed to allow the engines to be erected in the centre of the ground floor, with lathes and other machines under the gallery, and fitters' bench work on it. The timber construction of this building is an interesting anachronism, for cast iron had long been in use for columns; it may be that the foundry was not equipped for such large castings, and the builders preferred to use local materials.

There was a characteristic shape and plan to different kinds of industrial building. The corn-mill was often almost square in plan in response to the fact that the grinding stones were generally placed around the circumference of a larger circle, the great spur-wheel. The length of the paper mill, cotton or woollen mill, on the other hand, was several times its width. The brewery [Plate 47(b)], mint, bleachyard [Plate 47(d)], printworks, glassworks, pottery, or ironworks was often planned around a courtyard. Two- or three-storey buildings predominated although at the larger breweries the characteristic 'tower' had appeared by the end of the eighteenth century and was common by the mid-nineteenth century. Extensive stabling had to be provided for brewery dray horses and at potteries and glassworks kilns were often placed in the centre of the courtyard. In some industries, minting for example, a bastille-like plan was adopted for security and this was possibly important in other trades where secret processes had to be guarded; a number of glassworks in the Stourbridge area had this plan. In all these industries the power required was low but it was needed in small amounts in several different workshops. This favoured the retention of the horse wheel since individual power units could be easily installed at little cost although they consumed valuable space. There were separate horse wheels for malt grinding and for pumping the wort at many eighteenth-century breweries.

The materials used and the methods employed in the construction of early industrial buildings were traditional. Cone structures were already known [Plates 42(a), (b) and (c)],

10.17

WETHERIGGS POTTERY (*83/NY 555263 – 3 miles south-east of Penrith*). Built in 1855 by a Mr Binings, the pottery is now worked as a studio pottery by Harold Thorburn, who took over in 1952 although his father worked there before him. In earlier days the products included barm pots, salt kits, and drain pipes, but local markets declined and sales dropped until tourism provided an outlet for more ornamental wares such as slip-ware, flower-pots and mugs. Much of the original small equipment remains, but the electric kilns visible in the picture have replaced the earlier coal-fired one.

and multi-storey warehouses existed in the seventeenth century. The heavy wooden beams used in mill construction were capable of sustaining the weight of the machinery in use in the eighteenth and nineteenth centuries [*10.10* and *10.16*], and iron eventually replaced wood, not because of any structural weakness in wood but because iron was less combustible. The early cotton mills were generally thirty feet wide and could be spanned by a single unsupported beam. If additional width were required, as it was when mule spinning was adopted, timber or cast-iron supporting columns were used.

The widespread adoption of iron as a structural material was encouraged by a series of major factory fires which persuaded manufacturers of the need to make their premises fireproof. The first fireproof factory was built at Derby by William Strutt between 1792 and 1793. Paved brick arches replaced the traditional joists and floor boards, and hollow pots, looking like flower pots with lids, were used for the ceiling of the sixth storey. Cruciform cast-iron columns and wrought-iron tie-rods were used to support the arches but the beams, albeit protected by plaster and sheet metal, were of wood. A similar structure was built at Milford, and before either the Derby or the Milford building was completed Strutt began a six-storey factory measuring 190 ft by 31 ft at Belper, again using brick arches, wood beams, cast-iron pillars, and wrought-iron tie-rods.

The next stage in the evolution of the fireproof factory was the substitution of cast iron for the wooden beams formerly used. This was first accomplished in the Shrews-

183

10.18

WETHERIGGS POTTERY (*83/NY 555263 – 3 miles south-east of Penrith*). This steam blunger was built in 1855 but is still in a good state of preservation. The 14 ft diameter brick-lined trough is about 3 ft deep and hanging above it on a central axis are two heavy iron frames each with a number of tines reaching almost to the base of the trough. In operation this tank was half filled with a mixture of clay and water, which was then agitated by the blunger to put the clay into suspension. After allowing time for heavy particles to settle out, the resulting creamy liquid was run off into a sunpan (which still remains in situ), for natural evaporation of the water. Blungers of this kind were once widespread in smaller potteries; later, production was speeded up by heating the sunpan artificially.

bury flax mill of Benyon, Benyon and Bage which was built under Bage's direction in 1796 [*10.20, 10.21* and Plate 46(a)]. This mill, the first iron-framed building in the world, 177 ft long and 39 ft 6 in. wide, survives as a maltings. Between 1802 and 1804 the Benyon brothers and Bage built two new iron-framed factories, one at Leeds and another at Shrewsbury but neither of these survives. Bage's experiments helped William Strutt to decide in August 1803 to rebuild Belper North Mill (burned down in the January) as an iron-framed factory. This building still stands beside the massive red-brick factory of 1912. The Salford Twist Mill (demolished) was the next important step in the development of the framed building for in this factory the columns were circular and hollow. Steam was admitted to them from a boiler in the basement and they served as central heating pipes as well as being essential to the structure. This factory set the pattern for the fireproof factory of the early to mid-nineteenth century, but the framed industrial building with some important exceptions [*10.28–10.31*] did not become

10.19

10.19 shows the kiln, with iron strapping, surrounded by a drying-room. A minor defect of earlier kilns had been a tendency for heat to flow up the sides of the firing chamber to leave a cold cone in the middle. The Wetheriggs kiln (built in 1855 and in regular use until 1959) illustrates the final form of the circular multiflued kiln – with specially constructed flues built under its floor to avoid the formation of a cold area during firing. Eight large firemouths are spaced round the base of the kiln, tapering to small slits which cut through the kiln wall. Each flame was split, half to pass through triangular flues traversing the cupboards inside the firing chamber, the other half to pass under the kiln floor and rise up the central vent. This gave an even distribution of heat, but as much as six tons of coal were needed to bring the kiln up to 1100°C over a period of 36 hours; a further 2–3 days were allowed for cooling.

This pottery is an excellent example of a semi-industrialized concern of a size which was the fore-runner of the large potteries in the area around Stoke-on-Trent.

common until the latter part of the nineteenth century because it was considerably more expensive to build than the traditional structure [*10.16*]. Industrial buildings were still partly constructed of wood in the present century [*10.4–10.6*].

The basic factory form was a response to the function that the building was to serve. The main problem was to provide sufficient space not only to house the machinery but also to arrange it in the most satisfactory way in relation to the source of power. The need for regular motion and the necessity of avoiding undue loss of power through friction meant that long shafting had to be eschewed if possible. The standard width of the Arkwright cotton mills was clearly dictated by the size of the machinery which they were intended to hold. Within the space provided a row of water frames could be fitted on either side of a horizontal shaft, leaving adequate side-aisles for the machine operatives. The length of a rope walk, on the other hand, was obviously determined by the length of ropes to be made. The amount of light required in the building was also

185

10.20 and 10.21
THE FIRST IRON-FRAMED FACTORY IN THE WORLD (*118/SJ 499139 – Ditherington, Shrewsbury*). *10.20* shows the method used to fix the beams and columns together. The details were exposed when it was necessary to undertake some constructional work for the maltings now occupying the building – always a valuable time for the archaeologist to be around. *10.21* is a detail of a roof member joint – note the considerable similarity to the joints on the Iron Bridge. [See also Plate 46(a).]

a possible factor influencing the width since, except for the top floor it was not possible to have overhead lighting. But the great variation in the amount of natural light in the early cotton factories suggests that this was not a factor of paramount importance.

Functionalism extended beyond the basic dimensions to the peculiar adaptations necessary for certain industries. The long dormer windows, so characteristic of the west of England textile mills, were required by burlers who inspected and repaired the cloth; the iron plates noticeable in the walls of some metals factories are not the terminating point of a tie iron but are the means by which work benches for heavy machines were fixed to the building. The lucam, housing a hoist is characteristic of the corn-mill and maltings [*10.27*]; the louvred window is typical of the tannery and maltings. Despite these functional adaptations industrial buildings were interchangeable just as the early water-mills had been. Factories were erected by speculative builders who were pleased to let or sell them to any manufacturer irrespective of trade; buildings erected for one purpose were often used for something entirely different later on. One Birmingham brewery was converted to a nail factory in the early nineteenth century and, in the same period, pottery works in north Staffordshire were advertised for sale, as being suitable for conversion to iron foundries.

It has usually been assumed that if an industrial building was functional it was plain although not necessarily dull. This is true up to a point, for many plain factories survive. The Pennine lead-smelting mills and the Cornish ore-crushing plants are unadorned while Sir Robert Peel's cotton mills at Tamworth are very austere. But on the other hand there are industrial buildings which are sometimes almost flamboyant.

186

10.22

COTTON MILLS, PAISLEY (*60/NS 486635 – near Cart Basin, Paisley*). Several very fine mills were built here towards the end of the nineteenth century. The Anchor Mills of J. & P. Coats are magnificent six-storey red-brick Renaissance blocks; the Atlantic (1871–72) in the west is united with the Pacific (1874–75) in the east by a central tower (1882–83). Internally they have wooden beams and floors supported by cast-iron columns which also drain the roof. *10.22* shows Mile-End Mill (1899–1900), of five storeys in brick, with two towers; it was designed by W. J. Morley of Bradford.

10.23

AVON MILLS, MALMESBURY (*157/ST 936869 – on the river Avon in Malmesbury*). This elegant stone-built factory, originally a woollen and then a silk mill, dates from the late eighteenth century. Note the narrowness of the block, a characteristic of such early mills.

Plate 45(a)

MALT KILNS, MISTLEY OLD MALT-INGS (*150/TM 109319 – adjacent to Mistley High Street*). The maltings were erected between 1807 and 1828, most of them remaining in active use until 1967. On the ground floor at the far end of each two-storey building is an open tank, in which the barley was steeped in water; a number of these tanks still have their original hand pumps. The tile-surfaced working floor carried the germinating grains, which were later dried in the kilns shown in the plate. Each kiln was fired by an anthracite grate, with pierced earthenware tiles supporting the grains. The original swivelling cowls were replaced after the First World War, and the present louvred tops put in their place. These maltings give an excellent picture of this industry before the advent of mechanization.

Plate 45(b)

RHODES BREWERY, THIRSK (*91/SE 429821 – in Kirkgate, Thirsk*). This operated as a brewery from 1803 until the end of the century, after which it became a bottling plant. It is now used by a firm of builders. None of the plant remains, but the original steeping room shows evidence of the tank, and the louvres which are still visible externally give a clue to the building's former function. This size of brewery would have been supplied by a malt kiln of the size shown in Plate 45(a).

Plate 45(c)

EDGE RUNNER – ALBERT MILL, KEYN-SHAM (*166/ST 658679 – at the lower end of Keynsham*). Albert Mill was a logwood mill, the last commercial load leaving in November 1964. [See Plate 26(a) for an external view.] A logwood chipper is still in place behind these edge runners, which are shown as an example of less usual machinery operated by water-power. Their present diameter is 4 ft 8 in., but they are known to have worn down several inches within living memory. When installed in the 1870s it took eleven horses to haul them from Bristol. The large spur gears above originally had the usual wooden teeth.

Plate 45(d)

SWINEFORD COPPER MILLS (*156/ST 691689 – 4 miles north of Bath*). This is a fine complex of industrial buildings, the larger part dating from the 1840s. Two undershot water-wheels are still in position, with shafting of a later date when the building was converted into a flock mill. The headrace was used at one time as a loading basin, for the Avon is still navigable well above here.

Plate 46(a)

THE FIRST IRON-FRAMED FACTORY IN THE WORLD (*118/SJ 499139 – in Ditherington, Shrewsbury*). In 1796 Charles Bage designed this flax-spinning mill built for Benyon, Benyon & Bage. Brick jack arches span between the cast-iron beams, which are supported on cast-iron columns. It is not strictly an iron-framed building in the modern sense, for the walls carry part of the load, and there are no longitudinal beams – only a series of wrought-iron ties to take up any unequal thrust from the arches. The fireproof structure in this form proved very successful in the nineteenth century, although the maximum width allowed by such a method of construction is only about 50 ft. The building is currently in use as a maltings (originally Jones's Maltings, but now Allied Breweries). The photograph shows the special columns designed to carry shafting for power transmission. Originally there were many more windows than now remain, for it was essential to block up the majority to control the temperature of the germinating malt. This is a building of fundamental importance. [See also *10.20* and *10.21*].

Plate 46(b)

SMITHFIELD MARKET (*160/TQ 318816 – London E.C.1*). With the growth of urban areas new or improved markets were required to provide large-scale marketing and storage facilities for agricultural products. Smithfield, the centre of the London meat trade since 1852, was set up on an already ancient market site, which had been paved as early as 1614. The first two sections of the present building were opened in 1868. Designed by Horace Jones, the main feature is the central avenue shown in the plate. This roadway is 50 ft wide, between double piers which carry the richly moulded elliptical arch and pediment of cast iron. The sides of the roadway are separated from the market by an open space. Where the central avenue is intersected by the public road, gates (25 ft high by 19 ft wide) of attractive ornamental cast iron close off the market. The whole building is a most interesting exercise in covering a large area using cast iron; even the street lamps are supported by cast-iron brackets.

These reflect the tastes and aspirations of manufacturers keen to rise in the social order. Although Arkwright's first factory at Cromford was plain, Masson Mill [*10.25* and Plate 47(a)] is in fine Palladian style. Wye Mill at Cressbrook, built in 1815, is a classic example of the factory as country house. Josiah Wedgwood's Etruria façade was Palladian, while Enoch Wood, a Burslem potter, gothicized his factory to the extent of crenellating the top of each kiln. Clearly these factory owners recognized the need to be accepted by the 'county', and one way of achieving this was to compliment the aristocracy by building factories within the framework of existing country-house styles. Adornment of a factory in this way was also a method of advertising. By the mid-nineteenth century when the steam-driven factory meant in many cases an urban site, when factory masters were less interested in being accepted by the aristocracy, and when the factory was altogether bigger, conscious architectural style, with some notable exceptions [*10.22* and Plates 48(a) and (b)], became rare [Plate 48(c)].

INDUSTRIAL HOUSING

Manufacturers searching for available water-power sites during the early years of the Industrial Revolution were drawn to remote, hilly areas away from good transport facilities and centres of population which could supply the labour force for the factory [*10.26*].

Some manufacturers offered higher wages in order to attract factory workers to these isolated sites, and in those industries where the labour force was composed chiefly of women and children, a few manufacturers consciously set about providing jobs for men so as to draw families to the district. Even if the labour force could be supplied from local villages and towns incentives were needed to tempt domestic workers who were reluctant to give up their quasi-independence for factory work. One of the chief incentives used to attract a labour force was the provision of good housing.

Shortly after Richard Arkwright built his first mill in Cromford he began to erect the housing in North Street [Plate 41(b)]. This comprised two terraces of three-storey stone houses, the living quarters allotted to individual families being two 12 ft square rooms arranged one on each of the two lower floors. The top storey of each terrace was

10.24

JOSIAH WEDGWOOD'S ETRURIA
FACTORY

10.25

MASSON MILL (*111/SK 294573 – 2 miles south of Matlock*). The mills at Cromford represent the first successful water-powered cotton factories in the world, for it was here that Richard Arkwright was able to apply water power to carding and spinning in sequence, as a continuous process carried out under one roof. Masson Mill, the last of Arkwright's three in the area, was built about 1784 on an excellent site by the river Derwent. Impressive water works and an unusual down-curved weir still exist at the rear of the buildings, and water power is used to turn a turbine.

10.26

NEW LANARK (*61/NS 881424 – 1 mile south of Lanark*). This is the outstanding industrial monument of Scotland. Although the eleven water-wheels which once worked here have now gone, the great lade remains. The boiler house and large chimney have also gone, but although the mills have been extensively modernized their exteriors remain unaltered. A housing association has been formed to modernize the houses while preserving their external appearance.

continuous and consisted of a long, stocking frame shop, for at this time only the preparatory processes and spinning were carried out at the mill. Two-storey housing was built along the road to Wirksworth, and an impressive inn in the Palladian style was erected in the centre of the village. A school and chapel were added later. Arkwright's houses and those built by the Strutts at Belper and Milford, the Evans at Darley Abbey, Samuel Oldknow at Mellor, and David Dale at New Lanark [Plate 41(c)] were superior to the houses in many of the growing industrial towns or, indeed, in many agricultural districts. Farey commented in 1813 on the 'vast numbers of neat comfortable cottages' erected by the Derbyshire cotton spinners and remarked that 'they must have had a great influence on the general style and condition now observable in the (agricultural labourers') cottages' of the district which were far better than those in the south.

The housing was certainly superior but with some few exceptions (such as the Evans of Darley Abbey) the manufacturer charged a rent of between two and five shillings a week for houses costing between £50 and £100 each, which gave him between 5 per cent and 10 per cent interest on his capital investment and he had no problems of rent arrears, for the rent was deducted at source. But housing was valuable to the factory master in other ways. Absenteeism was a constant problem and many factory operatives tended to be migratory, staying in one job for a few weeks then moving on to work in another factory. Once a good house was provided the threat of dismissal became a successful deterrent to absenteeism and it was generally acknowledged that once a wife had been given a good home she would not let her husband move on.

There were other less measurable benefits for the manufacturer who provided good housing. The labour force was thought of as a sort of living machinery which had to be well ordered and regulated just like its mechanical counterpart in the factory. Good living quarters were a necessary factor in keeping the human machine in a suitable condition for work. Robert Owen of New Lanark explained the profits to be expected from spending money on living machines: 'Your time and money so applied, if directed by a true knowledge of the subject would return you not 5, 10, or 15 per cent for your capital so expended but often 50 and in many cases a hundred per cent.' Unfortunately he did not divulge how he measured this. Owen made numerous welfare provisions besides housing at New Lanark including a New Institution for the Formation of Character and a school (which survive) where he put into practice his advanced ideas on education.

But Arkwright and Owen seem to have been exceptional for few other early factory masters attempted to build townships of the scale of Cromford and New Lanark; indeed Arkwright did nothing like this at any of his other water-powered factories. Factory villages did, after all, consume large amounts of capital that might be required for the factory itself. Generally a couple of rows of houses was all that was deemed necessary. Houses can be found at many water-powered textile factories in Lancashire, Yorkshire, and the Midlands. They are much less common in the west of England textile area because the factories were built near existing villages and townships.

Although the late eighteenth- and early nineteenth-century factory village reached its highest point of development in the textile industries, rows of houses were equally common at many other kinds of industrial site. Housing remains at a number of Shropshire water-powered furnace and forge sites such as Eardington near Bridgnorth and many South Wales ironmasters provided housing like that at Bleanavon. Housing was common at many early breweries and good rows survive at Boroughbridge, Yorkshire,

10.27
SNAPE MALTINGS (*137/TM 392575 – 3½ miles south of Saxmundham*). This superb range of buildings incorporates elements dating from 1859 to 1952, although not all of them are to be seen in the plate. Excellent wooden details are abundant, and the dwelling on the left is in perfect harmony with the industrial units further along. The original buildings were erected for Newson Garrett, father of Elizabeth Garrett Anderson. This group is a most important site, not least for its sheer beauty. At the rear is the concert hall converted for the Aldburgh Festival.

10.28, 10.29, 10.30 and 10.31

ROYAL NAVAL DOCKYARD, PORTS-MOUTH (*180/SU 630005 approx.*). *10.28* is of the interior of the No. 6 Boathouse which was originally built as a Masthouse in 1843–45. The building is remarkable for its cast-iron columns and massive cast-iron under-trussed beams, each to carry 40 tons distributed load.

10.29 is of Marc Isambard Brunel's Scoring Machine, of about 1803, made by Henry Maudsley. This machine is at present in No. 6 Boathouse, but was made for the Blockmills [see *10.30*], as part of the machinery for making pulley-blocks for the Fleet. Marc Brunel (father of Isambard Kingdom Brunel) successfully set up one of the earliest mass-production lines in the world. Many of his ingenious machines are still in use today.

10.30 shows the interior of the main hall of the Blockmills, erected by Sir Samuel Bentham in 1803–8 to house the block-making machinery of Marc Brunel. The overhead shafting and pulley wheels are original, and although the buildings are at present used as a store, it is hoped that they may be restored to their original layout with original machinery re-installed as a fitting memorial to this considerable early achievement.

10.31 is of No. 3 Ship Shop, built 1845–49 to a slight modification of a design submitted by John Rigby and George Baker in 1844. The impressive arrangement of the slender curved braces springing from upright columns to support the light framework of the roof is of considerable importance in the history of building techniques, being far advanced for its time. Originally, both ends and sides were open, and there were Building Slips on which vessels were constructed.

It must be emphasized that these buildings are not generally accessible to the public, and the author is indebted to the Admiral Super-intendent of the Dockyard for permission to visit and photograph (and for permission to publish the photographs) and to Mr. R. Sutherland Horne, Dockyard Historian, for generous help in conducting round and providing information about the buildings.

and Stratton St. Margaret, Swindon, Wiltshire. There are rows of houses at many collieries, since mines were often opened at some distance from the nearest village. Stone Rows, Moira, Leicestershire, was built for the miners at Moira Collieries in 1811; Portland Row (demolished) was built in 1826 for workers at Selston Collieries.

A new kind of industrial township, the company town, emerged in the early to mid-nineteenth century. With the exception of New Lanark, Cromford, and a few others, the early factory village comprised little more than a few unplanned rows of houses, but the new townships were planned from the outset. Provision was made for mechanics' institutes, hospitals and schools.

One of the first of the new company towns was Goole. In 1819 a proposal was made for a deep water channel between the Aire and the Ouse, and in 1822, when two wet docks were planned, the Navigation Company asked the engineer to suggest the layout of a township. Streets were planned on a grid pattern and in 1825 the building of Goole began. The contract for much of the work went to Jolliffe and Banks, a large firm of civil engineers. Buildings clustered around the north and south extremities of the docks and hindered the future development of the docks along the river front. As in a number of early planned towns the original grand design was not fulfilled, only a portion of it being built, since urban development required large injections of capital. Nevertheless the Company provided a church, school, literary and scientific institu-tion, and a supply of gas for the town. The original housing, plain and dull, has been largely demolished in recent years [Plate 41(a)].

194

Plate 47(a)
MASSON MILL, CROMFORD (*111/SK 294573 – 2 miles south of Matlock*). This attractive mill (of which the central bay is illustrated), was built by Richard Arkwright, probably in 1784, on the banks of the river Derwent. Cotton doubling is still carried on here.

Plate 47(b)
BULLARD'S ANCHOR BREWERY (*126/ TG 231088 – in Coslany Street, Norwich*). Built chiefly in the 1860s, the Anchor Brewery lies beside the river Wansum. The buildings here are of domestic size, forming a most charming group.

Plate 47(c)
PERTH WATER WORKS (*55/NO 121232 –in Perth burgh*). Built in 1830 and now disused, it has a dome of cast iron designed to look like stone. Inside is a steam engine made in Kircaldy at the turn of the century. Efforts are being made to preserve this outstanding industrial monument, of relatively early date.

Plate 47(d)
BLEACHFIELD, SCONE (*55/NO 105297 – 4 miles north of Perth*). The Stormontfield bleachfield has this fine three-storey bleaching house, dating from about 1820, still in use. Linen bleaching before the introduction of chlorine used to be a very lengthy process, requiring a lot of capital and extensive land and water lades. Bleachfields were numerous in Perthshire, especially along the river Tay, and this bleachworks is an excellent example of the quality of building which may still be found.

Plate 48(a)

JARROLD'S WORKS, NORWICH (*126/TG 235092 – in Cowgate, Norwich*). Built as a yarn mill to the design of Richard Parkinson in 1839, this remarkable building is now occupied by Jarrold's printing works. Bales were dropped down the turret. The blank tympana over the third floor windows are a motif familiar in Georgian houses in Norwich.

Plate 48(b)

MALTINGS, MISTLEY QUAY (*150/TM 324319 – 1 mile west of Manningtree*). By the beginning of the nineteenth century a trade was established for the supply of malt from favourable areas to breweries in towns and cities. Mistley was well situated in the centre of a good barley growing area, with facilities for sea-going and inland water transport. This resulted in considerable-sized premises being erected, by the later part of the century. These maltings are typical of their kind, with strongly-modelled details and typically Victorian red and yellow panelled brickwork.

Plate 48(c)

MALTING KILNS, IPSWICH DOCK (*150/TM 167437 – Dock Street, Ipswich*). Ipswich Dock has many buildings concerned with grain in one form or another, and the considerable scale of these kilns indicates the advantages of water-borne trade for such bulk cargoes. The tidal river Orwell is immediately in front of the buildings, so that quite large ocean going vessels can be accommodated. The dormer windows are an unusual feature, and the functional aspect of the architecture comes through strongly in this group.

Plate 48(d)

NEW LANARK (*61/NS 882425 – 1 mile south of Lanark*). Robert Owen built his 'New Institution' for the gainful education of young and old, but he was a paternalist rather than a socialist. His profits, interestingly, were greater than those of less humanitarian employers. He had great belief in the therapeutic use of music and dance, and recitals by the village children were a common entertainment for the visitors who flocked to New Lanark after Owen had made it the European showplace for all interested in social reform and education. In 1816 there was a population of 2297, living in what can still be seen – a complete factory village of the industrial revolution.

Goole is the canal town *par excellence*. Stourport was a product of the canal age, but as far as is known the housing was built by private developers rather than by the canal company. But at many canal junctions and termini (Shardlow and Great Driffield for example) rows of cottages were built for wharfingers, warehousemen, and lock keepers.

Early in the railway age, in the 1840s, three new towns were created: Ashford (S.E.R.), Swindon (G.W.R.), and Wolverton (L.&B.R.), each built around a centre of railway engineering. In each case there was a settlement already existing, varying in size from the market towns of Ashford and Swindon to the insignificant hamlets of Wolverton and Eastleigh. The railway towns were, however, separate geographically and had a separate identity from the outset. The early housing at Wolverton consists of unadorned two-storey terraced dwellings in reflecting pairs while that at Ashford and Swindon makes more concession to architectural style. At Swindon there were different houses for different grades of workers; they all hint at Gothic with small gables and deep painted window reveals. The smallest houses are terraced two-storey dwellings in reflecting pairs with recessed front doors at angles of 45 degrees enabling each pair to share a small porch [Plate 41(d)] – ideal for neighbourliness on a wet day.

These railway towns of the 1840s heralded the developments carried out in Yorkshire during the 1850s and 1860s by Sir Titus Salt, Col. Edward Akroyd, and the Crossley family, all textile manufacturers. The model housing at Copley built by Akroyd between 1849 and 1853 bears some resemblance to the Swindon housing although the Copley houses are back-to-back.

The most ambitious company town is undoubtedly Saltaire. Financed by one man between 1853 and 1863 it epitomizes the mid-nineteenth century desire to raise the moral tone of the working classes. Sir Titus Salt installed his mill workers in architect-designed cottages built in the Italian style and laid in neat rows facing a park [*10.32*]. The street clutter of a working class area was discouraged by the provision of a laundry while education was recognized as the means of elevating the young – stone lions representing vigilance and determination sit outside the school built in 1868.

10.32
SALTAIRE

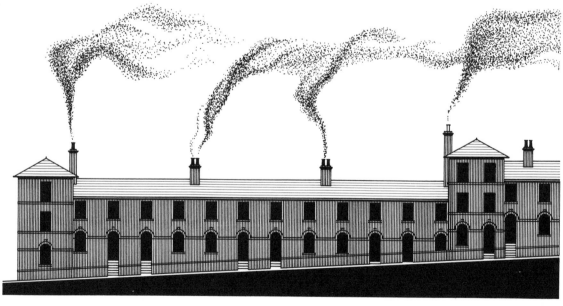

Although the layout of late nineteenth- and early twentieth-century model factory villages such as Port Sunlight, Bournville, and New Earswick shows an appreciation of the intermixing of the rural with the urban landscape which the earlier company towns lacked, the railway towns and the developments by Salt at Saltaire and the Crossleys at West Hill Park, Halifax were, perhaps, more realistic. They acknowledged and came to terms with the fact that because of the price of urban land high-density housing was a necessity. At the same time they showed that this could be achieved in good dwellings built at reasonable cost, in a manner that is aesthetically pleasing and planned so as to encourage a sense of community.

FURTHER READING

ASHMORE, O. *Industrial Archaeology of Lancashire* (Newton Abbot: David and Charles, 1969)

BUTT, J. *Industrial Archaeology of Scotland* (Newton Abbot: David and Charles, 1967)

CHAPMAN, S. D. *The Early Factory Masters* (Newton Abbot: David and Charles, 1967)

CHAPMAN, S. D. AND CHAMBERS, J. D. *The Beginnings of Industrial Britain* (London: University Tutorial Press, 1970)

HILLS, R. L. *Power in the Industrial Revolution* (Manchester: Manchester University Press, 1970)

NIXON, F. *Industrial Archaeology of Derbyshire* (Newton Abbot: David and Charles, 1969)

RICHARDS, J. M. *The Functional Tradition in Early Industrial Buildings* (London: Architectural Press, 1958)

TANN, J. *Gloucestershire Woollen Mills* (Newton Abbot: David and Charles, 1967)

TANN, J. *The Development of the Factory* (London: Cornmarket, 1971)

TARN, J. N. *Working-class Housing in Nineteenth-Century Britain* (London: Lund Humphries, 1971)

Index

Index